Policing the Markets

Set against the backdrop of the recurring waves of financial scandal and crisis to hit Canada, the US, the UK and Europe over the past decade this book examines the struggles of securities enforcement agencies to police the financial markets. While allegations of regulatory failure in this realm are commonplace and well documented in policy and legal scholarship, James W. Williams seeks to move beyond these conventional accounts, arguing that they are based on a limited view of the regulatory process and overlook the actual practices and dilemmas of enforcement work. Informed by interviews with police, regulators, lawyers, accountants and investor advocates, along with a wealth of documentary materials, the book is rooted in a uniquely interdisciplinary social science perspective. Peering inside the black box of enforcement, it examines the organizational, professional, geographical, technological and legal influences that shape securities enforcement as a distinctly knowledge-based enterprise. The result of these influences, Williams argues, is the production of distinct vision of financial disorder which captures certain forms of misconduct while overlooking others, a reflection not of incompetence or capture but of the unique demands and constraints of the regulatory craft. Providing a very different, and much needed, account of the challenges faced by regulators and enforcement agencies, this book will be of enormous interest to current research on enforcement, regulation, and governance both within and beyond the financial realm.

James W. Williams is an Associate Professor at the Department of Social Science, York University. He has written numerous articles on the policing of economic crime and the governance of financial markets, appearing in journals such as *Economy and Society* and the *British Journal of Criminology*.

Policing the Markets

Inside the Black Box of Securities Enforcement

James W. Williams

Routledge
Taylor & Francis Group
a GlassHouse Book

First published 2012
by Routledge
2 Park Square, Milton Park, Abingdon, Oxon OX14 4RN

Simultaneously published in the USA and Canada
by Routledge
711 Third Avenue, New York, NY 10017
A GlassHouse Book

Routledge is an imprint of the Taylor & Francis Group, an informa business

British Library Cataloguing in Publication Data
A catalogue record for this book is available from the British Library

Library of Congress Cataloging in Publication Data
Williams, James, 1972–
Policing the markets : inside the black box of securities enforcement / [James Williams].
p. cm.
Includes bibliographical references and index.
ISBN 978-0-415-69146-8 (hbk)—ISBN 978-0-203-13488-7 (ebk)
1. Securities industry—Law and legislation. 2. Securities. I. Title.
K1114.W55 2012
346'.0922—dc23

2011030801

ISBN: 978-0-415-69146-8 (hbk)
ISBN: 978-0-203-13488-7 (ebk)

Typeset in Baskerville
by RefineCatch Limited, Bungay, Suffolk

MIX
Paper from responsible sources
FSC® C004839
FSC www.fsc.org

Printed and bound in Great Britain by
CPI Antony Rowe, Chippenham, Wiltshire

In loving memory of my dearest mother
Maureen Williams
1943–2009

For Audrey and Kai

Contents

Preface

As a study of securities enforcement and the policing of financial markets, this book is relevant to a number of different audiences with distinct concerns, interests and points of view. This ranges from those directly engaged in the field, whether as investors, enforcers or professional intermediaries, to policy analysts and media commentators, to academics working not only in the immediate area of financial crime and regulatory studies but also more distantly related fields including socio-legal studies, economic sociology and the study of professions and organizations. One of the difficulties in treading this course and engaging with these myriad audiences is that some readers may experience a sense of frustration with things going not quite as expected. Indeed, given that the book is informed by a theoretical framework forged from a number of academic literatures, it may be viewed by those in the field as too theoretical, as insufficiently attuned to the more pressing matters of policy and reform, and as overly circuitous in its approach and manner of argument. For these readers, I would urge patience in moving through the more theoretical sections of the book. While at times abstract and seemingly removed from the field of inquiry, these provide the frames of reference upon which many of the substantive findings depend and through which they have been interpreted and made meaningful. These theoretical footings also inform a series of, if not recommendations, at least potential policy moves that may prove useful in advancing the future enforcement agenda.

There is also the issue that, for those deeply concerned with the problems facing securities regulation and for whom a systematic overhaul is the only reasonable option, the book's approach and conclusions may not be bold enough, while remaining overly sympathetic to those at the heart of the enforcement enterprise. This is especially true for those in the advocacy community, who are extremely passionate about what they view as the injustices of the enforcement process and the need for a fundamental rebalancing of policy and practice to better reflect the interests of the small investor. To this I can say that, in seeking out the viewpoints of a number of interested groups and peering inside the enforcement box, I have made an effort not to choose sides, to provide as balanced a view as possible within the limits of my own outsider's perspective and to focus less on the manifest politics of this field and more on the actual details of enforcement practices. This is not to suggest that the analysis unfolding in the pages to follow is somehow anemic or beholden to the status quo; far from it. Instead, it seeks to provide a more nuanced view that can only come from a place in the middle of things.

Acknowledgements

All research is a matter of intrusion and this study is certainly no different. Indeed, the fact that it draws extensively from interviews with those in the field, many of them busy professionals in their own right, speaks to the burden placed on respondents who were asked to give generously of their time with the promise of little direct benefit in return. While confidentiality provisions bar them from being recognized by name, I want to extend my heartfelt thanks to all of those who participated in the study and who kindly tolerated my trespassings. Without their involvement, this book would not have been possible. As the research enterprise also comes with significant financial and logistical demands, I am further indebted to the financial support provided by the Social Sciences and Humanities Research Council of Canada, as well as the tireless efforts of a number of research assistants who worked with me over the course of the project. These include Brigitte Cecckin, Tia Dafnos, Suzanne Day, Augustine Park and Elizabeth Wong. For many of the theoretical and conceptual insights of the book, I owe thanks to dialogues with colleagues such as Chris Andersen, Randy Lippert and Laureen Snider. Most importantly, I would not have survived the long process of researching and writing this book without the love and support of my wife Audrey Tokiwa and her family, as well as my son Kai who arrived midway through the project and added more than his fair share of spice to the process. I also want to recognize the love and support of my father Wayne Williams, my sister Alysha Kropf, and especially my mother Maureen Williams, who passed away while this book was being written and to whom I will be eternally grateful for the faith that she always had in me and for the quiet strength that she brought to all aspects of her life.

Introduction

Policing the markets?

During his 10 September 2009 testimony before the US Senate Banking, Housing, and Urban Affairs Committee, Harry Markopolos, a seasoned financial analyst turned forensic investigator, said of the SEC: 'They couldn't find ice cream in a Dairy Queen' (Markopolos 2009b: 21). Offered as a searing indictment of the agency's handling of the Bernie Madoff affair, this is symptomatic of a much deeper and abiding scepticism regarding the abilities of enforcement agencies to police the markets and respond to financial misconduct in its various forms and guises. In view of the numerous bubbles, scandals and meltdowns to have plagued the markets in recent years, the notion that securities enforcement is ineffective and in desperate need of repair is a mantra that has been repeated in a number of other jurisdictions including Canada, the UK and Australia, spurring endless commentaries and much political handwringing on how to right the enforcement ship.

This book is inspired by these very debates, taking the 'problem' of securities enforcement as its primary focus.[1] However, in resisting the enchantments of this dense forest of accounts and the reigning orthodoxy of regulatory dysfunction articulated by those at both ends of the political spectrum, it seeks to chart a very different analytical course. The book is less interested in striking the standard evaluative pose, excoriating agencies for their misses, fumbles and injustices and attributing these to either incompetence or capture, and is dedicated instead to examining the specific influences, logics and contingencies that shape the enforcement process as a distinctly social enterprise. Informed by contributions from sociology, philosophy and politics, the staking of this analytical ground requires a fundamental reframing or reproblematization of enforcement itself, a recognition that it is not simply geared to the generation of cases or the production of compliance with the law, albeit these remain its manifest aims, but rather the production of knowledge of, and about, the markets. By examining securities enforcement as a knowledge-based enterprise and charting the conditions and constraints governing the terms of its engagement with the financial world, the book offers a very different view of the challenges facing enforcement agencies in their bid to police the markets. This introductory chapter sketches the basic contours of this approach, including the various literatures, considerations and methodologies that inform the study, and notes the potential pitfalls associated with analysing a terrain positioned so close to the heart of finance.

Financial insecurities and regulatory failures

For anyone with even a modest interest, let alone stakes, in the markets, the early 2000s were tumultuous indeed. Beginning with the collapse of the technology bubble and the bankruptcies of former stock market darlings Enron and WorldCom, and rising to a crescendo a mere eight years later with the implosion of the sub-prime market, investors witnessed deep and sizeable losses to their portfolios and retirement savings, with side-effects extending into many corners of the economy.[2] These market meltdowns, punctuated by a number of more run-of-the-mill scandals, such as the Madoff Ponzi scheme triggered a seemingly endless parade of commentaries and reports, a veritable explosion of discussion about the markets and the problems of regulation notable not only for its volume and degree of consternation, but also its extension beyond the traditional base of the financial news into a variety of cultural sites. The mere fact that one of the most hyped editions of Jon Stewart's comedy program *The Daily Show* featured an interview with MSNBC's Jim Cramer speaks to these larger ripples.

Within these accounts, a recurring theme that unites commentators with very different investments in, as well as relationships to, the markets is the failure of regulators to detect these problems and to take the requisite preventative or remedial action. While few countries have been left unscathed, this regulatory interrogation has been especially pointed in Canada where no less than three major studies, sporting auspicious titles such as 'The Wise Persons Committee to Review the Structure of Securities Regulation in Canada' (2003), 'The Task Force to Modernize Securities Legislation' (2006) and 'The Expert Panel on Securities Regulation' (2009), have concluded that Canadian securities enforcement is lax, ineffective and in desperate need of repair.[3] In the sober assessment of one such report: 'If a basic purpose of securities regulation is to protect investors, Canada's system is falling short' (Expert Panel 2009: 2). It is these commentaries and discussions of regulatory failure that provide the impetus for this book. However, rather than simply adding its voice to this chorus of boos, one of its objectives is to recognize the limitations of these accounts themselves and their tendency to produce a rather narrow and somewhat caricatured view of the enforcement enterprise. A key premise and starting point for this analysis is thus that the 'problem' of regulatory failure is itself part of the problem.

Understanding enforcement: the 'problem' of regulatory failure

While it is difficult to dispute the claim that securities regulation and enforcement have fallen short in a number of important respects and are in need of at least some degree of repair, closer scrutiny of these assertions of regulatory failure reveals some interesting tendencies and limitations. First, despite its superficial coherence and seeming unanimity, even a modest effort to drill down into this discourse reveals very different interpretations of exactly what is meant by 'failure' or 'ineffectiveness'. For members of the industry and their legal counsel, the issue is not so much inaction on the part of enforcement agencies but perceived inefficiencies, unfairness and bias in the regulatory process itself. Here regulators are chided for their failure to take on the 'right' types of cases, namely those involving clearly egregious offences which cast aspersions on the markets as a whole, while subjecting so-called legitimate industry players to overly aggressive and unfair regulatory encroachments (eg Cory and Pilkington 2006). These problems of unfairness and inefficiency, we are told, are exacerbated by the sheer number of agencies with stakes in the enforcement game and thus the multiple and overlapping sources of regulatory scrutiny, a 'regulatory burden' which contributes to 'coordination difficulties' that impede investigations and create 'potential injustices to respondents' (WPC 2003: 30; see also Carscallen et al. 2003; Crawford 2003; Osborne et al. 2004). In contrast, from the perspective of retail investors, the issue is not the burdensome nature of regulation but the failure of regulatory agencies to investigate and provide restitution in cases of misconduct brought forward by investors (SIPA 2004). Ineffectiveness is thus gauged according to a logic of remediation and is based largely on the ability to recoup losses. These contrasting critiques reveal an enduring ambiguity as to the mandate and scope of the regulatory enterprise, the meaning of 'regulatory failure' and the range of interest and normative positions on which these claims are staked.

A second limitation of the discourse of regulatory failure is that these protests are waged on the basis of a rather limited understanding of the enforcement process itself, with criticisms directed to the handling of, or failure to handle, individual cases. Here the main fodder for critique comes from efforts to sift through agency caseloads and proceedings with an eye to critical missteps or inappropriate outcomes, as well as the identification of misconduct reported through other channels, such as the media, civil actions and investor testimonials, but not taken up by regulators. This focus on easily discernible outputs and on 'the case' as a primary unit of analysis is understandable given the limited access granted to outside observers and the absence of alternative measures of regulatory activity. However, the result is a tendency to reduce enforcement to a series of inputs (eg regulations; personnel; and resources) and outputs (case dispositions), with little insight provided into not only what actually goes on in the enforcement divisions of the major agencies, but also the kinds of challenges they face on a daily basis. Enforcement thus remains largely unexplored and unexplained, with aspersions cast on the basis of limited, case-based generalizations rather than a more nuanced view of the regulatory process.

Third, there is a tendency in the discourses of regulatory failure to attribute identified flaws in the handling of cases along with observed patterns in regulatory outputs to the influence of particular and often highly personalized interests. From the perspective of the regulated, case outcomes reflect the aggressiveness of enforcement staff, combined with an underlying sense of bias that precludes their fair treatment. Consistent with this individualized frame, regulatory lapses are further attributed to a lack of expertise and judgment on the part of enforcement personnel. In contrast, for external stakeholders, such as investor advocates and other commentators, the issue is bias of a different sort. Regulators are seen as hopelessly conflicted and beholden to the very industry they seek to regulate, hence their failure to take seriously the concerns of small investors and to act appropriately in responding to their grievances. The notion that regulators are 'co-opted by the industry' (Investor Advocate #2: 4) is a common refrain that is also shared by some members of the media, who point to an enforcement apparatus which, by virtue of these allegiances, is destined to yield disappointing results: 'So what are the reasons for this dismal track record? One factor that can't be overlooked is the cozy relationship between the corporate community, their law firms, and Canada's thirteen securities commissions' (Livesey 2008: 45). Despite their obvious differences, each of these accounts thus remains invested in the notion that securities enforcement is primarily interest-based; that is, it is driven by narrow sets of interests that function to produce outcomes ultimately consistent with those interests.

While one might expect these policy and practitioner literatures to be grounded in exactly this kind of politics of accounts, and to be somewhat limited in their understanding of the enforcement enterprise, similar tendencies are evident in the academic literature, albeit assuming a slightly different form. This is certainly true of the contributions of those working from the perspectives and institutional affiliations of law, accounting, finance and economics, publications that dominate the academic landscape and engage with similar questions of failed enforcement, excessive burdens and regulatory inefficiencies. Stepping outside of these more specialized literatures into the social sciences, the problem is the relative dearth of offerings with only a handful of noteworthy contributions providing a more nuanced view of securities enforcement as a distinctly social enterprise (eg Shapiro 1984; Stenning et al. 1990; Condon 1998; Snider 2009). And yet, not only is this literature thin in volume but it remains ensconced in a similarly narrow problematic of regulatory (in)effectiveness, with the limitations of enforcement framed according to the epidermis of discernible inputs and outputs and 'the case' remaining a primary frame of reference and datum to be explained and accounted for. There is also a tendency in many of these accounts to conceive of enforcement in terms of a series of levers or drivers, ranging from particular interests and ideologies to larger structural exigencies. Snider (2009), for one, attributes the failings of enforcement, defined in terms of a lack of charges in high profile cases, to the role of 'corporate power' in shaping the 'common sense' view of regulators, such that the activities of the larger players are excluded from the regulatory tent. This notion of embedded interests and accommodative postures yields an image of corporate power determining case outcomes in a manner akin to metal filings placed over a magnetic field. Thus, while drawing attention to its social features, enforcement remains somewhat decontextualized, or perhaps overly contextualized, in these accounts, bound to the problematic of accounting for agency outcomes and geared towards a finite set of regulatory drivers.

Moving further afield and tapping into the much larger and more well established literatures on regulation, governance and corporate crime, analyses continue to be framed in terms of the outcomes, outputs and case logics of the regulatory process and, in particular, the task of 'demonstrating how enforcement frequently fails to produce compliance and how this can be explained' (Lange 1999: 553). This overriding concern with a particular problematic of legal (non-)compliance has had the twin effect of: (1) privileging law as a primary frame of reference and legal deviation as the thing to be accounted for, with many accounts treading perilously close to a kind of legal formalism (Lange 1999); and (2) tethering contributions to debates over how best to achieve this compliance, with some opting for a more conciliatory or 'responsive' stance (Braithwaite 2008; Baldwin and Black 2008) and others advocating for the deterrent effect that can only come from the full force of legal sanctions (Pearce and Tombs 1999; Tombs 2002). And yet, often overlooked in these accounts are the actual working practices that underlie regulation as a multi-faceted enterprise and in respect of which the question of compliance is an important but in many ways secondary concern. Admittedly, this is an overview painted with very broad strokes, as authors such as Hawkins (2002), Lange (1999), Reichman (1992) and McBarnet (2004) have indeed offered more in-depth and finely grained views of the practices and social world of regulators. And yet, even here, the emphasis remains on the problematic of compliance versus non-compliance, the tracking of case dispositions, and a highly institutionalized view of regulation as the work product of individual agencies.

Notwithstanding fundamental differences in approach, politics and perspective, what emerges from this brief survey of the research literature is that many of the existing contributions to the study of regulation in general, and securities regulation and enforcement in particular, remain bound to the distinctly normative enterprise of accounting for past failures and producing 'better regulation' in the future. This is an endeavour that embeds the regulatory process in a definitive legal and institutional form and treats regulation a bit like an engine producing, or failing to produce, cases in accordance with a particular mechanical logic that, more often than not, traces back to the influence, power and authority of the regulated. Within these accounts, regulation is thus reduced to a kind of 'black box'. What matters most are its inputs and outputs, while limited attention is paid to the details, materialities and vicissitudes of the regulatory process itself.

As an attempt to pry open this black box and examine the distinct features of enforcement as a particular type of regulatory project, this book endeavours to set aside or bracket the questions of effectiveness, outcomes and drivers (that is, the 'why') and instead focus on the details (that is, the 'how') of securities enforcement. There is also an explicit effort to resist the tendency to simply see in enforcement the machinations of financial capital or the manifestations of larger needs or interests. Positioned in the shadow of finance, there is no denying that securities enforcement is shaped by the gravitational pull of the industry with financial interests penetrating deeply into the regulatory fabric. The challenge is to recognize these influences without reifying them, to examine the ways in which they are themselves mediated by and through the localized features of enforcement practice. While the regulated may never be far from the minds of enforcement staff, it is also important to appreciate the influences exerted by factors such as the unique nature of the markets as regulatory objects, the reliance on various technologies and computer programs to detect and interpret signs of financial disorder, the turf battles between agencies each seeking to assert or defend their jurisdiction and their place in the regulatory game, as well as the need to work within the conventions governing the production of evidence and to satisfy the formatting demands of the regulatory process as a distinctly knowledge-based enterprise. Given the limitations of the existing literature, this task of opening up the black box of enforcement and engaging with these various contextualities and contingencies requires a very different set of theoretical tools, the main features of which are outlined below.

Opening the 'black box': theoretical currents and analytical frames

The first of these theoretical currents flows from the insights of science and technology studies and, in particular, Actor Network Theory (ANT) (Latour 1987, 1999, 2005, 2010; Callon 1998; Law 2002). Inspired by ethnographies of the research laboratory, this tradition seeks to expose the social features and practical contingencies underlying the seemingly technical domains of science and technology, while resisting the tendency to lapse into totalizing approaches that see in scientific practice the workings of larger structural logics or interests. The emphasis is thus on the specific, localized and material practices through which science is performed and constituted, made and remade. The interest of ANT scholars in subjecting technical domains to critical scrutiny, while avoiding 'macro-social' explanations, is evident in their use of the term 'black box', a concept invoked by cyberneticians 'whenever a piece of machinery or a set of commands is too complex. In its place they draw a little box about which they need to know nothing but its *input* and *output*' (Latour 1987: 2; emphasis added). ANT scholars thus seek to open up these black boxes, to examine their seemingly unimportant technical details and inner workings, all the while eschewing the sociological inclination to 'mobilize gigantic forces, to detect dramatic patterns emerging out of confusing interactions, to see everywhere in the cases at hand yet more examples of well-known types, to reveal behind the scenes some dark powers pulling the strings' (Latour 2005: 22). Another key insight from this tradition is a recognition of the agency exercised by both human *and* non-human actors and thus the role of technologies, documents and devices in shaping social practice: 'In addition to "determining" and serving as a "backdrop for human action", things might authorize, allow, afford, encourage, permit, suggest, influence, block, render possible, forbid, and so on' (Latour 2005: 72). Aspects of this approach have inspired two more substantively grounded literatures that are directly relevant to securities enforcement and provide essential supports for this book.

The first of these, and the second core theoretical current, involves research in what is variously described as the 'social studies of finance', the 'sociology of financial markets' or 'cultural economy'. Drawing inspiration from ANT, as well as various post-structuralist and Foucauldian approaches, one of the key streams within this larger body of work involves an attempt to engage with the technicalities and materialities underlying the domain of finance. Framed in juxtaposition with political economy and, in particular, the International Political Economy (IPE) literature, this tradition seeks to counter the 'mystification of finance and the financial world as an unknowable and, importantly, undoable center of power and domination' (Aitken 2006: 79–80) and thus its 'representation ... as a homogeneous and clearly bounded system' (de Goede 2005: 149–50). In resisting the treatment of finance as a 'black box' (MacKenzie 2005), contributors have pointed to the need to denaturalize and repoliticize this domain by examining the specific and often mundane ways in which finance is performed through various technologies, calculative devices and representational media (de Goede 2003, 2005; Langley 2008a; Aitken 2007; MacKenzie 2009; Preda 2009a). Authors working in the larger cultural economy tradition have also drawn attention to the social, cultural and spatial characteristics of markets, including their enactment through networks of social relationships and interpretive communities that are geographically bounded, an urban geography of finance that problematizes the notion both of a homogenized form of capital and the purely virtual nature of financial transactions (eg Leyshon and Thrift 1997). Markets thus possess not only social but also spatial attributes, therein bearing the imprint of a critical socio-spatial contextuality.

The insights of Latour and Callon have also percolated into the study of law and legal governance. This is evident in recent contributions to the socio-legal studies literature and, in particular, the work of Mariana Valverde (2003, 2005, 2006, 2009; Levi and Valverde 2008) and Annelise Riles (2000, 2005, 2011), both of whom draw from ANT in opposing what they see as grand theorizing around questions of law, legality and governance. Following on the heels of Latour, Valverde in her various contributions resists the tendency to conceive of law in terms of a coherent institutional form driven by larger socio-political interests and logics. Rather than 'explaining legal processes by reference to some invisible underlying structure that is imagined as having "needs" and functions' (Valverde 2003: 29), she urges us to think in terms of the workings of legal networks that combine human and non-human actors, including people, texts, architecture, documents and concepts, and which are constituted through localized practices and knowledge effects. Attention is thus drawn to dynamics such as the production of documents and strategies of documentation, a key aspect of the materiality of legal cases and evidence of law's status as a '*documentary network* through which the social is arranged and assembled' (Levi and Valverde 2008: 818, original emphasis), as well as legal technicalities such as jurisdiction which have a critical bearing on governance arrangements (Valverde 2009). Thus, Levi and Valverde (2008) urge socio-legal scholars to 'open the "black-box" that tends to erase the process through which objects are produced and which compels us to lazy attributions about our world' (823). Riles (2005) likewise invokes the concept of the black box as a means of drawing attention to what she refers to as the 'technical dimensions of law' (975), and thus the value of talking 'not just about people and epistemes, but about technical legal knowledge itself – about the theories, the models, the arguments, the techniques' (984–5). Rooted in the processes, networks and actors through which the world is constantly being assembled and of which law is an essential part, the emphasis for these authors is thus on how forms and attributions of legality are imposed on the world (Levi and Valverde 2008: 806).

A third theoretical current, one that actually intersects with and informs each of those discussed above (see Rose and Valverde 1998; de Goede 2005; Aitken 2007; Langley 2008a), is associated with the work of Foucault and the tradition of governmentality studies. Grounded once again in the eschewal of grand narratives and structural imperatives, Foucault is concerned with the links between contemporary forms or relations of governance and the practices of knowledge production. Here governance is seen to hinge on the localized discourses and modes of intelligibility through which individuals and populations are defined as problematic and are thus constituted as objects of governance (Foucault 1991; Miller and Rose 2008; Dean 2011). This informs Foucault's interest in questions of knowledge and knowledgeability and his emphasis on modes and dynamics of problematization (Rose and Valverde 1998). One concept that is especially relevant to the present study is that of 'discursive formation', which refers to the rules or conditions governing the production of discourses of and about the social world, that is, what can be said, when and by whom and, ultimately, what counts as being 'true' (Foucault 1989). This concept is critical to the 'politics of knowledgeability' that underlies enforcement and which is outlined throughout the course of this book.[4]

The final theoretical current represents a significant departure from the first three as it takes as its core problematic the reproduction and legitimation of the social order, a more conventionally structuralist approach that would seem to fit squarely into the frameworks critiqued by the likes of Latour, Callon and Foucault. Rooted in the work of Pierre Bourdieu and his seminal concepts of 'field', 'habitus' and 'capital' (Bourdieu 1984, 1986, 1993; Bourdieu and Wacquant 1992), this perspective is valuable in highlighting the extent to which social practice hinges on attributions of status, credibility and symbolic authority that are inscribed within and read off such things as credentials, personal contacts and connections, and embodied signs of authority including speech and dress. This forms the basis for Bourdieu's understanding of power as fundamentally symbolic in nature with the effectiveness of social performances dependent on the possession of what he refers to as symbolic capital, one of the many concepts to be flushed out in the chapters to follow. Following from his appreciation of the spatial features of the social world and a sense of referentiality that is not unlike that of Latour, Bourdieu is interested not only in the nature of symbolic capital and its implications for social practice, but also the extent to which it is unequally distributed between individuals occupying different positions in what he refers to as social fields. Indeed, one of his key contributions is his argument that the social world is organized in terms of a series of distinct yet intersecting social fields, each of which is hierarchically structured and defined by relations of conflict and struggle between those occupying dominant versus subordinate positions. Mapping the social topography of enforcement as a particular social field, including relative positions of advantage and disadvantage and lines of conflict and struggle, is thus an important aspect of this analysis.

Certainly, Bourdieu's work is not without its limitations, chief among which are its structuralist tendencies and its failure to appreciate the contingencies of social practice (eg Valverde 2005, 2006, 2009; Levi and Valverde 2008). And yet, his approach is invaluable in capturing the politics and power relations operative in various regions of social space, and is thus helpful in offsetting what even the staunchest supporters of ANT admit are deeply empiricist tendencies and a neglect of questions of power and politics (Levi and Valverde 2008). Moreover, the emphasis on symbolic authority as a feature of effective social performances suggests that part of what is essential to the materialities and technicalities of interest to Valverde, Riles and others hinges on the symbolic authority of those responsible not only for their development and institutionalization, but also their ongoing production and use *as* technicalities. Thus, while recognizing the limits associated with its structuralist tendencies, and opting for the more flexible use of its core concepts, Bourdieu's work serves as a valuable complement to the first three perspectives and is critical in drawing out the unique politics and legitimacy struggles at play in the fields of finance, law and, ultimately, securities enforcement.

Framed in terms of these various theoretical currents, the task of opening up the black box of securities enforcement and examining its inner workings requires a fundamental shift in perspective, a move away from the normatively inspired concerns with effectiveness, outputs and outcomes and the search for regulatory drivers, and a focus instead on the specific details, technicalities and politics underlying this particular regulatory space conceived as a social field. Following the ANT tradition and its influence on both the social studies of finance and socio-legal studies, this includes an appreciation for the 'technical' features of the enforcement enterprise: the role of documents, assessment forms, detection technologies and risk metrics, as well as legal conventions such as privilege, disclosure and jurisdiction. These are the non-human actors populating the enforcement field. This theoretical current also speaks to the need to conceive of enforcement not as a passive process of registering and responding to incidents of market misconduct, whether in a proactive or reactive mode, but as a force in its own right actively constituting and performing the very distinctions between legitimate and illegitimate financial activity, and thus shaping the activities of market players as they seek to manage their conduct such that it remains in-bounds and on-side. As with financial theorems and calculative devices, enforcement is itself directly implicated in the performativity of the markets.

Pursuant to this, the social studies of finance and the broader cultural economy tradition point to the need to take the markets seriously as regulatory objects and to frame the study of enforcement in terms of a much more sophisticated understanding of their social features and technical properties. The notion that the markets are dependent on situated performances and practices that are social as much as they are technical, and which possess their own vulnerabilities and discontinuities, draws into question the completeness of finance's influence over enforcement. It also suggests that the challenges encountered by enforcement staff may have more to do with the distinctly social, cultural and geographical features of markets as social networks and interpretive communities, rather than decontextualized and abstracted centres of financial and political power. Thus, considerable effort is made in this book to provide a more complete view of the markets and to frame the activities of enforcement agencies in terms of their position within, or more accurately their distance from, these centres of finance.

While firmly implanted in these questions of materiality and performativity, and thus the more finely grained practices of regulation, opening up the black box of enforcement also requires an appreciation of the unique power relations and forms of politicking operative within this sphere. Here the work of Bourdieu is helpful in conceiving of enforcement as a distinct social field constituted in terms of the relative positions of, and relationships between, the agencies, organizations and individuals with stakes in the regulatory game. A key task is thus to chart the respective positions of these players in this larger field, as well as to examine the forms of conflict that inform these relationships, a 'wide angle' view of regulation (Nader and Nader 1985) that will help to overcome the more narrowly institutionalized view of enforcement that follows from a reliance on studies of individual agencies (eg Shapiro 1984; Condon 1998).

Another key contribution from Bourdieu stems from his interest not only in fields and their social and relational properties, but also in the notion that the practices within these fields are geared towards and are dependent upon the possession of specific forms of social authority, credibility and legitimacy. This suggests that enforcement may itself be framed in terms of social performances and interactional encounters involving regulators, respondents and various professional intermediaries. This is consistent with the view of socio-legal and regulatory scholars that much of the substance of regulation consists of struggles over the interpretation of alleged violations, as well as forms of bargaining and bluffing unfolding in the shadow of the law (Reichman 1992; McBarnet 2004). Assuming that these kinds of social performances indeed hinge on attributions of credibility and legitimacy, the question inevitably arises as to the differences in symbolic authority on the part of the various regulators relative to other players, and the effects of these differences or deficits on their engagements in the enforcement field. The importance of legitimacy also draws attention to the role of professionals and attributions of professionalism in the enforcement process, and to the efforts on the part of regulatory agencies *as* organizations to protect their own credibility and to manage the institutional risks that invariably come with the rather curious mandate of protecting the integrity of the markets.

Informed by these theoretical currents, the ultimate objective of this book is to understand how the enforcement project, as a point of intervention in the markets and site of financial regulation, is rooted in a particular kind of knowledge work, or what is referred to as a 'politics of knowledgeability'. The focus is on the criteria governing what counts as legitimate regulatory knowledge and thus the conditions, constraints and contingencies that are imposed on, or more accurately, embedded within the enforcement enterprise as an attempt to 'know' and to speak 'the truth' of the markets, not by virtue of any kind of structural accommodation, but rather the parameters underlying this particular field of engagement. These include: (1) its relationship to, and distance from, the markets as electronically mediated yet inherently social, cultural and geographical spaces; (2) its reliance, by virtue of this distance, on a series of technologies, devices and reporting channels to identify and assess misconduct; (3) its subjection to the evidentiary and formatting demands of the regulatory process; (4) its engagements with legal professionals who seek to shape its understanding of events, and who must be convinced of the merits of its claims; (5) its grounding in particular mandates and organizational logics; and (6) its unfolding within a wider field of individual, professional and organizational conflict and struggle. What is most interesting about these conditionalities and constraints, to be fleshed out in the chapters to follow, is the extent to which they contribute to the production of a particular 'regulatory vision'; that is, a performative and discursive rendering of the markets that has the effect of highlighting certain forms of disorder while at the same time concealing others and which, in so doing, draws and redraws the very boundaries between legitimate and illegitimate activity on which 'finance' and 'the markets' depend (Preda 2009a). Refined through an analogy with the 'camera obscura', a different kind of black box, and framed in terms of a process of reinvestment rather than reproduction, this regulatory vision reveals the practical workings of the politics of knowledgeability and their translation into a form of epistemic engagement with the financial world whose very complexities the book seeks to unpack.

Questions of method: researching securities enforcement

This move inside the black box of enforcement is informed by the results of a five year study of the Canadian regulatory system. A relatively small market compared with the US, UK, Europe and Asia, Canada may seem an unlikely choice for a major study of securities enforcement. However, there are a number of unique features of this national context that make it an ideal laboratory for examining the details, practices and politics of enforcement. These include: (1) the high profile of securities regulation over the last several years and the depth of concern regarding the 'effectiveness' of the regulatory system; (2) its status as one of the few jurisdictions in the world without a national securities commission, with enforcement provided instead through a number of provincial agencies, thus offering a unique perspective on inter-agency tensions and forms of politicking; (3) the smaller scale and greater concentration of financial and enforcement activities making them more accessible and more readily observable; and (4) the opportunities for financial misconduct, and the distinct enforcement challenges, that accompany a smaller marketplace. In each of these respects, the Canadian context throws into relief many of the essential dimensions of securities enforcement, while its similarities with other jurisdictions allow for the generalizability of the results.

In approaching this particular research site, a number of considerations came into play. The first involved the general parameters of the study. Given the interest, following from Bourdieu, in framing securities enforcement in terms of a social field defined by different positions and players, the study sought to include in its ambit not only the enforcement units of the major regulatory agencies, but also a number of stakeholder groups, including the securities professionals responsible for managing the relationships between regulators and regulated, members of the media and representatives of various shareholder and advocacy associations.

A second consideration had to do with the geographical scope of the study. While recognizing the diversity that comes with having 13 provincial and territorial securities commissions, a decision was made very early on to focus on two primary jurisdictions: Ontario and British Columbia. These were natural choices given that Ontario is the home jurisdiction for the Toronto Stock Exchange (TSX) and boasts the largest number of issuers and market participants, with the major banks and brokerage houses clustered in the financial district of downtown Toronto. The Ontario Securities Commission is thus by far the largest and busiest of the provincial securities commissions, often assuming the role of de facto national regulator. Similarly, BC and the financial district of Vancouver are home to a vibrant venture capital market and sport the second largest securities commission in the country. Of the remaining jurisdictions, one notable absence is the province of Quebec, which houses the country's principal derivatives exchange (Bourse Canadienne de Produits Dérivés) and whose securities commission (the Autorité des Marchés Financiers) is known to be especially aggressive in its enforcement activities. While references are made to Quebec where appropriate, this was not identified as a primary research site given access and language barriers, as well as the very different legal tradition of the province drawing into question its comparability to other jurisdictions.

A final consideration involved a question not of space but rather time. Spurred by the market turmoil that began in the early 2000s, one of the hallmarks of securities regulation has been the tremendous rate of change with new institutional structures and legislative initiatives emerging seemingly on a monthly basis. Just one example of this state of flux came towards the end of this study when two key self-regulatory agencies, the Investment Dealers Association and Market Regulation Services, merged to form a single SRO, the Investment Industry Regulatory Organization of Canada (IIROC). Two points follow from this. First, this book represents a cross-sectional snapshot of the regulatory infrastructure at one particular point in time (2004–2008). Given that much of the research was carried out prior to the merger, this is a viewpoint that includes the IDA and RS as separate agencies. Second, it is often the case that these kinds of structural adjustments occur with very little change to actual working practices. For example, in the case of the merger, all indications are that the enforcement units of the IDA and RS have simply been parachuted into the new agency and are operated largely by the same people, with very similar processes and with the same degree of autonomy.[5] All of this is to say that the insights provided by this book into the working practices of securities enforcement remain relevant, notwithstanding ongoing renovations to the regulatory infrastructure.

With this groundwork in place, the research itself was informed by three core methodologies. The first, documentary and archival research, was used to analyse a variety of source materials, including: (1) the work product of the various enforcement agencies, namely proceedings and settlements, policy statements and speeches; (2) conference presentations by regulators and members of relevant stakeholder groups; (3) policy and research reports; and (4) a legion of media commentaries and op-ed pieces. Beyond yielding ample fodder through which to address questions, such as agency mandates, the scope of regulatory activities and areas of debate and controversy, the sheer volume and range of materials pointed to the fact that securities enforcement is not only about the generation of cases but also the production of documents, a distinctly papered medium through which agencies strive to manage their public face and shape the parameters of public debate and discussion. These documentary materials also provided a comparative dimension to the study, yielding insights into enforcement practices in a number of other national contexts including the US, the UK and Australia, although these comparisons are offered only in passing and do not represent an explicit focus of the study.

Foregrounding these various documentary sources, the central thrust of the research consisted of semi-structured interviews with representatives of the various enforcement agencies, including both current and former members, as well as a number of stakeholder groups. The respondent pool was thus drawn from: (1) police and Crown Attorneys; (2) securities commissions in BC and Ontario; (3) self-regulatory organizations; (4) law and accounting firms; (5) investor and shareholder advocacy groups; and (6) the media.[6] Individuals were initially selected on the basis of their formal position and/or status within these groups, with additional respondents solicited using a strategy of snowball sampling. This selection process yielded a total of 93 respondents (see Table 1.1), with the bulk of interviews conducted between November 2004 and December 2008, primarily in Toronto, Vancouver and Ottawa. The interviews were loosely structured, ranged from half an hour to two hours in duration, and in all but nine cases were digitally recorded, transcribed, and then analyzed for key themes.[7]

These contacts yielded a number of preliminary observations. First, the majority of respondents were male, white and middle-aged, a demographic that was especially pronounced in the practitioner communities, with women better

Table 1.1 Distribution of respondents

Provincial Crown Attorneys	2
Police	21*
Ontario Securities Commission (OSC)	13**
BC Securities Commission (BCSC)	1
Former OSC	2
Former BCSC	2
Investment Dealers Association (IDA)	6
Mutual Fund Dealers Association (MFDA)	1
Market Regulation Services Inc. (RS)	5
Former RS	2
Lawyers	28***
Accountants	2
Consultants	3
Journalists	2
Investor advocates	2
Shareholder activists	1
Total	**93**

*All of these 'police' respondents are affiliated with the RCMP's Integrated Market Enforcement Team (IMET), the primary investigative body responsible for policing securities crimes in Canada. In addition to 14 police investigators and senior police administrators, this group also includes two embedded Crown Attorneys from the federal Department of Justice, two accountants working under contract, and three individuals with industry experience serving as analysts and subject matter experts.
** Three of these respondents were interviewed during their secondment to IMET.
*** Eleven of these respondents have direct experience in the regulatory world, either through formal secondments or full-time staff positions.

represented on the regulatory side, including a number of key management posts. When asked about this gender gap, respondents noted the greater opportunities in the regulatory world, as well as more flexible work schedules. Differences were also evident in the social and educational backgrounds of respondent groups. The most stark contrast was between current and former police officers, many of whom entered the force immediately after high school and worked their way through the ranks, and legal counsel who boasted extensive post-secondary credentials. Second, the personal biographies of respondents revealed a distinct professional network with frequent movement between regulatory and practitioner communities, an indication of the professional rather than simply institutional roots of enforcement. Finally, there were some interesting differences, particularly in the case of Toronto, in the physical location of the interviews themselves, as most of the securities professionals resided in the downtown financial district with members of the SROs located close by. In contrast, the OSC and especially the police were positioned much further afield, geographical variations that may simply reflect different tolerances for expensive commercial real estate but which also hint at the distinctly geographical features of this regulatory space.

These interviews were supplemented with attendance at a number of regulatory and legal conferences sporting such grandiose titles such as 'Securities Superconference'.[8] A form of participant observation, this offered a glimpse into the less public and in many respects more informal aspects of the enforcement enterprise, a viewpoint made available in a forum that was open to the public yet clearly intended for regulatory and legal insiders. Of particular interest were the moments when speakers departed from their notes and offered jokes, anecdotal comments and less scripted responses to audience questions. These conferences also yielded insights into: (1) key personalities in the field; (2) points of conflict and controversy; and (3) status differences between police, regulators and lawyers, with these differences manifested in terms of language and dress, as well as personal styles and interactional dispositions. Thus, as with the interviews, the conferences were valuable not only in terms of their varied content but also their insights into the practitioner communities and personalities inhabiting the field of securities enforcement.

Structure and organization of chapters

Having surveyed the basic lay of the land, the balance of the book is organized as follows. Living up to the promise to take the markets seriously, Chapter 1 examines the characteristics of financial markets as distinctly social and cultural spaces, constituted through a range of technologies, discourses and interpersonal networks, and situated in specific geographical locales, namely urban financial centres. A number of trends relating to the structure and organization of the markets, and their implications for the enforcement project, are also discussed. Chapter 2 then broaches the question of regulation and, following a brief account of the history of securities regulation, examines the principles, mandates and logics that inform the regulatory enterprise. Particular emphasis is placed on the inconsistencies and contradictions underlying the regulatory mandate, and the extent to which agencies seek to manage these contradictions through the production of signs of organizational accomplishment and competence loosely coupled with practices on-the-ground.

Informed by this sketch of the markets and the regulatory system, Chapter 3 moves on to frame securities enforcement in terms of a social field in the sense intended by Bourdieu, mapping the positions that make up this field and examining the relationships and forms of conflict and struggle that ensue between the various players. Attention is also devoted in this chapter to the legal encodings of this regulatory space and, in particular, the extent to which individual agencies are enabled or restricted in their vision of the markets and thus their regulatory reach by virtue of their legally mandated jurisdiction. Remaining with Bourdieu, Chapter 4 argues that the positions in the enforcement field may be understood not only in organizational, but also individual terms, as they correspond with differences in social and symbolic capital and thus attributions of status and credibility. These forms of social distinction, themselves expressions of the social, biographical and physical distances between police, regulators, professionals and the markets, are used to explore the place of expertise in the enforcement enterprise, an allegedly technical attribute that upon closer scrutiny turns on forms of social competence and attributions of symbolic authority. The consequences of these gaps in 'expertise' include forms of risk aversion and perceptions of regulatory unreasonableness.

Following these discussions of mandate, jurisdiction and expertise, the next two chapters delve more deeply into the enforcement process itself. Chapter 5 examines the technologies and channels through which troublesome market activities are first detected and identified, and the types of logics, narratives and formatting demands that are then brought to bear in determining whether or not they merit conversion into official cases. Chapter 6 remains with the enforcement process, although the emphasis is less on the origins and assessment of cases and more on their subsequent legal framing and disposition. Particular attention is paid to the interactions between regulators and legal counsel, as much of what passes for enforcement consists of forms of posturing and bargaining with lawyers and their clients. It is in this context that the differences in confidence, credibility and regulatory authority noted in Chapter 4 are most clearly brought to bear on the regulatory process.

Chapter 7 brings together these various influences and examines their contribution not only to the selection of certain types of cases, to the exclusion of others, but also the production of a particular regulatory vision. The chapter explores the various aspects of this vision, including its gaps and blind spots, and advances the 'politics of knowledgeability' as an analytic that is useful in accounting for the selective nature of enforcement without resort to the usual regulatory drivers. The book then concludes with a tentative return to the policy arena, examining the struggles waged by investor advocacy groups to shift the terms of the enforcement debate and highlighting a number of possible footholds for advancing the policy agenda.

Notes

1 While 'securities enforcement' refers specifically to the formally designated units responsible for detecting and responding to breaches of securities laws, it is in practice impossible to draw a clear line between this and other 'policing' functions performed by securities regulators. A case in point is compliance units which are similarly geared towards the detection of violations, albeit in a more educative than punitive mode. The analysis of securities enforcement undertaken in this book is thus informed by the connections and blurred boundaries between this and related regulatory functions, and the significance of enforcement as a point where *distinctions are made* between 'technical breaches' and 'market misconduct'.

2 One of the most notable of these reverberations was the near collapse of General Motors, pushed to the brink of bankruptcy not only by the erosion of the auto market but also by its inability to finance the massive losses to its defined benefits pension program, a testament to its own exposure to the markets and its less than conservative approach to investing the retirement savings of its employees.

3 The fact that the Canadian regulatory system has sustained such intense scrutiny may be surprising to some given the international acclaim Canada received for emerging relatively unscathed from the sub-prime crisis. However, this was largely a reflection of

tighter *federal* banking regulations. Securities regulation, an area of *provincial* jurisdiction, has long been and remains an area of concern.

4 What is notable about Foucault's work, relative to the ANT tradition, is that it expands the frame of analysis beyond the microscopic details and technical materialities of institutional practices into the realm of discourse where emphasis is placed, among other things, on the oppositions between normality and abnormality, inclusion and exclusion, that lie at the heart of discourses and which are constitutive of their knowledge or truth effects (Foucault 1989).

5 Reflecting this sense of regulatory inertia, one respondent anticipated that: 'With the exception of senior staff at the organization there's really not going to be any change at all. I kind of just see them being their own department and they'll be doing the same thing, operating underneath the same roof for a change' (IDA #2: 8).

6 While there are a handful of interviews with members of the industry, this group was not explicitly targeted in the study given their limited first-hand experience with enforcement agencies, other than in a compliance context, and their hesitation to speak candidly about matters of regulatory interest. Rather, industry views were captured through interviews with legal counsel who are their primary representatives and who are better positioned to speak both to specific cases and to larger issues in the industry. Industry viewpoints were also probed through the accumulated documentary materials.

7 In the interests of confidentiality and anonymity, all direct quotes from the interviews are cited through references to the primary occupation or institutional position of the respondent at the time of the interview, followed by the page number of the transcript from which the quote was taken. Thus, for example, individuals from the private sector working with the police under contract are included in the police pool, as this best reflects their position in, and perspective on, the enforcement field (see Table I.1). In cases where respondents have been seconded to other agencies, and thus possess more than one institutional affiliation, they are identified based on their formal, full-time positions. It should also be noted that, while there are a number of respondents from the private sector who have worked as regulators in the past, only those who have held recent positions, and whose comments are directly informed by these positions, are identified as 'former' regulators.

8 My participation in these conferences was entirely transparent. I made no effort to conceal my identity or institutional affiliation during the registration process, and I made it clear during my interactions with other delegates that I was conducting research on securities enforcement in Canada. It should also be noted that while the book contains a number of quotes taken from these conferences, the identities of the speakers are not disclosed with the references limited to the titles and dates of the conferences themselves.

Chapter 1

Market matters

Introduction

One of the great ironies of research on financial regulation and securities enforcement is the failure to take markets seriously. Indeed, this is an issue in the larger regulatory literature which tends to frame questions of regulation primarily in terms of law and legal departures while devoting less attention to the unique attributes of regulatory objects themselves. This approach may be tolerated, or at least is much less problematic, in areas of regulation such as industrial pollution or workplace health and safety where there is at least a certain discernible materiality to the practices in question. However, it creates serious difficulties in the context of securities regulation. Financial markets are unlike most other areas of economic activity, constituted as they are in terms of the circulation of 'symbolic property' (Ericson and Haggerty 1997: 199) and the distinct layerings of materiality and virtuality. This first chapter seeks to fill this gap by examining the features of financial markets as a particular type of regulatory object, one that is far removed from the conventional view of finance as a rational space of economic exchange with emphasis placed instead on the social, geographical and technological embeddedness of markets as fields of play. This is the ground on which securities regulators must tread and which shapes both the possibilities and constraints of the enforcement enterprise. Given the foreignness of finance to the uninitiated, this task begins with a brief primer on the markets.

A brief primer on financial markets[1]

As a quick perusal of any basic economics or finance text will reveal, financial markets are defined in terms of formal centres of exchange in which investors come together to buy and sell stakes in a variety of financial products or 'securities', including stocks, bonds, commodities and derivatives. These transactions take place in a variety of fora, the most recognizable of which are the organized exchanges which represent the primary institutional form of the markets and are divided into various areas of specialization. There are dedicated exchanges dealing primarily or exclusively in equities, commodities and derivatives. In addition to the formal exchanges, there are also a number of other trading venues including:

(1) alternative trading systems (ATSs), which trade exchange-listed securities independently of the exchanges themselves based on the promise of superior price discovery and trade execution, among other perks; (2) the 'dealer market', which consists of trading in fixed-income products such as bonds, asset-backed securities and money market instruments; and (3) the 'over-the-counter' (OTC) market, where parties engage in private or 'off board' transactions while benefiting from minimal listing requirements and a decidedly light regulatory touch. Collectively, this 'confederation of markets' (Reichman 1993: 67) is integral to the economy financing corporations and governments, hedging risks and operational liabilities, as well as determining the value of companies and other financial entities in the form of published prices.

In addition to their varied morphology, there are a number of additional attributes that define financial markets and distinguish them from other forms of market-based exchange. First, in contrast with producer and consumer markets, 'Financial markets are not primarily concerned with the production of goods or with their distribution to clients, but with the trading of financial instruments not designed for consumption' (Knorr Cetina and Preda 2005: 4). These financial instruments are abstract, intangible and largely virtual in nature, representing 'claims on future states of the world that they embody: rights to dividends from a corporation, to interest payments from a government and so on' (MacKenzie 2007: 357). This trading on the basis of possible futures is relatively straightforward, in theory if not necessarily in execution, in the context of bread and butter products such as equities and bonds but becomes much more complex in the case of items such as derivatives whose value is determined through an intricate layering of different product futures and thus seemingly remote lines of financial fate.

Second, the transactions that make up financial markets are embedded in a dense interactional network consisting of a variety of players and intermediaries. At its most basic level, this includes issuers, the companies whose stocks (ownership stakes) or bonds (debt obligations) are issued for purchase and sale and the investors who buy and sell these financial stakes. These players are then surrounded by a host of middlemen (the gendering of which is appropriate here) responsible for organizing and executing these transactions and providing advisory services in return for which they receive a commission or percentage of the transaction's value. This includes: (1) the investment banks who underwrite and issue new offerings; (2) the broker/dealers and financial advisers who execute the trades and offer advice on trading strategies and investment portfolios on behalf of retail and institutional investors; and (3) a cast of supporting professionals, ranging from the analysts and ratings agencies who value securities and rate corporate debt, to the lawyers and accountants who oversee corporate financial reporting and advise on the legal ramifications of deals and transactions. Thus, 'creating and distributing a securities product combines a diverse set of actors and organizations into a single network organized around a particular, related product. Each actor has to be both responsive to the deal and also to the larger constellation of actors that embed his or her work' (Reichman 1992: 255).

Third, following from the abstract and future-oriented nature of financial markets, information is a key determinant of value as products are priced on the basis of available information regarding both the product in question and larger economic conditions and circumstances. This linkage between information and financial value informs one of the most influential and long standing philosophies of investment activity, the 'efficient market hypothesis'. This theory holds that the prices of stocks and other financial products perfectly reflect all available information in the marketplace and that, as a result, it is impossible to 'beat the market' by searching for under- or over-valued stock: 'The implication of the hypothesis is that shares are fairly priced, at any given moment, and so it is impossible, at least for the amateur investor, to find "bargains" and so beat the market with any consistency' (Condon et al. 2005: 221). While ostensibly a theory of value, the efficient market hypothesis is also grounded in a view of the markets as highly rationalized spaces of economic exchange with investment decisions rooted in the assessment of objectively available market information, hence the status of investors as rational calculators and investing as an eminently rational activity (Preda 2009a). There is also a subtle normativity to this position as the markets are conceived as being entirely transparent and thus absent the informational asymmetries that would advantage some players over others. This fits with the view of markets as extensions of political democracies and is consistent with narratives of the evolving democratization of finance (Erturk et al. 2007). It is thus the presumptively rational nature of the markets and investing that is the hallmark of the efficient market hypothesis and which continues to inform the cultural imaginings of finance.

Cultural spaces and social spaces

Despite their deep penetration into professional and public consciousness, these representations of rational and transparent markets have come under fire in recent years in the form of behaviouralist theories of finance. Developed by finance scholars as a competing theory of investing, behaviouralist theories challenge the efficient market hypothesis on the grounds that it neglects not only the less rational dimensions of investing, including the impact of investor bias and herd instincts, but also fundamental asymmetries in the availability of information and thus buying and selling opportunities (Langevoort 2002). While this approach certainly opens the door to the social rather than purely economic roots of financial markets, it remains grounded in a rather narrow, individualized and ultimately economistic approach to investing.

For a much broader view of the social side of the markets and investing, a natural place to look would be the social sciences. And yet the relationship between sociology, and other social science disciplines, and the financial markets may best be described as one of benign neglect (Adler and Adler 1984; Baker 1984; Knorr Cetina and Preda 2005; Preda 2007). This oversight stems from a range of possible factors, including a belief that the markets are best left to economists, a view of finance as an overly complex and esoteric area of inquiry (Miller 2001; Preda 2007), a greater interest in producer and consumer markets (Knorr Cetina and Preda 2005) and/or the notion that, amidst a disciplinary orientation towards demystification, the influences of financial interests and dominant forms of political power on this social domain are so transparent as to be uninteresting. Moreover, where the markets have been taken seriously, most notably work in a political economy vein, there is a tendency to subscribe to a view of finance that is not all that different from that of orthodox economics, a point made by de Goede (2005):

> The current literature in the broadly defined field of political economy insufficiently considers the socially and politically constructed nature of money and finance. In fact, many authors assume finance to be an autonomous sphere with clearly defined boundaries and take for granted the unproblematic existence of money, banknotes, credit, financial instruments, etc. as a material starting point to their inquiries (xxv).

Thus, with a handful of notable exceptions (eg Baker 1984, 1990; Abolafia 1996, 1998), social science scholars have devoted very little attention to financial markets and, to the extent that they have engaged with this domain, have tended to reify and rationalize finance in a manner that makes them rather awkward bedfellows with the economists.

Fortunately, this situation has changed quite dramatically of late with the emergence of what is variously described as 'cultural economy', 'the social studies of finance' or 'the sociology of financial markets'. Situated within the larger tradition of economic sociology, and building on earlier contributions from authors such as White (1981), Granovetter (1985), and Fligstein (1996), this diverse body of work is grounded in an appreciation for the distinctiveness of finance and financial markets as a particular social and institutional site. Most critically, rather than approaching the markets as reified, hyper-rational domains catering to the interests of financial capital conceived as a relatively singular and homogeneous actor-subject, this tradition seeks to examine both the social, cultural and geographical dimensions of the markets, and the contextualities, contingencies and vulnerabilities of finance as 'knowledge-producing webs of social relationships' (Preda 2007: 507). Emphasis is thus placed on the discursive labours through which the markets are actively constituted and reproduced *as* rational, natural and scientific domains, on the grounding of finance in everyday practices of investing (Aitken 2007; Langley 2008a), on the unique forms of sociality underlying the markets and the role of interpretive communities in driving market exchanges (Knorr Cetina and Bruegger 2002) and on the 'materiality' (MacKenzie 2009) or what Beunza et al. (2006) refer to as 'the *technicality* of financial markets: the role played in those markets by technologies and by systematic forms of knowledge; the concrete, material practices of trading, risk management and regulation' (721, original emphasis). By exposing the material practices, interpretive dynamics and discursive performances at the root of finance, that is the work of production that underlies the markets, the objective of these authors is both to repoliticize that which appears natural and taken for granted (de Goede 2005) and to highlight points of vulnerability that unsettle the financial order of things. Having sketched the basic contours of this admittedly broad tradition, there are three key lines of research that are directly relevant to the study of securities enforcement undertaken in this book.

Interactional/Interpersonal

The first analytical tack involves the notion that financial markets are, at their root, complex social and informational networks. The most obvious manifestation of these social features of the markets are the forms of networking and interpersonal relationships that provide access to information that may not be available to the general public, or at least not available in a form conducive to profit-making opportunities:

> The social organization of Wall Street … reveals little resemblance to the neoclassical imagery. The prevalence of network ties and the premium on inside information make market operations far from the ideal of individual utility maximization with perfect information. Indeed, stock markets across space and time are rife with political interventions, social networks, and power considerations.
>
> (Lie 1997: 343)

This extends well beyond formally sanctionable activities such as insider trading to include what is euphemistically referred to as 'information leakage', as well as the more innocuous circulation of various bits of information, impressions and rumours. Rooted in a very different view of finance as a world of hunches and guesswork, and investing as the leveraging of relatively small and often imagined informational advantages (Abolafia 1996; Lie 1997; Leyshon and Thrift 1997; Thrift 2000; Zaloom 2003; Beunza and Stark 2005), the markets thus consist of socially constituted informational networks with information flows circulating through and across established relationships. As we will soon see, this complex layering of the informational and the social creates challenges for regulators lacking this more finely textured view of the markets.

A second insight offered by this tradition is that investment and trading decisions hinge not simply on the availability of information but on its interpretation as common or shared knowledge. As noted by Abolafia (1998) in a seminal contribution that prefigures the cultural economy tradition:

> Once information has been gathered and sorted, traders employ a networking routine to see how others are perceiving the same or different information. They are in contact with a network of brokers, traders, salespeople, economists, and informants in government agencies. Traders are generally aware that it is

> not the correctness of the interpretation that counts, but rather the degree to which others will read the same information the same way (75).

Similar insights emerge from more recent ethnographic accounts of exchanges and trading rooms, which reveal that traders are regularly confronted with 'informational ambiguities' (Zaloom 2003: 61) and must thus contend with the task of 'figuring out how to pull meaning from interminable streams of numbers' (Pryke and du Gay 2007: 344; see also Zaloom 2003; Beunza and Stark 2005; Preda 2009b). These interpretive challenges have become more rather than less acute in recent years given the growing availability and volume of digitized, real-time market data (Pryke and du Gay 2007: 345; Knorr Cetina and Bruegger 2002; Sassen 2006; Zaloom 2006; Pryke 2010) and changes to the very organization of the markets. What were previously face-to-face exchanges are now highly automated digital networks where trading occurs under a cloak of anonymity through buy and sell orders matched automatically using sophisticated electronic trading systems (Zaloom 2003, 2006). Here social relationships and interpersonal networks, or what MacKenzie (2004) refers to as 'social connectivities' (83), remain crucial as informational ambiguities are negotiated through collective forms of 'interpretive work' (Sassen 2006: 359) or 'communities of interpretation' (Beunza and Stark 2003: 141). This interpretive labour hinges on the ability to make use of various cues and forms of intellectual shorthand as well as to impute motives to on-screen transactions, that is, to infer the 'socially relevant attributes' of trading activity (Preda 2009b). The markets are herein constituted as a kind of shared 'narrative space' (Zaloom 2003: 267), a further testament to the inherently social features of the markets even in their most digitized and thus 'asocial' form.

Geographical/Spatial

The notion that market transactions are dependent on localized interpretive communities and forms of social connectivity also figures prominently in a second research tradition in the sociology of markets. Emerging from the work of cultural and economic geographers, this is a stream that emphasizes the importance of place or space to the operation of financial markets which, despite their increasingly electronic form and global reach, nevertheless remain grounded in specific geographical locales. For evidence of this, authors such as Leyshon and Thrift (Thrift 1994, 2000; Thrift and Leyshon 1994) and Sassen (2004, 2006) point to the enduring status and significance of international financial centres such as New York, London and Tokyo:

> Empirically what stands out in the evidence about the global financial markets after a decade and a half of deregulation, worldwide integration, and major advances in electronic trading is the extent of locational concentration and the premium firms are willing to pay to be in the major centres. Large shares

of many financial markets are disproportionately concentrated in a few financial centres.

(Sassen 2004: 233)

This is certainly the case in Canada where the activities of the major banks and financial institutions are concentrated in a four block stretch of Bay Street in what is widely recognized as the financial district of downtown Toronto. The cultural geographers attribute the stability of these highly localized urban financial centres to the irreducible value of social contacts and connections which offer not only sources of information but also forms of social reflexivity, the 'interpretations and inferences that come with bouncing off information among talented, informed people' (Sassen 2004: 238) and which are only sustained by the kinds of face-to-face exchanges that occur in the meeting rooms and restaurants of the financial district (Thrift 1994; Thrift and Leyshon 1994; Sassen 2004). As noted by Thrift and Leyshon (1994), while there is a 'disembedded electronic space ... there is also a re-embedded set of meeting places (from restaurants to trading floors) where many of the practices of the first space have to be negotiated ... These meeting places become soups of reflexivity, where people work hard to present themselves' (311–12). Markets are thus defined by their geographical moorings with the social features of markets as information orders dependent on the forms of 'spatial agglomeration' (Sassen 2005: 26) that financial districts provide. For Thrift (1994), 'International financial centres will continue because they satisfy essential communicative/interpretive needs that cannot be met through electronic communication. There will be no "end to geography"' (352). This of course begs the question of enforcement's own spatial and geographical roots.

Calculative/Performative

A third course of analysis focuses less on the interactional and interpretive side of the markets and more on what authors such as MacKenzie (2009) refer to as their materialities. This includes the various mechanisms, devices and technologies through which the markets and finance are constituted and performed on a daily basis. Examples include recording technologies such as the stock ticker (Preda 2006), market indices including the Dow Jones Industrial Average (de Goede 2005), calculations of realized rates of return, standard deviation and net asset value per share so critical to personal investing or 'popular finance' (Aitken 2006, 2007; Langley 2008a), audit technologies (Power 1997, 2004; Miller 2008),[2] as well as a range of financial formulas and theorems including those used to determine pricing and predict risk (MacKenzie 2006, 2009). As noted by Beunza and Muniesa (2005): 'The financial space is cluttered with a myriad devices through which actors at stake seek to inform and perform value. Newswires, trading systems, financial analysts' reports, pricing models and various kinds of charts and figures cohabit with lawsuits, regulatory debates, advertising campaigns, trade unions, academic conferences, and professional lobbies' (633).

What is critical is that these devices do not passively record the market's movements or discover hidden properties which can then be exploited in the interests of profit-seeking. Rather, they represent part of 'the material and discursive assemblages that intervene in the construction of markets' (Muniesa et al. 2007: 2), and are part-and-parcel of the practical orderings and discourses that act to produce economically relevant activity (Law 2002: 21; Preda 2002, 2006; MacKenzie 2006; de Goede 2005; MacKenzie et al. 2007). As noted by MacKenzie (2006) in his adoption of the metaphor of an engine rather than a camera, financial theorems and other market devices do not capture the reality of market activity in a way that is then useful for trading, but actively constitute the materiality of the markets by bringing these activities in line with the presuppositions of the theories themselves. These devices are also critical to the enactment of the markets as objective and rational spaces, a kind of natural universe following specific laws of motion that can be discovered and tracked using the right observational strategies, 'From radically unknowable and aleatory, financial markets are transformed into an object of systematic investigation' (Preda 2009a: 111). As noted by de Goede (2005) with respect to the emergence of the Dow Jones index in the late 1800s:

> Perhaps the most important step in the imagination of the financial market as an independent mechanism with its own laws and regularities was the development of stock price averages in the late nineteenth century. The construction of the Dow Jones ... has to be understood as a technology that did not simply represent financial reality but fundamentally transformed the operation of modern credit practices making it possible to imagine the financial market as a coherent entity (101).

A similar point is made by Preda (2006) in his historical account of the stock ticker, a technology that allowed for new visualizations of, and thus engagements with, the markets: 'price variations became visualizations of market transactions and objects of symbolic interpretation. The ticker made market exchanges visible as they happened, disentangled them from local conversations, and transformed them into something that is both abstract and visible in several forms to everybody at once' (775). Directly informed by contributions from actor-network theory (ANT), particularly the work of Callon (1998), this perspective requires that we pay close attention not only to the role of situated human actors in accessing and interpreting the informational ambiguities of the markets but also the distinct forms of agency exercised by market technologies and calculative devices themselves and thus their place in the everyday workings of the markets.

Discursive/Cultural

A fourth aspect of the cultural economy literature that is consistent with the notion that markets are defined by their performative features involves a recognition of the discursive undertones of the markets and their contribution to the legitimation of finance and investing. Departing once again from the political economy literature and the presumption that the legitimacy of finance is unproblematic and more or less assured in capitalist economies, attention is instead devoted to the historical contingencies underlying the markets. This is a 'fragile history' (de Goede 2005: 200) defined by numerous points of rupture and uncertainty with the mainstream acceptance of investing as a legitimate practice and social endeavour indebted to a range of cultural, financial and legal discourses. According to de Goede (2005), a key transition point came in the late 19th century during which time investing was more sharply distinguished from gambling, thanks in large part to cultural and legal discourses that demonized the latter as morally objectionable and valorized the former as an eminently rational and indeed socially virtuous pursuit defined by calculable risks. As noted by Preda (2005), this also included a shift in the cultural figure of the investor from a treacherous and sinful gambler to what he describes as an 'investor scientist' dedicated to discovering the universal laws of the markets.

This cultural and discursive fabric remains essential to the legitimacy of the markets today with a key role in the contemporary context played by the news media and in particular the financial press, which has morphed from a mere footnote to the daily news to dedicated, 24 hour news channels (Leyshon and Thrift 1997; Leyshon et al. 1998; Clark et al. 2004). Offering a continuous stream of commentaries and prognostications, these popularized accounts further glamorize and glorify the markets as democratized spaces essential to the wellbeing of the nation at the same time as they reaffirm a belief in the markets as inherently rational and apolitical centres of financial exchange (Frank 2000; Clark et al. 2004; Selden 2006). Thus, 'the press and television have become powerful ordering forces in the modern international financial system' (Leyshon et al. 1998: 306) and represent a 'new form of discursive power in the financial markets' (Clark et al. 2004: 290). Operating alongside these media accounts are a seemingly endless supply of self-help and how-to guides, government pamphlets on saving and investing and advertising materials, which further solidify the view of the investor as a prudent, responsible subject obligated to plan for their own financial future (Aitken 2006, 2007; Langley 2008a) and investment advisers as staid professionals offering wisdom, guidance and advice. Collectively, these accounts make up the discursive fabric of the markets and investing and are essential sites through which finance is constituted, performed and legitimated.

The matter of enforcement

Through this foray into the cultural economy literature, we have arrived at a very different understanding of finance and the markets than is typically provided at the hands of both classical economics and political economists. Markets are far from the highly rationalized engines of financial exchange envisioned by these accounts and they lack the imputed homogeneity of interests and the qualities of naturalness and inevitability, products of their representation rather than their reality. Instead, they are complex social and cultural spaces constituted in terms of interpersonal relationships, information flows and transactional networks, as well as a host of devices, technologies and discourses through which they are performed and reproduced hour-by-hour and day-by-day. They are also tied to social connections that emerge from the concentration of activities in particular urban geographies, and thus the formation of distinct knowledge-based communities. In this respect, markets both extend across time and space and yet are aggregated along particular interpretive and epistemic currents. While these insights may be interesting in-and-of-themselves, they are critical for our purposes suggesting that enforcement efforts are directed towards a particular kind of regulatory object, the features of which will invariably inform, shape and hinder these efforts themselves. With this in mind, there are a number of core insights emerging from the social, geographical, technological and discursive dimensions of the markets that have a critical bearing on the enforcement enterprise.

Networks

The first insight is that enforcement agents must contend with the reality that the markets and finance are defined in terms of social networks. The financial transactions that make up the markets are constituted through a constantly shifting set of relationships and information streams extending across time and space. These relationships may be well established or ephemeral. They may involve conflicts of interest, divided loyalties and forms of collusion that may or may not run afoul of existing laws. Here regulators face the daunting task of having to penetrate these networks with the specific nature of the connections between two individuals or accounts often determining the legitimacy of a given transaction. They are also dependent on documentary and data-based footprints which may or may not be available and they must ascertain not only the flow of information, funds and transactions but also the social identities of those concerned. The difficulty of course is that the close and informal social ties that underlie market transactions create conditions of secrecy and complicity that mitigate against the very forms of visibility required by enforcement agents. There are thus fundamental questions regarding the ability of regulators to ascertain the social features of financial transactions with the distinct intermingling of the social and the financial constituting a key investigative barrier. The complexity of these underlying networks also begs the question of the regulatory division of labour, that is how regulators divide responsibility for the governance of this diverse financial space and its footings in myriad products, exchanges and institutional hubs (eg banking, insurance, brokerages), and the limitations that these configurations invariably create.

Spaces

Second, as indicated by the cultural geographers, regulators must contend not only with the social, but also the spatial and in particular the geographical features of the markets. Many of the social relationships and information flows discussed above possess a nodal quality as they flow through and are shaped by geographically defined urban financial centres. This impacts the movement of information through contacts and connections, as well as its intelligibility or digestibility as the epistemic communities that cluster within these geographically defined spaces provide collective frames of reference through which the markets and their movements are made sensible, akin to the knowledge that an increase in interest rates or a negative jobs report will move the markets in a particular direction, but possessing a much more specific and distinct form. This social topography of the markets raises critical questions as to the ability of regulators to position themselves within these spaces, to forge contacts and to tap into existing interpretive communities. To the extent that enforcement agencies and their staff are removed from these socio-geographical enclaves, their ability to access localized market networks and draw from these centres of discursive authority may be impaired. In this respect, their position in both *social* and *physical* space is an important consideration.

Materialities

Third, the practice of enforcement will invariably be shaped by the materialities of the market. Constituted in terms of a 'socio-technical network' (Beunza and Stark 2003; see also, Callon 1998), both the reality of and the regulatory engagement with the markets is dependent on computers, software, technological capacities and supports, as well as non-computerized 'technologies' including worksheets, forms, audits and all manner of records and documentary recordings. One of the key issues here is that, despite the fact that the markets are more transparent and visible than ever, this with the move to electronic trading and the ability to access trading data in real-time, regulators are invariably limited to a rather narrow set of indicators through which they must gauge market movements and discern signs of disorder. An important question is thus how these technologies and materialities shape the enforcement enterprise as regulators are confined to the virtual or documentary skin of the markets and yet must penetrate beneath the surface and probe their social innards. This is a task made especially difficult given that they are also obliged to work within the confines of a legal regime that imposes its own set of material constraints including evidentiary requirements, testimonial formats and standards of proof that require extensive documentary labour and a degree and form of access to the markets that enforcement staff may ultimately lack. The materialities confronting regulators are thus constituted both 'inside' and 'outside' of law.

Discourses

Moving beyond the more immediate substrate of the markets, the regulatory project is also shaped by the manner in which finance and investing are represented in academic and popular discourse. This influence takes a variety of different forms. First, it is the imagined characteristics of both the markets and investors that sets the stage for the regulatory project, including the objectives and appropriate scope of enforcement efforts. Thus, the ascendancy of the efficient market hypothesis (Selden 2006) and the cultural image of the investor-scientist (Preda 2005) have contributed to a regulatory system that, at its core, is dedicated to transparency and disclosure as prime directives rather than a more active role as arbiter of the quality and worth of offerings. Were markets shorn of their seemingly natural efficiencies and investors seen as unsophisticated and in need of protection from sharp practices, the regulatory system would look very different, as would the acceptable range of regulatory motion. Second, the practice of enforcement is shaped by cultural narratives that conceive of wrongdoing in terms of moral culpability and individual blameworthiness. According to this logic, the most serious offences are those that involve deliberate misconduct on the part of marginal or 'rogue' figures[3] preying on 'innocent' victims, an attributional frame and moral register that informs the criteria brought to bear on enforcement cases and supplies the forms of narrativity essential to successful outcomes.

Finally, there is the reality that regulation is itself part of the discursive fabric of the markets. It is a means of responding to misconduct at the same time as it is a source of documents and commentaries that reinforce our collective belief in the safety of the markets as well tended spaces of investment and exchange. Engaged in the production of both cases and accounts, enforcement is itself a kind of discursive project, one of the 'strong nodal points of (discursive) authority' (de Goede 2005: xxiii) through which our faith in the markets is reproduced and reaffirmed. As we will soon see, it is the credibility and legitimacy of enforcement agencies themselves that is central to this process.

Morphologies

A final set of market-related influences stems from changes to the structure and organization, or morphology, of the markets. One such shift is the aforementioned move from face-to-face to electronic markets, as well as the availability of digitally packaged and real-time market data, a transformation that has accorded a greater visibility to the markets while at the same time increasing the demands on regulators in terms of processing and interpreting this information. Another notable development is greater levels of concentration and consolidation in the financial sector (Moran 1991; Minns 2001). On the 'sell side', single sector firms have given way to large financial conglomerates which combine banking, securities and insurance under a single roof, a sharp break from the past where the financial industry was organized according to distinct sectors or 'pillars'.[4] This has had the effect, among other things, of fuelling the growth of the mutual fund industry as the entry of the banks has dramatically expanded the market of potential investors and offered a new-found sense of security and credibility (Reynolds 2005). Forms of consolidation are also evident on the 'buy side' of the market, the most obvious of which is the increasing size and influence of institutional investors such as mutual funds, pension funds and hedge funds (Zey 1998; Harmes 2001; Minns 2001). This growth has been fuelled by the privatization of pensions and social security programs (Clark 2000, 2003; Langley 2008a), as well as the incentives provided by government-run tax shelters such as the Canadian RRSP program.[5] Beyond dramatically increasing the stakes of regulatory action, these changes have contributed to the deepening of conflicts of interest while creating new incentives and opportunities for gaming the market. They have also reduced the size, scope and, ultimately, the visibility of market networks leaving fewer footprints to be identified and tracked by regulators.

The rapid growth of the institutional sector in particular has spurred a number of additional developments which have further muddied the regulatory waters. The first is an incessant drive towards innovation and the development of new products and services. With fund managers holding ever greater amounts of investable capital, and returns from more conventional investments such as stocks and bonds dampened by historically low interest rates, there is an ever greater demand for new products offering higher than average returns. The investment banks and brokerage firms have been more than happy to oblige, offering a seemingly endless supply of new, or newly re-engineered, and increasingly complex products. This is significant as many of these products fall under permissible market exemptions and are thus subject to limited regulatory oversight while their complexity is itself a drag on regulatory efforts. As noted by one respondent, 'product innovation has been very impressive and a constant challenge for regulators because new products tend to be more complicated or more esoteric, and it's very difficult for a lot of these people to develop the knowledge base to deal with them' (Consultant #1: 2).

A second trend worthy of note is the emergence and rapid growth of new forms of trading. Included here are the aforementioned alternative trading systems, which have surged in both number and volume and now represent serious competitors to the established exchanges for trade and order flow. Similar expansion is evident in the 'over-the-counter' (OTC) market, which is significant given that these transactions are entirely private and are thus removed from the public markets altogether. Combined with the growth of anonymous trading, whereby favoured clients are given direct access to broker terminals allowing them to trade without the knowledge or intermediation of individual brokers, the result of these developments is the increasing fragmentation of the markets creating additional difficulties for regulators unable to peer across and into these various currents of exchange. The larger repercussions of these changes are noted by a long-established regulator: 'Recent global developments in both regulation and market structure underscore the blurring of lines between conventional exchanges, ATSs, financial intermediaries, and markets. New products, new players, new trading systems, and new technologies must be matched by a new approach to regulation' (Wolburgh Jenah 2008). With agencies so far slow to respond, the enforcement of these shifting spaces of finance remains a key challenge.

Conclusion

By way of this detour through the cultural economy and sociology of markets literatures, the practice of securities enforcement has been cast in a very different light. Rather than a distinct institutional form bounded by specific legal obligations, it would appear that the possibilities and limits of enforcement are shaped through the characteristics of the markets as particular kinds of social spaces. Here the question of *how* enforcement unfolds in practice must contend with the networks, spaces, materialities, discourses and morphologies through which the markets are themselves performed and reproduced. These unique features are significant to the extent that they shape the production of regulatory knowledge and thus impact the very *knowledgeability* of the markets. Viewing these attributes in the context of questions of knowledge and conditions of knowledgeability is thus critical to developing a more nuanced understanding of securities enforcement. While this must necessarily be informed by an appreciation of the power and influence wielded by financial capital, the complexities of the markets as social, geographical, technological and cultural entities suggest that this accounts for only part of the story, drawing into question approaches that rely exclusively on invocations of capture and/or accommodation. A final implication of this engagement with the markets is that enforcement and finance cannot be viewed as fundamentally separate domains with regulation conceived as something that is *done to* the markets, whether as an external force polluting the market's natural efficiencies or as a necessary corrective to its inevitable excesses. Rather than distinct realities, one economic and the other legal, regulation and the markets must be viewed as mutually constitutive (Burk 1988; Stenning et al. 1990; Shearing 1993; de Goede 2005) with enforcement representing part of the very fabric of the markets: 'Regulation is not something done to a market by watchdogs ... but is rather an integral feature of the market, undertaken by those involved in it. Regulation does not merely control a market. It constitutes it' (Stenning et al. 1990: 116). It is these fundamental interconnections and their spatial, cultural, technological and discursive roots, which inform the analysis of securities enforcement to follow, starting with the philosophies and mandates that enliven the enforcement project.

Notes

1 Technically, the markets discussed in this chapter and which define the formal mandates of securities regulators are 'capital markets' – that is, markets devoted to raising investment capital through the sale of equity or debt-backed securities and the subsequent trading in these securities in the secondary market – as opposed to, for example, 'money markets', which involve trading in short-term debt or 'derivatives markets', which are based on contracts used to hedge risk. However, in recognition of the blurring of 'capital', 'money', and 'derivatives' markets, as was evident in the US sub-prime crisis, along with the move by regulators in Canada, the US and Europe to bring derivatives under the umbrella of securities regulation (Anand 2010), the broader term 'financial markets' is used in this and all future chapters.

2 While work on the calculative devices of accounting and auditing is not formally associated with the social studies of finance, there are some interesting parallels including the notion that the audit does not simply reflect the financial condition of a company but rather actively constitutes it, what Power (1997) refers to as the process of 'making things auditable' (87). A similar sense of performativity is evident in the work of Miller (2001) who argues that: 'As one of the preeminent means of quantification in certain Western societies, accounting accords a specific type of *visibility* to events and processes, and in so doing helps transform them' (393, emphasis added).

3 The reference to 'rogues', and in particular the cultural figure of the 'rogue' broker, is a commonly employed linguistic device used in both industry and regulatory parlance to signal the egregiousness of misconduct, its clear and incontrovertible departure from normal market practices and the limited responsibility of the larger organization in which it occurs. It is thus indicative of a particular language of culpability and politics of blame and is part of the cultural mythology of white-collar crime (Poveda 1994).

4 In Canada, these 'pillars' included: (1) chartered banks; (2) trust companies and credit unions; (3) insurance companies; and (4) securities dealers with the erosion of the four pillars dating to legislative amendments in 1987 and 1992 which removed restrictions barring other financial institutions from owning more than 10 per cent of a broker/dealer. Following these changes, the big banks quickly assumed controlling interest in the largest brokerage houses in the country. This trend is by no means unique to Canada. The US repeal of Glass-Steagall in 1999, the depression era law that separated commercial from investment banking, contributed to a similar wave of consolidation in that country's financial sector.

5 The Registered Retirement Savings Plan (RRSP) was proposed by the federal government in 1957 as a means of levelling the playing field between individuals who had employer-sponsored pension plans and those who did not (*Globe and Mail* 2010). Since then the program has grown into a key investment medium and a major source of revenue for the financial industry.

Chapter 2

Mandates and mantras of securities enforcement

Introduction

The move from the markets to the enforcement enterprise begins with the recognition that securities regulation and enforcement are fundamentally delivered by and through organizations, and thus bear the imprint of organizational logics and interests. In light of these organizational horizons, this chapter documents the principles and expectations that inform the larger project of securities regulation and examines their impact upon, and their translation into, the operational mandates and working practices of enforcement units. With regulators expected to protect the integrity of the markets at the same time as they are exhorted not to rule with too heavy a hand lest investors abandon national markets for more favourable regulatory climes, of particular interest are the points of tension and contradiction within these mandates and how these tensions are subsequently managed by regulatory agencies *as organizations*. Drawing from the wider organizational literature, a key question for the chapter is the extent to which the management of organizational appearances becomes an overriding concern, yielding a public face for these agencies that may be somewhat out-of-sync with the daily realities of enforcement on-the-ground. This is an analysis that begins with the historical context and evolution of securities regulation from its roots in the financial turmoil of the early 1900s.

Securities regulation comes to the fore

While the distribution, purchase and sale of interests in corporations, governments and commodities dates back to the early 1600s, with fraud dating back equally as far, financial markets did not assume their modern form until the late 1800s and early 1900s with the emergence of organized exchanges in the nascent financial centres of London and New York. Spurred by government bond markets and a growing number of industrial and financial stocks,[1] these exchanges operated largely in the absence of formal regulation relying instead on gentlemanly persuasion, the limits of which were revealed in the prevalence of deceit, manipulation and outright fraud throughout this period (Geisst 2004). This state of affairs persisted well into the 1920s (Smith and Walter 2006), notwithstanding campaigns to crack down on bucket shops,[2] which were seen not only as a source of competition for the exchanges but also a threat to their legitimacy as they were less easily distinguished from gambling and thus fed into deep-seated suspicions of speculative trading (de Goede 2005; Preda 2005).

The emergence of securities regulation

This situation of relatively free and unfettered markets changed dramatically in the early 1930s following the market crash of 1929 and the ensuing Great Depression (Burk 1988). Given the scale of the losses, their disastrous economic repercussions and their roots in a variety of nefarious practices, this represented one of the first moments in which the markets and the question of market regulation became sufficiently politicized so as to warrant state intervention. Through the legislative measures that followed in 1933 and 1934, a new regulatory architecture was erected in the US, the most visible manifestation of which was the Securities and Exchange Commission (SEC), the federal agency tasked with enforcing the newly enacted securities laws. While not without its detractors, and immediately confronted by efforts to dilute its founding legislation and mandate, the establishment of the SEC was a watershed moment in the regulation of financial markets, which were thus reconstituted as legitimate sites of regulatory scrutiny.

Similar developments unfolded in many other national contexts, although not necessarily at the same pace or with the same level of conviction. In Canada, securities legislation was enacted in a number of provinces in the 1920s and 1930s, although this was framed primarily in terms of fraud prevention rather than market regulation, a period which included the founding of the Ontario Securities Commission in 1931.[3] Not surprisingly, these developments had minimal effect as Canadian markets enjoyed considerable autonomy throughout the 1930s, 1940s and 1950s (Armstrong 2001),[4] with regulatory efforts not ramping up until the 1960s following a series of financial scandals and a growing fear of market infiltration by organized crime groups. These events spurred the expansion of the OSC which, with the passage of the Ontario Securities Act in 1966, assumed a much more active role in market regulation. By way of various Royal Commissions and federal-provincial conferences, the 1960s also saw the first federal police involvement in market enforcement in the form of the RCMP's Commercial Crime program.

Notwithstanding these different rates of growth, the legislative developments of the 1930s initiated a legacy of securities regulation that played a critical role, particularly in the wake of the Great Depression, in legitimating the markets and constituting them as both *regulatable* and *well regulated* spaces safe for public investment (de Goede 2005). This regulatory function remains critical today as it continues to attract significant resources and attention and, more importantly, is one of the first rallying points in times of crisis. And yet, despite these developments and assertions of regulatory effort, the practice of securities regulation remains mired in a series of ambiguous and contradictory logics as well as recurring debates as to the appropriate mandate and scope of the regulatory enterprise. In order to understand these tensions and their impact, it is necessary to examine in greater detail the mandates of securities regulators as they have evolved from their roots in the 1930s and how these mandates are defined, framed and actualized in the daily work of regulatory officials.

Mission improbable: The logics and principles of securities regulation

Informed by the turmoil of the past and the desire to curtail abuses that would bring the integrity of the markets into disrepute, the mandates of securities regulators are rooted in a number of core principles and organizing logics. These are outlined in statutory legislation which provides agencies with their authority, powers and jurisdiction, as well as public statements, declarations and commentaries through which this mandate is continually reshaped, reaffirmed and defended, all in the name of investor confidence, market integrity and the promotion of economic growth and prosperity. Reflecting the myriad interests at play in this arena and the highly politicized nature of regulation itself, one of the most notable features of this regulatory mandate is its internal tensions and contradictions. These assume a variety of different forms.

Disclosure versus oversight

The first of these tensions involves the core logic and raison d'être of securities regulation and the question of whether the regulatory enterprise should be geared to policing the quality of offerings, with those deemed to be of low value excluded from the public markets, or instead to guaranteeing transparency with the investing public responsible for making decisions as to the soundness of individual investments. These approaches hinge on very different interpretations of both the nature of the markets and the attributes and sophistication of investors. The former assumes that markets are replete with nefarious practices and poor quality offerings, and that investors are naïve and unsophisticated, thus requiring a degree of protection. In contrast, the latter is rooted in a faith in the antiseptic qualities of information and the ability of rational investors to identify questionable investments if they are simply provided with the right data. Interestingly, it was the first view that dominated early approaches to securities regulation. Bolstered by the frauds and scams that were a regular feature of the markets in the early 1900s and an openly sceptical attitude towards the growing crowds of newbie investors (Geisst 2004), the emphasis of these first legislative efforts was on fraud prevention and enforcement as driving regulatory principles and the passage of what were commonly referred to as 'blue sky laws' (Armstrong 1997, 2001). Named for securities of questionable worth that promise the 'blue sky', these laws empowered officials to vet new offerings with those deemed to be of low or questionable quality barred from the public markets. This kind of active guardianship is in fact what many people still believe to be the mandate and core function of securities regulators.

Starting in the 1930s in the US and in the 1940s in Canada, this approach was largely abandoned as the blue sky laws were replaced by a system based on the logics of disclosure and informational transparency (Shapiro 1984; Armstrong 2001; Selden 2006) mandating that 'the [regulator] would not act as a judge about whether or not a company would succeed, but leave it to the investor to make an informed decision on whether to put up money' (Armstrong 2001: 42). Rather than oversight, the emphasis was on ensuring that investors were provided with timely disclosures of material information relating to the status and operations of publicly traded companies with regulation geared to remedying informational deficiencies (Selden 2006). It is no coincidence that this reliance on disclosure as a core regulatory principle came on the heels of the shifting representations of the markets and investing noted in the previous chapter. Thus, the progressive rationalization of the markets, the emergence of the efficient markets hypothesis and the notion that the markets are bound to a kind of natural and self-regulating equilibrium gave credence to the belief that the purpose of regulation is simply to facilitate natural market tendencies. Equally important was the shift in the view of the investor noted by Preda (2005) from someone who needed protection from the inevitable excesses of the market to the rational investor-scientist who could, with the properly disclosed information, make accurate determinations as to the value of securities on their own behalf. Regardless of the obvious flaws in this reasoning, including the inability of most investors to make sense of disclosed information and to assume the required degree of engagement in managing their financial affairs (Langevoort 1996; Black 2006; Selden 2006), this disclosure-based logic continues to hold sway. The result is not only dissatisfied investors who feel that regulators should be doing more to protect their investments, but also the devotion of scarce organizational energies to the task of monitoring disclosure practices and cajoling violators into correcting faulty disclosures rather than taking on potentially more serious problems in the marketplace: 'In short, as far as regulation is concerned, transparency enhancement seems to be the only game in town' (Blyth 2003: 245).

Protective versus remedial

A second point of mandate-related tension involves the question of whether the goal of regulators is primarily protective or remedial in nature. From the point of view of individual investors who have lost money as a result of alleged misconduct, the expectation is that the regulators will assist them in recovering these funds by investigating their cases and providing restitution or other forms of pecuniary remedy:

> Individual investors who have lost their savings due to the misconduct of regulated market participants are most interested in being compensated. They conceive of the securities regulator's role in protecting investors as helping them to be made whole and they are interested in seeing

> securities regulators play a greater role in facilitating compensation for their losses.
>
> (Puri 2005: 8)

That restitution should be a core part of the regulatory mandate is not inconsistent with practices in other jurisdictions. For example, the SEC frequently directs extracted fines and penalties to the compensation of individual investors. Moreover, it is in no way prohibited by existing securities legislation with Canadian regulators possessing a fair amount of discretion and latitude in how they opt to proceed in terms of the disbursement of fines.

And yet, despite regular calls for a greater emphasis on restitution, the long-standing position of those in the regulatory community is that their mandate is not to provide remediation for the losses suffered by individual investors but rather to take action to protect the wellbeing of the markets as a whole:[5] 'The regulatory regime is not designed to resolve [investor disputes] because theirs is a micro problem and the regulators are macro solutions. And the OSC perceives its mandate to be to police the markets in broad terms and to set policy and enforce policy. It's not there to micro-manage' (Lawyer #13: 2–3). According to a senior OSC official:

> There hasn't been a lot of consideration given to the possibility that securities commissions would reinvent themselves into vehicles for pursuing civil lawsuits on behalf of individuals who have been hurt. That certainly is not the jurisdiction that governments anywhere have granted to securities commissions. The primary responsibility is a forward looking market protection responsibility.
>
> (Dialogue with the OSC 2007)

When challenged on philosophical grounds, regulators often fall back on what they see as the nightmarish logistical challenges of restitution: 'The time and expense that goes into proof of civil claims to show causation and to show the quantum of damages in a way that courts can be sufficiently satisfied so that repayment of money can be made is quite huge. We're not structured that way' (Dialogue with the OSC 2004). This is reiterated by a member of the IDA who notes that it is 'really difficult to calculate and evaluate the loss. Quite honestly it would take up so much resources that it would be very difficult. And then there's the allocation issue. How many clients should be allocated the funds?' (IDA #5: 6). In resisting restitution, regulators also point to the availability of other options such as arbitration and civil suits notwithstanding their practical limits and limited accessibility for the average investor. Again, the result of these tensions is a sizeable expectations gap around what regulators are expected versus willing to deliver, a key lightning rod for enforcement's critics.

Preventative versus disciplinary

Another notable source of tension that flows from the collective versus individual orientation of the regulatory system involves the question of whether deterrence is a valid consideration in enforcement actions and, in particular, decisions around appropriate sanctions in individual cases. While one might imagine that the ability of regulators to mete out penalties that are punitive in nature and designed to send a message regarding the impropriety of conduct is a given in the securities world, this is in fact a source of considerable debate. For example, commentators such as Condon et al. (2005) have asserted that the underlying philosophy behind regulatory sanctioning should be the protection of societal interests rather than the punishment of individual faults. Treading on less philosophical and more strategic ground, legal counsel challenge the justification for deterrence on the grounds that it not only contradicts the protective and preventative mandate of regulators but also unjustifiably brings securities commissions into the orbit of criminal law, thus blurring the distinction between regulatory and criminal domains. In a seminal case on this issue, *Cartaway Resources*, the BC Court of Appeal held that a sanction based on general deterrence was beyond the public interest jurisdiction of the BC Securities Commission and that the commission could only sanction a respondent to the extent necessary to restrain future misconduct. A collective sigh of relief went through the regulatory community when this decision was overturned by the Supreme Court of Canada, which held that general deterrence is indeed an appropriate factor to be considered by securities regulators.

What is especially interesting about this debate is the artificial tension that is presumed between the mandates of protecting the integrity of the markets and punishing wrongdoing. In theory, these would appear to be mutually compatible and internally consistent objectives. And yet, as revealed by the comments of former OSC chair David Brown: 'The huge myth about the OSC is that we're all about securities fraud. Our mandate is investor protection and fostering market integrity, which is a different mission' (in Willis 2005: B8). A similar sentiment follows from the eschewal of comparisons between the OSC and the likes of Eliot Spitzer in the US: 'Mr. Spitzer is a law enforcement official. His mandate is to bring lawbreakers to justice. The OSC is a regulator. We have a mandate to promote the integrity of the capital markets' (Dialogue with the OSC 2004). Strange that the objective of bringing law-breakers to justice is so clearly differentiated from that of fostering confidence in the integrity of the markets. These kinds of distinctions clearly speak to the ambiguity at the heart of the regulatory mandate and the political stakes at play in how this mandate is carved up across the enforcement spectrum.

Market integrity and investor protection versus market efficiency and global competitiveness

A final and in many respects overarching point of tension in the mandate of securities regulators is a fundamental contradiction in its guiding principles. On the one hand, regulators are required to bolster investor confidence and market integrity through an active enforcement regime that intervenes to prevent and punish a range of abuses. However, on the other hand, there is an expectation that this pursuit be tempered by a concern for the impact of these activities on the efficiency and liquidity, as well as the competitiveness, of the markets. This need to strike a delicate balance between the promise of safe, transparent and well regulated markets and the promotion of liquidity, efficiency and innovation in market transactions has long been recognized as a core feature of financial regulation (Stenning et al. 1990; Reichman 1991, 1993; Levi 1993; Abolafia 1996) and is directly expressed in the formal mandate of agencies such as the OSC which seeks: 'To provide protection to investors from unfair, improper or fraudulent practices and to foster fair and efficient capital markets and confidence in capital markets' (http://www.osc.gov.on.ca). In one of his many legislative submissions, former OSC chair David Wilson posed the dilemma in the following terms:

> We strive to find the right balance when it comes to regulation. We clearly cannot have markets that have little or no regulation … On the other hand, we shouldn't over-regulate. Weighing down the markets with too much regulation in an effort to reduce investor risk simply creates a market that's inefficient and not competitive with other capital markets around the world.
> (Wilson 2008)

These tensions are also a centrepiece of reports on securities regulation in Canada and the US[6] where they are invoked, typically in the first few pages, to highlight the need for restraint as a core regulatory principle: 'Securities regulation must protect investors and promote market integrity, while achieving effective regulatory outcomes without imposing unnecessary compliance burdens' (Expert Panel 2009: 6).

There are a number of insights and implications that emerge from this discursive framing of regulation. First, the very juxtaposition of integrity and efficiency positions these regulatory objectives in terms of a zero-sum game in which gains in the former are invariably made at the expense of the latter. This kind of dichotomization is a regular feature of market and financial discourse (Williams 2008a) and reproduces the seemingly natural opposition between law and the markets, this despite the fact that a strong enforcement regime has actually been shown to decrease the cost of equity and increase the liquidity of markets (Bhattacharya 2006: 139). It may thus be the case that this dichotomy is more imagined than real:

> I do not think it's a dual mandate. I think that the … role of protecting investors includes the need to make sure that the market is operating fairly and efficiently. The regulators are reading it as 'Protect investors. Have a fair and efficient capital market'. And they say that to have a fair and efficient capital market, you have to do things that may shortchange investors. I don't buy that.
> (Consultant #2: 10)

Second, the belief that any improvements to regulation and enforcement will invariably be accompanied by potentially burdensome costs to the markets has resulted in an increasing reliance on cost-benefit analyses, and thus the requirement that proposals for regulatory change satisfy a cost and efficiency-based litmus test if they are to be favourably received. These are included not as mere considerations amongst a larger batch of criteria, but rather fundamental principles driving the policy-making process. As noted in the terms of reference for a major review of the regulatory infrastructure in Canada: 'We recommend that the guiding principles of regulatory conduct include the need for regulation to be cost-effective. We also recommend that they reflect the need to facilitate innovation and maintain the competitiveness of Canada's capital markets' (Expert Panel 2009: 12).

From a regulatory standpoint, these kinds of cost-benefit calculations are not particularly helpful and often lean towards the consideration of costs rather than benefits. The recollections of a former regulator are especially telling on this point:

> Cost-benefit analyses are really quite misleading. They're difficult to do. You can generally get a handle on the costs, although not with the scientific accuracy that you would hope, but you can virtually never get a handle on the benefits. Because the costs accrue to one party and the benefits accrue to another. And brokers look at the cost-benefit analysis, 'well it's going to cost us this, this, and this. But what are the benefits? There are no benefits to us.' And we kept saying 'well yeah but the benefit is to investors or to the reputation of the marketplace.' And we put out these cost-benefit analyses knowing that they were going to get torn apart ... It became a bit of a mugs game and highly political.
>
> (Former OSC #1: 7–8)

A similar dilemma of quantification and calculability confronts regulators in their efforts to communicate their activities and effectiveness in numerical form. As noted by Hawkins (2002): 'one of the major problems which regulatory organizations must constantly confront is how they can establish and display their success in combating the problems they were set up to control' (8), a sentiment echoed by a former senior manager at the OSC who noted that: 'We are under tremendous scrutiny to say how we measure ourselves' (Securities Litigation 2006). The fallback for regulators, particularly enforcement units, is to invoke stock indicators of regulatory activity such as the number of open files, proceedings and administrative orders initiated over a calendar year, or the value of fines levied through the enforcement process. This very tactic was used by former OSC chair David Wilson during questioning before a legislative committee: 'On a generic basis, I'd say that we are not unhappy to have 250 open investigation files. It proves, in numerical terms, that we are very active and busy' (Wilson 2008). The limitations of this kind of quantitative benchmarking are noted by Puri (2005) who asks: 'If more cases are opened, closed, or settled over previous years, is enforcement any more effective? It may be that simpler or more complex matters were taken on' (24). The added difficulty for regulators is that, in the absence of meaningful indicators of enforcement activity, critics invariably fall back on loose impressions of regulatory effectiveness gleaned from anecdotes and the statements of 'opinion leaders'; hence the '*perception* both in Canada and abroad that serious misconduct in Canada too often goes unpunished' (WPC 2003: 26, emphasis added).

However, it is not only the quantifiability of regulatory activity and its benefits that bedevils regulators, but also the question of the groups to whom these benefits should accrue. Despite the imputed universalism of the investor-subject, the population making up the universe of investors is in fact incredibly diverse, ranging from retail investors, to day traders, to pension and hedge funds, to brokerage firms engaging in their own proprietary trading, with each of these groups possessing different sets of interests and stakes in both the markets and the regulatory system: 'The commission has got a lot of interest groups to deal with and what is right for one is not right for the other' (Lawyer #15: 8). This balance of interests becomes even more complicated when other stakeholders such as issuing companies and non-investors are added to the mix, thus further problematizing 'the public interest' as a guidepost for the regulatory system. A perfect expression of these tensions emerges in cases where regulators face the prospect that, in taking action against senior management, they may harm shareholders, the 'real' victims, by triggering a loss of confidence in the company and a sell-off of its stock. This Catch-22 is nicely illustrated by a member of the OSC: '[Strong enforcement] could be counterintuitive. Do you want big failures of Canadian corporations? Doesn't that tell you that the capital markets may be weak here if you have major failures?' (OSC #4: 4). In the words of a senior legal counsel: 'in any context you have to ask yourself at the end of the day, if your interest in the public capital market is protection of shareholders' interests and creation of value, are shareholders ultimately going to be helped or harmed by what's going on?' (Lawyer #19: 1–2). The result of these different constituencies and interest groups is that securities regulators operate on the basis of 'divided loyalties' (Yudelman 2001: 21) with some groups asserting that regulators such as the OSC are 'out of control' and 'far too aggressive', while others ask 'where is enforcement?' and inquire as to why they 'seldom track down any wrongdoing' (Dialogue with the OSC 2004).

Seeking to free themselves from the horns of this dilemma, regulators find little guidance from the terms of their mandate and core concepts such as 'public interest', 'investor confidence' and 'market integrity'. Given the different constituencies to which regulators are beholden, '"protecting the public interest" turns out to be an equivocal and ambiguous concept that means different things in different contexts' (Stenning et al. 1990: 117). Similarly, 'Market confidence is … an inter-subjective construction that has a tenuous relationship to market fundamentals but does not have any precise, calculable metric' (Blyth 2003: 257). As revealed in another major report on the Canadian regulatory system, these terms are often used in combination with one serving to define the other in a kind of semantic tautology: 'Capital market integrity can be thought of as a level of general confidence in the functioning of the market. Integrity is closely related to investors' perception of the fairness of the markets' (Task Force 2006: 29). Clearly the problem here is that, despite their near incessant invocation through market commentaries and regulatory discourses, these terms are inherently ambiguous and thus resistant to any precise definition. They are 'performative mythical [entities]' (Hertz and Lepinay 2003: 23), semantically porous and infused with different and frequently contradictory meanings (Reichman 1991; Williams 2008a). Ironically, it may be this very ambiguity that informs their value. Like empty vessels, they can be filled with a variety of different interpretations and used to justify very different kinds of positions while, by virtue of their resistance to definition and clear quantification, they benefit from a built-in unfalsifiability. Thus, both a campaign of deregulation and the boosting of enforcement resources may be argued positively to impact 'investor confidence'. This speaks once again to the shifting discursive sands on which regulators must stake their positions and the endurance of metrics that privilege cost as the primary criterion in the assessment of future regulatory moves.

Mediated messages

As challenging as these competing mandates and expectations may be, those in the regulatory world must also contend with another critical yet often overlooked force: the media. By virtue of its position as both a conduit for the views of other stakeholders and an audience and interest group in its own right, the media has come to play a pivotal role in securities enforcement as both a pressure point and filter between regulators and the markets, at times invoking and at other times reshaping the many different sides of the regulatory mandate. The most noticeable aspect of this role follows from the media's position as one of the most vocal critics of the regulatory system, regularly offering opinions on the failure of enforcement agencies to take action in response to larger problems in the marketplace, such as insider trading, as well as to individual cases of sufficient notoriety to garner media attention. In the Canadian context, the leading edge of these critiques have been comparisons with enforcement activities in the US. This gaze south of the border was especially severe following the Enron and WorldCom scandals as the wave of 'perp walks' produced by US officials was viewed as a decisive condemnation of the responsible parties and a clear sign of that country's intolerance for financial shenanigans. In contrast, the enforcement response to a number of home grown scandals appeared slow and uninspired.[7] The following commentary is typical:

> Right now, the general consensus is the enforcement system is ailing, if not completely dysfunctional … While the likes of Enron's Jeffrey Skilling and Tyco's Dennis Kozlowski are behind bars with lengthy sentences, in Canada the landscape seems strewn with cases where few have been successfully prosecuted, or are instead being pursued by American regulators and enforcers rather than their Canadian counterparts.
>
> (Livesey 2008: 44)

These types of critical accounts have had a very real impact on stakeholder opinions in Canada. For example, during the 2005 proceedings of the Standing Senate Committee on Banking, Trade and Commerce, one senator made direct reference to US successes commenting that: 'We have still seen a lot of orange suits on the news, but not so many in Canada' (13: 112). And yet, the irony is that many of these comparisons are manifestly unfair, or at least inaccurate, conflating the regulatory with the criminal justice system and neglecting fundamental differences in the tools available to American versus Canadian investigators. For example, many media commentaries overlook the rather significant fact that Eliot Spitzer was acting on behalf of the Attorney General's Office of New York rather than the SEC and was empowered by a provision, the Martin Act, unique to New York State.[8] Criticisms of enforcement would thus more fairly be directed to the police rather than the securities commissions. However, even here the comparison is not entirely just as it overlooks the cultural and legal differences between these respective criminal justice systems, including the fact that Canada is one of the few jurisdictions where the police lack subpoena powers placing them at a significant disadvantage relative to their American, British and Australian counterparts. Nevertheless, these 'mis-comparisons' remain a thorn in the side of regulators:

> I think if the press hated us less it would have helped. To be frank, I think they've set up a straw man. I think they're very lazy in their analysis of what the SEC does versus the DOJ. I agree that there's much more aggressive conduct on the part of American prosecutors and the SEC, but that's not to be tolerated in Canada. So it's like a cultural difference that they ignore. And a confusion of the roles in the US. The DOJ is much stronger than Canadian criminal securities enforcement. I'm not sure there's a huge difference between the OSC and the SEC.
>
> (OSC #6: 6)

Judging from the comments of another member of the OSC's enforcement division, this may be less a matter of laziness or misinformation, than manipulation:

> We're constantly being compared to Mr. Elliot Spitzer in the States. I've been on media calls where we'll say to them 'We're not Spitzer, you can't compare us. Because Spitzer is criminal'. And we've had reporters say, 'I know that that's your answer but I don't care, I want you to answer this about Spitzer'. So the problem is this is a very complex area and if you have people who aren't willing to be educated on it, you can't respond to the criticism.
>
> (OSC #10: 10)

Beyond these more pointed lines of critique, which from a regulatory standpoint are frustrating yet eminently refutable, the media also exerts a far more subtle influence on regulators, shining a spotlight on enforcement efforts, dramatizing key missteps and heightening the stakes and potential costs of different regulatory manoeuvres:[9] 'I always say the OSC is *like litigating in a fish bowl.* It's a lot of pressure' (OSC #9: 11, emphasis added). As noted by another respondent: 'You are under tremendous scrutiny. Even for even the smallest of cases that you do' (OSC #10: 16). One former regulator went so far as to suggest that this media awareness and concern with positive publicity impacts the very decisions around which cases will be pursued and to what degree:

> I can't tell you enough how important the media is in this entire equation ... the media will largely decide how big a case is going to be ... So the media runs with the story on page one and the regulator better be there or somebody's going to be asking 'where are we?'. So the regulators' response is probably proportionate to the page they're on in the [newspaper] ... I never fully appreciated it until I got to the OSC just how powerful the media is. And in this particular area of law, they are extraordinarily powerful such that I am prepared to say that they have a significant impact on the day-to-day agenda.
> (Former OSC #2: 12)

The media is thus an essential barometer according to which enforcement activities are examined and evaluated, representing an irreducible part of the regulatory conscience.

And yet, from a regulatory standpoint, not all of this is negative as the media may also serve as a useful ally, helping to dramatize regulatory activities through their reporting on enforcement cases and proceedings. This publicity provides an important source of strategic leverage in individual cases as respondents are keen to avoid the damage to individual and organizational reputations wrought by negative publicity. The media is also used by regulators as a window into the industry, offering a means to assess emerging issues in the markets, to gauge industry and public opinion and to judge the impact of various regulatory actions on the marketplace. The media is thus not only a critic but also a kind of discursive sounding board according to which regulatory moves are contemplated, framed and plotted. This more positive side of the media relationship is alluded to by a senior enforcement official at the OSC:

> I've always been of the view that the media is a friend. We're not a public company that can spend money on advertising. We only have one way to get our message out. And whether it's criminal prosecutions or this business, a big chunk of the business is about deterrence and unless the public knows what you're doing you don't get the deterrence aspect out, so you have to rely on the media and it's important to have good relationships with them. Because either they're going to crap on you or maybe they'll try to tell your story properly.
> (OSC #12: 10)

However, here again regulators are placed in a very difficult spot as they have been criticized by members of the industry and the legal community who argue that this leveraging of media exposure constitutes an unfair advantage, forcing respondents to settle cases that are otherwise undeserving, simply to avoid the negative publicity associated with a more formal proceeding. Similarly, this reliance on the media as a means of publicizing their cases and bolstering investor confidence has spurred criticisms that the regulators are at best playing to the media, 'searching for trophies' and concerned with 'looking good' as much as 'doing good' (Lawyer #24: 4–5) and at worst assuming the role of 'market maker'. This latter critique was voiced by one prominent member of the legal community who faulted the OSC for its use of 'press releases as a regulatory tool', and for the fact that this type of regulatory activity 'puts the Commission in the place of becoming a market player in terms of influencing market prices' (Dialogue with the OSC 2004). On this point regulators are once again bedevilled by ambiguities in the meaning of core terms such as 'confidence' and 'integrity'. One would assume that, as one of the primary purveyors of signs of regulatory activity, and a key actor in the discursive universe that is constitutive of the markets, regulators *should be* actively concerned with their public image and their role in bolstering confidence in the markets. Not so, according to this same legal counsel: 'My problem is that it seems to me that confidence in the capital markets is being equated with confidence in the securities commission. And the trouble with that is that it's far too close to the commission being concerned about its public image rather than regulatory enforcement' (Dialogue with the OSC 2004). Regulatory dilemmas indeed.

'Impossible mandate'

In his highly influential study of police work, Peter Manning (1997) adopts the term 'impossible mandate' to describe the contradictions faced by the police in executing their mandate to control crime and protect public safety, foremost among which is the need to reduce rates of criminal behaviour while having little influence over the actual causes of crime. These tensions are not unlike the dilemmas faced by regulatory agencies as they struggle to find the right balance between an active enforcement regime and the promotion of efficient and competitive markets unhindered by excessive regulatory burdens. Complicating matters still further, they must negotiate this balance using benchmarks such as 'investor confidence' and 'market integrity' that are not only ill-defined and difficult to gauge, but which may be adversely affected by regulatory activities no matter how virtuous or well conceived:

> It is a double-edged sword … You have this very difficult balance between doing an effective regulatory job, which means ferreting out the proverbial bad guy and making sure the public is protected from him, and at the same time not creating what may be construed as an unnecessary chill in the marketplace or in some way discouraging the investment of capital in our markets. So that's one of the conundrums that they face and it's a difficult one. And that's why you'll see in some regimes there's no enforcement at all, if you

> look back historically ... you'll see sort of a very, very passive enforcement presence and that may in part be because on the enforcement side, no news is good news.
>
> (Former OSC #2: 4)

This minefield is made especially difficult to navigate given the decidedly schizophrenic relationship with the media, a necessary and valuable ally in signalling regulatory activity, sounding out harms in the marketplace and gauging the impressions of stakeholder communities and, at the same time, one of the most vocal and unreasonable of critics. Within this uncertain territory, regulators must be careful how and where they tread.

Another challenge impinging on the execution of their mandate is tensions within the agencies themselves as enforcement is only one division within a much larger organization across which the desired balance between investor protection and market competitiveness is bound to vary. To the extent that market problems are defined as the territory of other units (eg poor disclosure and compliance units), or management deems initiatives or cases to be in conflict with larger regulatory goals, the scope of enforcement activities may be further constrained:

> There's sort of a natural, internal tension between those people within the Commission who see their roles as facilitating the ability of individuals and entities to participate in the marketplace and the enforcement side of things. So one of the things that you run into is people in one area who identify problems and try to work with market participants to try to resolve those problems and sometimes compromising the potential for an investigation, sometimes stringing out ongoing harm with harmful effects to investors and so forth, is reflective of the tensions between the need for efficiencies in the marketplace on one hand, and investor protection on the other hand. So it's a delicate balance.
>
> (OSC #12: 1)

While experienced throughout the regulatory system, these kinds of tensions are especially acute as they relate to the police given not only the incommensurability of market enforcement with the traditional measures of police work (eg arrests; drug seizures), but also the unwillingness on the part of the larger police bureaucracy to invest scarce resources in a service line that is unlikely to yield much in the way of symbolic returns and with which the public is largely disengaged (Levi 1995).[10] Faced with this impossible mandate, the question not just for the police but for all securities enforcement agencies is what effect these tensions have on the organization, how are they managed or avoided, and to what extent they bring about a shift in emphasis from policing misconduct to organizational self-preservation.

Managing organizational appearances

Returning to the example of police work, one of the arguments advanced by Manning (1997) is that police agencies respond to their impossible mandate by engaging in a form of symbolic management whereby they seek to produce a carefully crafted representation of their work and signs of their effectiveness, largely for media and public consumption, notwithstanding their inability to deliver on these promises as a matter of practice. A case in point is the photo op of drug enforcement agents standing next to a cache of seized drugs. This conveys a powerful message of police activity, despite the fact that the seizure inevitably represents only a small fraction of the drug trade, will do little to stem the flow of drugs and was in all likelihood the product of a fortuitous tip rather than stolid investigative work. The result is a form of detachment, or what Manning (1997) refers to as loose coupling, between the symbolic face of the police and the daily mill of encounters and cases. These themes of symbolic management and loose coupling have long informed the organizational literature which has sought to move beyond the Weberian image of the organization as a rational, calculating bureaucratic machine, focusing instead on the uncertainties of organizational life and the efforts by organizations to establish policies, procedures and outward displays that allow them to *appear* legitimate (Meyer and Rowan 1977; DiMaggio and Powell 1983). As noted by Meyer and Rowan (1977), these rational myths and ceremonies are especially significant in environments where outputs are ambiguous and constituencies variable, the very hallmarks of securities regulation.

These notions of symbolic management and loose coupling are directly relevant to the activities of enforcement agencies as they go about managing their impossible mandate. In particular, they highlight the extent to which controlling the public face of the agency is a major managerial concern, one that is never far from the minds of enforcement staff. The importance of this symbolic labour is reflected in the comment from a lawyer and former senior manager at the OSC that they often felt like a PR specialist and, were they to move to the private sector, it would be with a PR firm rather than a law firm (Securities Litigation 2006). A similar sentiment emerges from the comments of former OSC chair David Brown: 'As the chief executive officer of the commission, *perception* is very important to me, and . . . *perception* can, if it's not addressed, undermine the credibility of the organization' (Brown 2004: F–922, emphasis added). These pressures have no doubt been heightened in recent years given the increasingly politicized environment of securities regulation along with demands that securities regulators, like most other organizations, provide clearer rationalizations and accounts of their actions.

Enforcement agencies have responded to this impetus to manage their appearances and guard themselves against external assaults in a variety of ways. The most obvious is their continued reliance on the media as a valued partner and means of dramatizing notable successes and new initiatives. However, of equal, if not greater, importance is their ongoing investment in the production of speeches, reports and commentaries, which cast the organization in as favourable a light as possible as an earnest and stout enforcer actively resisting the scourge of market malfeasance. In this vein, senior management make regular appearances at conferences and other public functions, outlining the threats currently menacing the markets and the steps taken to counter those threats. Always keen to emulate their rivals, enforcement agencies have also come to assume the mantle of larger institutional rationalities, particularly with respect to 'risk' and 'risk-based regulation', key watchwords for regulators in exactly this environment of heightened scrutiny (Black 2005, 2006; Hutter 2005; Rothstein et al. 2006; Power 2007). A perfect example of the mirroring of institutional logics, or 'institutional isomorphism', noted by organizational scholars (Meyer and Rowan 1977; DiMaggio and Powell 1983), this finds its clearest expression in the efforts of agencies to couch their activities in the language of risk and to adopt risk-based tools and devices. These range from the risk profiling applications used by the commissions and SROs to identify market actors that are 'at risk' for a range of regulatory problems, to more haphazard screening mechanisms such as those used to assess and prioritize incoming files: 'What we do at the commission is establish processes and procedures and risk-based approaches and screening mechanisms for determining which cases will be selected from the vast array of cases that could be pursued by enforcement' (Dialogue with the OSC 2004).

As a form of appearance management, this open embrace of risk-based regulation is interesting on a number of counts. In terms of benefits, risk profiling and assessment tools provide enforcement with a degree of transparency and thus a means of responding to recurring stakeholder demands for more information on priority setting and case selection. More importantly, they offer a way to rationalize the enforcement process itself which, it can now be argued, turns on objective criteria and the pursuit of the most objectively deserving (that is, 'high risk') cases, rather than more nebulous and potentially more politically objectionable criteria. Risk-based devices also provide a kind of built-in defensibility as decisions to pursue or not pursue individual cases can be justified according to the attributions of low versus high risk, thus yielding a 'defensible basis on which [the agency] can answer its critics and explain both the actions that it took and, more importantly, the actions it did not take' (Black 2006: 25; see also Hutter 2005). This addresses a key management concern: 'Something had to be done to change our process where we no longer had to take in everything. We needed to kind of *justify a reason* for saying "we can't do your file, it doesn't meet the threshold" or that sort of thing' (IDA #2: 4–5, emphasis added). The attractiveness of risk as an organizational and representational device thus stems from its ability to impose a degree of order on an otherwise ambiguous and uncertain process: 'Risk-based frameworks hold out the promise that the challenges and complexities of financial supervision can be rationalized, ordered, managed, controlled. Faced with that temptation, what regulator could resist?' (Black 2005: 179).

And yet, as we will see in Chapter 5, whether or how these risk-based devices actually impact the enforcement process remains an open question as they may 'add little that is new to the analytical capacities of the large regulators' (Power

2007: 91). When asked about this, a number of respondents commented that the tools were of limited practical use, although they did acknowledge their value in justifying decisions to both internal and external constituencies. Here we find the perfect illustration of the loose coupling between the symbolic face of agencies and their daily practices, whereby 'structural elements are only loosely linked to each other and to activities, rules are often violated, decisions are often unimplemented, or if implemented have uncertain consequences, technologies are of problematic efficiency, and evaluation and inspection systems are subverted or rendered so vague as to provide little coordination' (Meyer and Rowan 1977: 343). The adoption of these risk-based logics combined with their questionable impact on actual work routines also speaks to what a number of scholars have described as the growing preoccupation of regulatory agencies with managing risks to the institution itself rather than the societal risks that lie at the heart of their mandate (Hutter 2005; Rothstein et al. 2006; Power 2007). This suggests that, when faced with an impossible mandate, multiple stakeholders and an atmosphere of heightened scrutiny and unrealistic expectations, 'protecting the institution can become the overriding goal' (Rothstein et al. 2006: 107).

Conclusion

Since its emergence in the 1930s, securities regulation has developed quite rapidly with the proliferation of an extensive regulatory infrastructure and a host of laws and regulations designed to protect the integrity of the markets and provide a measure of transparency and fairness to market dealings. While the primary aim of this chapter has been to examine the different sides of this evolving mandate and their manifestation in terms of the competing logics and expectations to which regulatory agencies are beholden and which they seek to manage through dramatization and defensiveness in equal measure, the foregoing discussion also offers a number of unique insights into the enforcement project to be carried forward and further fleshed out in the chapters to follow.

The first of these insights involves the notion that what is ultimately most challenging about securities regulation, and which sets it apart from most other regulatory endeavours, is the combination of a highly politicized and exceedingly diverse task environment and the rather curious status of 'the market' as a regulatory object. Picking up on an analytical thread from Chapter 1, many of the aforementioned tensions in the mandate of securities regulators stem from the fact that, while regulatory efforts are ostensibly directed towards individual violators and victims, the former requiring sanction and the latter protection or compensation, the primary consideration for regulators is the wellbeing of 'the market' as an abstract collective; hence the rejection of deterrence and restitution as legitimate pursuits. When combined with the imputed attributes of markets as naturally efficient and investors as capably self-sufficient, the result is not only tensions in what might be expected of regulators relative to what they deliver but also a potential narrowing of the field of regulatory activity itself. A key question moving forward is exactly what this narrowing might look like and how these invocations of 'the market', shot through the regulatory mandate, impact the daily work of enforcement.

A second insight, intimated at the outset of the chapter, is that securities enforcement must be conceived as an organizational activity, that is, a set of practices performed *by* and *through* organizations possessing their own distinct logics and interests, rather than the mere actualization of a formal legislative or legal mandate. This is similar to the point made by Hawkins (2002), who notes that: 'Those who work in an organization are also subject to imperatives arising from membership of it, quite apart from those originating in their legal mandate' (5). Here the organization itself becomes a key variable, embedding particular interests and managerial concerns into the enforcement process including the need to manage scarce resources, to maximize efficiencies, to deal with constant turnover and other staffing issues and to prop up the legitimacy of the agency while staving off external assaults. The extent to which these organizational dynamics distract the attention of regulators while producing at times unanticipated and unintended consequences is addressed in a number of future chapters.

Third, following this theme of unintended consequences and unanticipated side-effects, another insight to emerge from this chapter involves the question of whether the strategies and devices used by enforcement agencies in the course of managing their impossible mandate are purely symbolic in nature, a mere superficial gloss on the enforcement process. Following on the heels of the cultural economists and their insights into the performativity of market devices, it is possible that these risk-based metrics and profiling tools exert a more subtle influence on the enforcement process, for example, through the enactment of implementation limits and blind spots (Black 2006) that artificially narrow the regulatory field of vision. As Black (2006) observes: '[risk-based regulation] is not simply a legitimation device that leaves underlying processes untouched; rather, it seeks to reshape those processes quite fundamentally' (21). A key question for future chapters is thus how these devices impact the enforcement process and whether they direct attention to certain market problems to the neglect of others.

Before moving on to these larger questions, there is another critical aspect of securities enforcement that needs to be addressed. This involves the politics that flow not from the larger environment of competing interests and stakeholder groups, but rather from the divisions within the regulatory field itself as the responsibility for enforcing securities laws is in fact divided between a number of very different agencies. This raises the question of how the mandates examined in this chapter are interpreted and defined by these respective agencies and the extent to which they contribute to a particular regulatory division of labour. It is this division of labour, and the underlying forms of conflict and cooperation, that is the focus of the next chapter.

Notes

1 Despite the prevailing view of the markets as creatures of private capital, their rapid growth in the late 19th and early 20th centuries was due in large part to government financing initiatives, including the purchase and sale of government bonds (Carruthers 1996; Geisst 2004; Braithwaite 2008). Starting in the 1800s, these bonds were purchased in lots and then distributed to the general public by bankers who received a commission for their part in the transaction.

2 These were coffee shops and street-side venues where members of the public were given the opportunity to speculate on exchange-listed securities without purchasing the securities themselves, a kind of unofficial shadow market.

3 Spurred by a number of scandals in the 1920s, the first securities statute in Ontario was the Security Frauds Prevention Act passed in 1928. This dealt with the licensing of stockbrokers and provided for investigations into securities frauds. Soon after, in 1931, the Ontario Government established the Securities Fraud Prevention Board to police financial dealings, which changed its name to the Ontario Securities Commission in 1932 (Armstrong 2001).

4 This is true despite the passage of the Ontario Securities Act of 1945, which has been described as Canada's first modern securities legislation (Neufeld 1972: 532–8; Condon et al. 2005). This broadened the ambit of the 1928 Security Frauds Prevention Act by introducing the concept of the distribution of securities to the public, as well as the requirement that issuers make public disclosures of their financial health and operations. However, the 1945 legislation relied heavily on self-regulation, providing for the delegation of certain regulatory functions to self-regulating bodies (Condon 1998; see also Armstrong 2001), thus dulling its regulatory bite. It should also be noted that much of the regulatory activity that did occur in the 1940s and 1950s involved nefarious sales practices (eg selling shares in penny mining stocks of dubious value and subject to various forms of insider manipulation), and was spurred by US concerns with salesmen based in Canada selling shares to Americans via phone and mail campaigns (Armstrong 2001).

5 There are exceptions. Securities commissions in Manitoba, Saskatchewan and New Brunswick are able to order compensation up to $100,000, while Quebec has a direct compensation system allowing investors to be compensated for up to $200,000 (Expert Panel 2009).

6 Notable US reports include those authored by the Committee on Capital Markets Regulation, the Commission on Regulation of US Capital Markets in the 21st Century, the US Chamber of Commerce, and a New York group which published a report entitled 'Sustaining New York's and the US' Global Financial Services Leadership', all of which argue that US markets have been weakened by recent regulatory reforms, with one committee concluding that: 'A substantial portion of the erosion in U.S. markets global and internal competitiveness … relates to insufficiently coordinated, costly and/or excessive market regulation and enforcement, public and private' (Committee on Capital Markets Regulation 2006: 3).

7 Comparisons with the US have become much kinder of late given the criticisms of the SEC over its mishandling of the Madoff affair (Markopolos 2010), and the failures of the regulatory system more generally with respect to the sub-prime crisis (Engel and McCoy 2011). The Financial Services Authority (FSA) in the UK has also recently come under fire for its 'light touch' to regulation, particularly in cases of insider trading (Enrich 2011).

8 The Martin Act of 1921 is a New York state law which gave the Attorney General the right to investigate any business operating in the state with the additional power to subpoena witnesses and publish the results of investigations (O'Brien 2005).

9 Interestingly, the relationship with the media is especially caustic in BC where a single columnist, David Baines, has regularly attacked the police and the BC Securities Commission for their failure to deal adequately with cases of securities misconduct, a

kind of populist fervour that has placed regulators on the defensive and instituted Baines as 'part of the enforcement mechanism in B.C.' (Lawyer #26: 10).

10 During one interview, a senior IMET manager commented that support from RCMP leadership has been inconsistent at best and that, despite positive public overtures, a number of IMET requests have fallen on deaf ears. A similar sentiment was relayed by an IMET investigator: 'I think some of the challenges lie from us internally as an organization ... I'm not so sure that a lot of the senior executives are buying in ... There's a lot of really good lip service paid to it. I don't know if what's said to us on paper is what's said after the fax is sent' (IMET #10: 12–13).

Chapter 3

Inter-agency politics and jurisdictional boundaries

Introduction

As complainants soon discover as they are shepherded through the various stops in the regulatory circuit, one of the hallmarks of securities enforcement is the sheer number of different agencies with stakes in the regulatory game. In the Canadian context, this decidedly motley crew ranges from the police, to statutory securities commissions, to self-regulatory organizations, to private agencies and advocacy groups, all participants in what is euphemistically termed the 'enforcement mosaic' (OSC #13). The sheer number and variety of players operating in this arena demands an analysis of the relationships between these agencies, the ways they each seek to deliver on the promised mandates of securities enforcement and the scope of their authority and jurisdiction. This chapter examines these very relationships using the work of Pierre Bourdieu and his concept of social field as a guide. Emphasis is placed on the relative positions and forms of conflict that define securities enforcement as well as its roots not only in social but also physical and legal space, a social geography of enforcement anchored by jurisdiction and couched in various social relationships and exchanges. However, before embarking on an analysis of the concept of social field and its resonance with the 'enforcement mosaic', the chapter begins with an overview of how inter-agency relationships have been treated in the existing research literature, thus setting the table for a deeper engagement with Bourdieu's own work and its role in extending and deepening the present course of analysis.

Surveying the field of securities enforcement

Within the regulatory literature, it is now accepted wisdom that the state is no longer the sole or even primary purveyor of regulatory services, with regulation conceived instead as a hybrid product of relationships between a number of different players or agencies spanning the increasing anachronistic public/private divide (Braithwaite 2008). This sense of diversity is perhaps best expressed in the juxtaposition of the more conventional 'hierarchical' (Scott 2001: 334) or 'command-and-control' (Baldwin 1997; Reichman 1998; Black 2001) view of regulation as the product of legal rules enforced through centralized state agencies, with one grounded in the notion of governance networks. Following a number of intersecting currents in the wider social science literature,[1] this embodies an understanding of regulation as fragmented, dispersed and decentred (Shearing 1993; Black 2001, 2002, 2004; Scott 2001, 2004; Schmidt 2004; Braithwaite 2008), as lacking a centrifugal force or organizing rationality and as enacted through complex lines of conflict and cooperation involving a variety of interested parties.

There are a number of benefits that ensue from this analytic of decentred or networked governance as a regulatory paradigm. First, it grounds questions of governance in terms of relationships not only between different agencies but also organizations. This organizational frame of reference, one that harkens back to the previous chapter, follows from the seemingly straightforward yet often neglected insight that 'economic regulation is … predominantly regulation by and through organizations' (Hancher and Moran 1989: 297). Second, it acknowledges the limited usefulness of distinctions cast in terms of public/private, regulator/regulated and state/market, emphasizing instead the role of 'networks that combine governmental and non-governmental actors in a variety of ways' (Black 2001: 110; see also Scott 2001; Picciotto 2002). Finally, the concept of 'networks' invariably raises the question of space as a core dimension of decentred governance. This is featured most prominently in the work of Hancher and Moran (1989) who use the term 'regulatory space' to capture the situated contextualities of regulation asserting that 'place matters in determining the nature of regulation' (279; see also Lange 2003).

Without a doubt, the metaphors of 'networked governance', 'decentred regulation' and 'regulatory space' resonate quite strongly with the evolving institutional structure of securities regulation, this given: (1) the key contributions of a number of different players; (2) the inability to clearly define or differentiate these agencies, particularly the SROs, on the grounds of their public or private status; and (3) the role of situated interactions and exchanges between these 'partners' in shaping enforcement practice. There is thus a certain analytical purchase to be had from conceiving of securities enforcement in terms of the relationships between agencies and organizations positioned within a larger regulatory network and thus of engaging in the kind of mapping exercise advocated by authors such as Julia Black (2002, 2004).

And yet, this perspective is not without its limitations, chief among which is the presumption that participants in these regulatory networks are engaged in a common enterprise and, by virtue of similar goals and interests, are drawn into various forms of cooperation. Resembling a kind of negotiated order perspective, the emphasis on coordination and commonalities of interest pays short shrift to the potential for conflict between regulatory players, of agencies working at cross-purposes and protecting their own turf. Again, one notable exception is Hancher and Moran (1989), who remain keenly aware of inter-organizational conflict and the struggle for institutional advantage. Second, with an emphasis on the decentring and fragmentation of power, what Scott (2001) refers to as the 'fragmented possession of key resources' (330), the networked governance perspective also scants the differences between agencies in terms of their relative status and the extent to which players enter the regulatory arena with different degrees and types of resources in hand. Finally, despite the value of questioning the boundaries between public and private, and the legally encoded distinctions between the authority and reach of different agencies, this tradition overlooks the extent to which these differences remain salient despite or perhaps because of their artificiality, and how they are used to defend organizational turf and protect perceived rights and privileges. In each of these respects, the networked governance perspective suffers from a degree of political myopia that clouds its view of the politics at play in governance networks. It is in this context that the work of Pierre Bourdieu is valuable, meshing nicely with the sense of diversity underlying notions of networked governance, while potentially offering a much deeper and more sophisticated understanding of the political contours of regulation as a distinct field of social practice.

Pierre Bourdieu and the 'enforcement field'

As a sociologist interested in questions of social reproduction and, in particular, how the dominant political order is reproduced through its connections to seemingly autonomous spheres such as law, education and art, one of the core insights offered by Bourdieu is that the social world is organized in terms of distinct social fields. These are defined as loosely institutionalized yet hierarchically structured universes of social action, characterized by a particular distributive logic and constituted in terms of dominant versus subordinate positions (Bourdieu 1991, 1993; Bourdieu and Wacquant 1992). This logic, and thus the arrangement of the positions within this social space, is expressed through the relative possession of a distinct form of capital unique to each field and valued for the status and influence it confers. These unequal endowments of capital, which could take the form of educational credentials, social connections or linguistic competencies, represent the terms and stakes of the struggles that define these fields themselves:

> A species of capital is what is efficacious in a given field, both as a weapon and as a stake of struggle, that which allows its possessors to wield a power, an influence, and thus to exist, in the field under consideration, instead of being considered a negligible quantity. In empirical work, it is one and the same thing to determine what the field is, where its limits lie, etc., and to determine what species of capital are active in it.
>
> (Bourdieu and Wacquant 1992: 98)

For example, the legal, or what Bourdieu (1987) refers to as the juridical field, is defined by the distribution of juridical capital, that is, the possession of educational credentials combined with various forms of experience, interactional competency and standing in the legal community, all of which translate into the ability or right to determine what counts as law.

Beyond their morphology and distributive logic, there are a number of additional properties that define social fields. First, while seemingly static in nature, fields are actually characterized by ongoing forms of conflict and competition between the occupants of these different positions, struggles that are waged not only over the possession of the capital at stake in each field but also the ability to define this capital in a way that best reflects the competencies of each group. It is these struggles that provide the moving force behind fields as inherently political, and politically contested, spaces. Second, despite being concerned with their role in the reproduction of larger structural relations, fields possess a relative autonomy. They are defined by a specific socio-logic and rules of practice that are distinct and irreducible to the broader field of class relations. Thus, fields are 'relatively autonomous, i.e. spaces of objective relations that are the site of a logic and a necessity that are *specific and irreducible* to those that regulate other fields' (Bourdieu and Wacquant 1992: 97, original emphasis). This notion of relative autonomy is critical in avoiding some of the more crudely structuralist readings of Bourdieu's work. Third, the boundaries of fields are ambiguous and are themselves stakes of the competitive struggles unfolding within them. In the case of law, the boundaries of the juridical field, that is where law 'ends' and other modes of ordering 'begin', are contingent on negotiations and struggles over the contents and imaginings of law itself. Finally, in addition to capital and field, a third concept developed by Bourdieu and germane to his understanding of social fields is that of 'habitus'. This refers to the embodied schemata and dispositions that emerge from one's position *in* a given field and which are reflected in one's perspective *on* that field (Bourdieu and Wacquant 1992). These are pre-reflexive and unconscious and contribute to the generation of social practices that tend towards the reproduction of the field itself.

Given its structural currents and concern with the problematic of social reproduction, Bourdieu's approach to social fields, along with his concepts of capital and habitus, is certainly not without its limitations, foremost among which is its static and somewhat deterministic quality (Valverde 2006; Latour 2010). Valverde (2005, 2006) for one is especially critical of Bourdieu's work and, in particular, his understanding of law which she argues resembles a 'loosely Marxist approach' (Valverde 2006: 594), a 'static, quasi-structural model' that overlooks the specificities of legal practice:

> The legal field is over here, the cultural field is over there, the economic field overlaps with both, and so on. And while the content of the legal field is of course specific, the general form of capital accumulation that goes on in the legal field is not presented as arising from the history of law itself ... The specific knowledge/power moves that characterize legal manoeuvres thus remain in the dark, blackboxed if you will.
>
> (Valverde 2006: 595)

In this respect, Bourdieu's approach is seen as distinctly at odds with the Actor Network Theory (ANT) tradition that informs Valverde's own work. Valverde (2005, 2006) is likewise critical of Bourdieu's conception of power as a competency or capacity for action embodied in individuals, rather than a product of networks, discourses and technologies as per a more Foucauldian slant. Thus, for Bourdieu, 'people are nothing but conduits for institution-specific or class-fraction-specific knowledges and norms' (Valverde 2006: 593). While these criticisms are drawn from a rather narrow slice of his overall theoretical corpus,[2] and thus may not do justice to some of the complexities of social fields as envisioned by Bourdieu, there is indeed a lingering structuralist trap that underlies his work and from which he is unable to free himself completely. Expressed through some of the more deterministic and arguably static shadings of his work, the result is a limited appreciation for the contingencies and localized politics at play in social fields which represent not only structural universes but also planes of knowledge and knowledge effects.

Despite these limitations, Bourdieu's core concepts of field and capital, along with his underlying theoretical framework, remain valuable on a number of levels. First, they provide a means of capturing the sense of regulatory diversity and decentring invoked by the networked governance literature, while recognizing that these relationships are characterized by conflict and struggle rather than simply cooperation and coordination. Second, grounded in an appreciation of the spatial features of fields as constellations of relative positions, a sense of referentiality that is not unlike that found in ANT, these concepts speak to the importance of social location and perhaps even more importantly relative social *distance* and *distinction* as not only defining features of regulatory fields as structural configurations, but also the staging on which regulatory politics are played out. Finally, while Bourdieu's testament to the relative autonomy of fields appears as a bit of a failsafe against charges of structuralism, the notion that fields possess distinct attributes and forms of motion while nevertheless refracting larger social, political and economic logics preserves a recognition of power as a key dimension of regulatory practice while skirting the instrumentalist trap. It is these situated politics and power relations that shape, and are shaped by, the materialities and knowledge effects recognized by Valverde and others. In adopting the field analytic as a useful way of mapping and teasing out the distinct features of regulatory domains, the task moving forward is to examine how securities enforcement may itself be conceived as a social field. This begins with identifying the players[3] occupying this field, the nature of their positions and the tenor and tone of their relationships.

'The players'

In light of the importance of space to Bourdieu's understanding of social fields, one of the first considerations in mapping securities enforcement is how to conceive of the positions that make up this field. In much of his own work, Bourdieu uses grids consisting of intersecting vertical and horizontal axes to plot different players and positions. However, a more accurate as well as more useful analytic in the context of securities enforcement is that of a bull's eye. That is, the field of securities enforcement is best understood in terms of a series of concentric circles with the financial markets located at the centre and the various regulatory bodies and stakeholder groups positioned along distinct yet overlapping bands moving outwards from this core. This scheme captures both the centrality of financial markets and the fact that the positions of the various players are best defined not only by their relationships to, but also, and more importantly, their social and physical distance from, the markets. It is these relative distances that inform the differences between players along with their status in and perspective on the enforcement field.

Police

With status and distance from the markets as the primary locational coordinates, it should come as no surprise that the agency positioned at the outermost limits of the enforcement field is the police along with the criminal justice system. They are the most distant from the regulated in terms of background, expertise and influence, their mandate and organizational attention is divided between a number of very different tasks, and they are dependent on referrals and assistance from players positioned closer to the centre. While the responsibility for investigating securities offences that violate criminal law is shared by municipal, provincial and federal police forces, each of whom may rightfully assert jurisdiction should an offence occur within their 'territory', in Canada the primary player in this arena is the Royal Canadian Mounted Police (RCMP). As such, the trials and tribulations of this particular agency provide a critical window into the position of the police more generally in the field of securities enforcement.

Despite its status as a federal policing agency with a history that dates back to the late 1800s and a well established presence in front-line policing and drug interdiction, the RCMP is a relative newcomer to the area of financial and securities investigations, first wading into these waters in 1967 with the formation of a small unit dedicated to policing crime in the markets. Prior to this, cases of securities fraud were handled largely through private forms of recourse or, in more serious cases, the fledging yet largely ineffectual provincial securities commissions and SROs. As noted in the previous chapter, the early to mid 1960s was a period defined by a series of high profile corporate collapses involving the misappropriation of shareholder funds and clear accounting abuses, as well as worries about the growing influence of organized crime on the markets. These concerns culminated in a decision by the federal government in 1966 to establish a series of securities fraud units to be staffed by highly skilled and well trained investigators possessing specialized expertise in accounting and law. While the intended focus was on market-related offences, the mandate of these units was quickly expanded to include suspicious bankruptcies and other forms of financial crime broadly defined, with securities investigations handled by specific units under the larger commercial crime umbrella. Notwithstanding the dilution of its original mandate, the RCMP did enjoy some notable successes in the years that followed, including a number of high profile convictions in the 1970s and early 1980s and a reputation for highly skilled and effective investigations (Palango 1998).

Unfortunately, this success was short-lived with the effectiveness of the units soon dulled by a deteriorating investigative capacity and ability to bring cases forward for prosecution that began in the mid-1980s and accelerated through the 1990s. This was due to a variety of factors, including the loss of experienced investigators to the private sector, federal cutbacks, shifting organizational priorities and more stringent procedural and evidentiary standards,[4] all of which dramatically increased the length and complexity of investigations (Williams 2005). While resources, expertise and legal changes no doubt played a key role in this deterioration, the comments of a senior RCMP officer hint at the politics that may have also played a part:

> I think also in corporate Canada there wasn't a great feeling that the police were needed downtown. Self-regulation was the way to go. You had the securities commissions in the different provinces that were getting comfortable with their roles. So criminal enforcement I think in some areas was viewed as bad publicity and not something that you necessarily need around here.
>
> (IMET #5: 1)

Granted, the RCMP did attempt to reassert itself in the securities business in 1995 with the establishment of the Securities Fraud Office, a joint initiative between the RCMP, the Crown Prosecutors Office and the BC Securities Commission. However, saddled with many of the same resourcing and operational challenges and plagued by high staff turnover, the plug was pulled on the initiative after just three years and no significant charges, an experiment that ultimately 'left a bad taste in the mouth of the securities commission and the Attorney General's Office. Everyone who participated said it was deemed a failure' (IMET #19: 1).

Despite a number of home-grown scandals in the late 1990s and early 2000s,[5] it was not until the much publicized collapses of Enron and WorldCom in 2002 that the RCMP was finally pressed to retry its hand at securities enforcement. Spurred by much hand-wringing around the potential for a Canadian Enron, the identification of criminal enforcement as a key weakness in the Canadian regulatory system, and quick action on the part of key organizational entrepreneurs within the RCMP,[6] the plan was to establish a coterie of highly specialized, multidisciplinary investigative teams consisting of experienced RCMP investigators, forensic accountants, members of the various regulatory bodies, representatives from the Department of Justice, market experts and a number of technical support staff. To ensure the maximum impact on the markets, the mandate of the teams was narrowly cast limiting them to large cases involving 'serious Criminal Code capital markets fraud offences that are of national significance and involve actions of publicly-traded companies with sufficient market capitalization to pose a genuine threat to investor confidence and economic stability in Canada' (Public Works 2006: 3). In addition to revamped human resource policies and clear performance benchmarks, the IMET program was also accompanied by an extensive legislative package deemed essential to its success including: (1) a new criminal offence of insider trading; (2) greater penalties for existing offences; and (3) a new type of warrant that would allow investigators to obtain documents and other data from third party record holders without having to secure a search warrant. With the requisite funding, structure and legal framework in place, the IMET initiative was rolled out with great fanfare in June 2003 with a series of news conferences and a travelling RCMP road show making regular stops on the conference circuit.

Following an initial wave of enthusiasm, delays in bringing charges especially in its most high profile cases have since caused the program to lose much of its lustre. The business press in particular have been extremely critical of IMET, castigating the agency not only for the paucity of charges, but also the departure of key personnel and internal politicking with the federal prosecution service. According to one editorial, the result has been a further loss of faith in the RCMP:

> If only someone could restore our faith in the RCMP, whose record on many of Canada's most prominent white-collar crime cases is looking increasingly dismal ... If IMET can't live up to its promise, it should be fixed or replaced. It's a sad fact that criminals appear to have nothing to fear from Canada's big crackdown on securities crime.
>
> (*Globe and Mail* 2006: A12)

A similar sentiment emerges from recent policy reports. One major report on securities enforcement in Canada concluded that: 'Media commentary and the concerns expressed to us by many of those with whom we consulted make it clear that the credibility of IMETs, for which there were such high expectations, is now at serious risk' (Cory and Pilkington 2006: 222). Not surprisingly, these views were echoed by key stakeholders with a senior securities litigator providing perhaps the most sobering assessment: 'I think it is probably generally accepted that IMET has been a failure. And it's coming apart at the seams' (Lawyer #9: 1). For their part, top ranking IMET officials have publicly acknowledged the lack of output and the failure to live up to expectations participating in a number of internal reviews (eg Public Works 2006; Le Pan 2007) and promising that these 'growing pains' would be overcome through the only currency that counts: charges in its largest cases.[7] While these struggles are not unlike those experienced by their counterparts in other countries,[8] the scale of these failures combined with erratic police commitments to market enforcement have contributed to a situation where the police occupy a distinctly marginalized position in the wider enforcement field, a self-fulfilling prophecy that has actually played out to the detriment of other players in the field.

Securities commissions

Taking another step towards the centre, we move from the police, who possess at best a peripheral involvement in the securities world, to the most prominent as well as most maligned player in the field of securities enforcement: the securities commissions. These are the statutory bodies created for the express purpose of enforcing legislation pertaining to all facets of the public markets. This is an exceedingly broad mandate, covering areas ranging from certification requirements, to primary stock offerings, to continuous disclosure, to corporate finance, delivered through a number of semi-autonomous units (eg 'market regulation', 'compliance and registrant regulation' and 'corporate finance'). While a range of regulatory functions are provided through each of these units, most of which revolve around a compliance-based philosophy of educating and/or cajoling issuers, firms and investors into complying with established regulations, the task of taking action against clear breaches of provincial securities laws falls to dedicated enforcement units sandwiched amongst these other divisions.

As the recognized enforcers of the securities world these units, which are themselves divided into a number of smaller operational groups including 'case assessment', 'investigations' and 'litigation', possess extensive powers to gather records and conduct interviews as well as the ability, through the settlement and hearings process, to levy fines, issue cease trade orders and seize assets. These powers have increased significantly in recent years[9] and, along with the move to self-funding,[10] have dramatically expanded the scope if not necessarily the effectiveness of the enforcement function. While enforcement actions are informed by specific breaches outlined in the various securities acts, including insider trading, manipulative or abusive trading and distributing a security without a prospectus, most commissions also possess a public interest power that allows them to take action in cases where the underlying conduct does not violate a specific rule yet is deemed contrary to the public interest. On the subject of powers and penalties, some commissions, most notably the OSC, have the added power to bring quasi-criminal charges and pursue cases through the criminal courts, while most others must either refer their cases to the police or convince a provincial Crown Attorney to lay a charge and prosecute the case on their behalf. Positioned as distinct enclaves within a much larger organization, these enforcement units possess their own distinct culture which follows in part from the unique mix of personnel. Whereas most other divisions are occupied by lawyers with backgrounds in securities law, the enforcement units are staffed by lawyers, accountants and investigators, including a significant complement of both former police officers and Crown Attorneys with the organizational culture thus infused with a distinct policing mentality.

While the Canadian regulatory system has been subject to a number of criticisms, the elephant in the room in most discussions, whether acknowledged or not, is the fact that Canada stands alone in organizing securities regulation along provincial lines with the result being that the aforementioned regulatory functions are delivered through 13 different securities commissions.[11] This has led to a sense of embarrassment, particularly on the international stage, and has precipitated much consternation about the lack of integration and consistency in this country's regulatory infrastructure. While the question of whether national commissions provide for a stronger enforcement function remains a matter of debate,[12] this arrangement has at the very least added a further layer of complexity to the Canadian regulatory system. Industry players and investors alike are required to deal with 13 different statutory regulators and thus 13 different mandates and institutional priorities. Regional politics are also hereby added to the mix, this despite efforts on the part of umbrella groups such as the Canadian Securities Administrators (CSA) to coordinate efforts amongst the various commissions and to establish a degree of consensus around regulatory policy on a national level. And yet, this sense of heterogeneity may be overblown. Despite the existence of 13 commissions, in practice the lion's share of regulatory and enforcement activity is undertaken by just four: the BC Securities Commission, the Alberta Securities Commission, the Ontario Securities Commission and the Autorité des Marchés Financiers in Quebec. It is thus unclear whether diversity is really a problem or simply part of the posturing and politics at play in the enforcement field.

Self-regulatory organizations

If the securities commissions are the grand overseers of the markets, powerful yet somewhat distant disciplinarians, a third player that is more directly engaged on the regulatory front-lines and positioned much closer to the heart of the markets are a handful of self-regulatory organizations or SROs. With roots dating back to the early 1900s, self-regulation in the securities industry has a long history in the US, the UK, Australia and Canada (Condon 1998; Armstrong 2001) and is 'crucial to an understanding of the historical operation of securities markets' (Condon 1998: 34). In contrast with the police and securities commissions, which possess a statutory authority and are guided by a clearly defined public interest mandate, the SROs are independent agencies governed by members of the industry itself. Their regulatory mandate and authority stems from a delegated responsibility passed down from the commissions to perform a host of tasks ranging from dealer registration, to oversight of sales and marketing practices, to the monitoring of trading on the various exchanges. This follows the age-old adage that regulation is best performed by those who are closest to and have the greatest knowledge of the markets, a posture that has long drawn the ire of investor groups who view this as regulatory capture in the extreme. While the SROs are overseen by the commissions and thus have been brought into the fold of the statutory system, the authority of the agencies themselves is contractual in nature,[13] derived from the requirement that all firms and individuals operating in the securities industry be registered members of the SROs and adhere to their bylaws: 'We regulate by contract, we have no statutory jurisdiction. It's strictly an agreement between us and our members' (IDA #1: 7). The SROs thus occupy a kind of no man's land between public and private spheres as they enjoy delegated authority from the securities commissions and are engaged in the performance of a public regulatory function. Yet, given the absence of statutory authority and their status as contractually constituted industry bodies, they are in many respects private entities or 'private interest governments' (Coleman 1989). In the words of one litigator: 'The IDA says they are acting in the interests of the public, but it's really a private contractual relationship between them and their members ... It's schizophrenic' (Lawyer #4: 7).

As noted in the introduction to this book, the SRO landscape has changed quite dramatically in recent years. Up until very recently, the three primary SROs in Canada were: (1) the Investment Dealers Association (IDA) responsible for regulating investment dealers and their employees and overseeing areas such as sales compliance, financial adequacy, business conduct and educational proficiency, (2) the Mutual Fund Dealers Association (MFDA), providing a similar regulatory function in the context of the mutual fund industry and (3) Market Regulation Services Inc. (RS), a not-for-profit agency tasked with monitoring trading on the various equity-based exchanges and alternative trading systems. While the authority of all three agencies was contractually derived, in the case of the IDA and MFDA these contracts flowed through membership agreements with firms and by extension individual dealers, whereas RS contracted with individual exchanges serving as their recognized 'regulation service provider'. The IDA, in addition to compliance and enforcement, also offered an arbitration service whereby aggrieved investors, rather than pursuing an expensive and time consuming civil suit, could seek a claim against an investment dealer with the ultimate judgment rendered by an independent arbitrator. However, mirroring trends towards SRO consolidation in other contexts, including the UK and US, in 2008 the IDA and RS were merged to form a single SRO, the Investment Industry Regulatory Organization of Canada (IIROC). While recognizing these changes, the discussion to follow in this and other chapters is directed to these agencies in their pre-merger form with the conclusions about each agency's struggles and dilemmas being entirely generalizable to the newly consolidated entity and acknowledgements provided in the case of notable exceptions.

To these three (now two) primary SROs, we can also add the exchanges themselves, which perform a self-regulatory function through the enforcement of their listing requirements including rules around capital adequacy and corporate governance. A final agency that can loosely be described as self-regulatory is the Ombudsman for Banking Services and Investments (OBSI), an investigative and adjudicative body that is funded by the industry and provides individuals with an alternative to the IDA (now IIROC) arbitration system.[14]

Advocates and activists

Moving beyond the formally designated confines of the regulatory system, another key position in the wider field of enforcement is occupied by a number of investor and shareholder advocacy groups. Reflecting the diversity of investors and their interests, these extend from shareholder rights agencies such as the Canadian Coalition for Good Governance (CCGG), to a handful of much smaller investor advocacy groups, such as the Small Investor Protection Association (SIPA). While the former advocate on behalf of large institutional investors, engaging in proxy fights and leveraging the weight of their membership to bring about reforms to corporate governance practices among other concerns, the latter are devoted to the more modest interests of retail investors agitating to bring about their fairer treatment at the hands of both the industry and regulators alike. Occupying a somewhat ambiguous position between these two groups is the Canadian Foundation for Advancement of Investor Rights (FAIR). A relatively recent arrival on the regulatory scene, this organization has fashioned itself as the 'national voice for investors on securities regulation and a catalyst for enhancement of the rights of Canadian shareholders and retail investors' (http://www.faircanada.ca), thus placing a foot in both shareholder advocacy and investor protection pools. These various groups represent important, yet invariably unequal, stakeholders of the regulatory system and serve as key points of contact between the police, commissions, SROs and the exceedingly diverse population of investors.

Advisers and intermediaries

Approaching the centre of the enforcement field and occupying the position closest to the markets is a coterie of professional advisers, including lawyers, accountants and consultants, that perform a variety of services on behalf of the regulated. A sign of the ever greater professionalization or 'expertization' of the markets, this includes offering advice on the legal and regulatory implications of transactions, conducting investigations and acting on behalf of clients in enforcement matters, engaging in policy-related advocacy work and working directly with the regulators through advisory boards and formal staff positions. Here the role of lawyers is especially intriguing. As a profession and as individual practitioners, they are positioned both within and outside of the regulatory establishment with regular movement across this border. They thus exert a unique influence from both ends of the regulatory spectrum. Moreover, given that they operate in a number of different legal fora, including regulatory, criminal and civil, lawyers also serve as importers and translators of legal principles across these domains. The drive to import standards from the criminal realm into regulatory proceedings is just one example of this cross-fertilization. While lawyers no doubt play the most active part in the enforcement field, accountants also represent key players, albeit more in an advisory than advocacy role. This ranges from advising companies on accounting matters, to establishing compliance programs, to undertaking forensic investigations in response to suspected abuses at client firms. To lawyers and accountants we can also add a small but influential group of consultants offering advice and serving as expert witnesses in regulatory and legal proceedings. Collectively, these diverse professional engagements reveal the field of securities enforcement to be structured not only in institutional or organizational terms, bound to the bureaucratic housings of individual agencies, but also through the workings of a series of crisscrossing professional networks or 'regulatory communities' (Meidinger 1987: 364). As nodes of expertise and symbolic authority, these networks play a critical yet often overlooked role in the regulatory system.

Issuers, brokers, traders and investors

At the very centre of the enforcement field, and the point around which the other positions are organized and defined, are the markets themselves. As discussed at length in Chapter 1, this extends from actors with direct stakes in the markets, namely issuers, brokers, traders and investors, to the various platforms, technologies, data streams and physical spaces through which the markets are performed and reproduced on a daily basis. Representing the basic source materials from which enforcement cases are built and, in the case of market actors, occupying the somewhat strange position of both regulatory target and primary stakeholder, it is important to note that this move into the markets does not represent an absolute break with the regulatory sphere or, put in slightly different terms, an absence of order. The markets are themselves defined by various informal mechanisms and modalities of control, ranging from peer pressure and the fear of ostracism, to financial leverage and moral suasion, to opportunities for 'pay back' between 'repeat players' (Gunningham 1991: 318). While it is certainly appropriate to be sceptical of these forms of 'control', they do speak to the unique vulnerabilities among different classes of investors as, for example, institutional investors are better positioned to take advantage of such informal controls while individual investors are forced to rely more heavily on the formal regulatory system. The result is not necessarily more or less abuse, but rather a kind of selection bias in the cases bound to 'make it' to the regulatory sphere.

Moving from the centre of the field back through to its outer limits, this mapping exercise has revealed securities enforcement to be extremely diverse, multifaceted and constituted in terms of a number of different dimensions. The first of these is *institutional*, or *organizational*, referring to the formally designated regulatory agencies and recognized stakeholder groups, a field of play that can be expanded to include international counterparts such as the FBI, the SEC and the Financial Services Authority (FSA) in the UK, all of which exert a critical influence on the Canadian enforcement system albeit from afar. The second dimension is *professional* and includes the various professional communities which, like the points of intersection in a Venn diagram, penetrate and yet extend beyond the confines of the enforcement field. The final dimension is *legal*. Not only is the enforcement field rooted in different forms of law, including statutory, administrative and contractual, it also abuts a number of neighboring legal sites, most notably the civil justice system. These offer another source of operational logics as well as additional avenues through which complaints may be resolved, therein diverting them from the regulatory system. What emerges from this overview is thus a distinctly three-dimensional rendering of the enforcement field as an institutionally, professionally and legally constituted space of intervention in the markets, a field whose boundaries are ambiguous and fluid, and which is underlain by a diversity of interests, players and logics. With this in hand, and following Bourdieu's lead, the task now becomes to move in closer and examine in greater detail the specific relationships that define and flow through these respective positions, that is, to understand the forms of conflict that ensue between the various regulatory players and the impact of these struggles on the enforcement enterprise.

Inter-agency politics and jurisdictional battles

One of the more enduring policy debates, and a factor often cited in critiques of securities enforcement, is the extent to which the regulatory system is characterized by overlap versus fragmentation. On the one hand, there are those who would argue that the securities commissions and SROs cover a very similar group of market actors and activities, thus imposing an excessive regulatory burden. This stems from multiple and overlapping regulations and compliance demands which are costly, consume scarce organizational resources and energies and generate inefficiencies on the part of regulator and regulated alike. In addition to the compliance burden, the regulated are also quick to point to the multiple proceedings to which they may be subject for any given violation including regulatory, criminal and, for the truly unfortunate, civil, a kind of regulatory 'piling on' that generates multiple forms of legal jeopardy and is seen to saddle the industry with excessive legal and regulatory risks (Lawyer #19).[15]

On the other hand, the regulatory system is faulted not for its redundancies but rather its omissions, as evidenced by variations in enforcement priorities across jurisdictions, coordination difficulties particularly in multi-jurisdictional cases and gaps between regulatory silos that sap 'enforcement virility' (Task Force 2006: 19), resulting in a system that is 'highly fragmented and therefore somewhat dysfunctional' (Lawyer #27: 1). In reality, these are different sides of the same coin as the existence of multiple regulators with common mandates creates the possibility of *both* overlapping expenditures of regulatory labour *and* different standards according to which these mandates are envisioned and executed, with some cases invariably falling between the cracks. Rather than posing the question of inter-agency relationships in these more abstract policy terms, the key is to examine the localized struggles, turf battles and jurisdictional tensions between agencies, each seeking to define their place in the enforcement field.

Turf-battles and inter-agency politics

In speaking with regulators and the police about their relationships with their fellow agencies, most were inclined to emphasize the positive aspects of these exchanges, including a high degree of cooperation, the absence of competition and an atmosphere of mutual respect. While this is likely true on a macro level, tensions were more evident in the course of daily interactions, thus revealing a vibrant regulatory politics: 'There's all sorts of interesting regulatory competition which doesn't improve efficiency . . . It's "I won't share information with him. I'm going after this one and they're going after that type of case"' (Lawyer #21: 8). This sentiment is reiterated by another respondent: 'It sort of surprises you that there is a lack of communication where you think for sure that they are talking to each other. And they do talk on one level, but it's more macro rather than micro' (Lawyer #6: 5). Much of this conflict, not surprisingly, involves how cases are assigned to and processed by the various agencies and thus the nature of the regulatory division of labour understood not as a static assignment of tasks, but rather a set of more informal considerations and decision-criteria brought to bear on specific cases. Typically these tensions are most evident around inter-agency referrals which, as noted by Emerson (1991) and Hawkins (2002), hinge on inter-organizational knowledge, including past practices and anticipation of how a case is likely to be received by other agencies in the referral chain. While one might imagine these transfers to be effected on the basis of relevant case features and appropriate sanctions, it is strategic decisions and institutional interests that often exert the strongest effects, including a desire to maintain control and to select the cases which best showcase the agency. Happenstance also plays a role as there are cases where assignments have been made on the 'finders, keepers' principle of which agency was first to come across the activity, although the securities commissions remain the bully on the block empowered to assert their jurisdiction whenever it suits them. It is these dynamics of case assessment and inter-agency referral, rather than more macro forms of organizational contact, that offer a critical lens into the politics at play in the enforcement field:

> I'd say there's a very interesting turf war going on and I think that if you accept that there's only so much regulatory pie to go around as people have started to expand their jurisdictional scope and sharpen their regulatory elbows, other regulators have had to try and push back.
>
> (Lawyer #12: 3–5)

These tensions and sharpening of elbows extend through three primary points of contact.

Police and crown attorneys

Returning to the outer limits of the enforcement field, one of the first forms of organizational tension and inter-agency politicking involves the police and prosecutors. A perennial theme in discussions of white-collar and corporate crime (Benson and Cullen 1998), the common complaint on the part of the police is that Crown Attorneys are often unwilling or at least hesitant to take on complex securities cases, given that they lack not only the requisite resources and expertise but also the institutional will. This follows from competing priorities and the low likelihood of conviction relative to the standard criminal fare dominating the provincial docket: 'The whole system is set up to handle social crimes and social crime is bad, really bad. People get killed in social crime. They don't get killed in my world' (Former BCSC #2: 14). Given the prevailing public concern with violent crime, white-collar investigations are undoubtedly a hard sell: 'It's the mindset ... some rich cat atop of Bay Street fleecing investors isn't necessarily seen as a priority in the courts compared to making the general Canadian public feel safer. So we're lucky if we're going to be the flavour of the month' (IMET #1: 8). This situation is made even more difficult in Canada, given the separation of the police and Crown[16] and the limited opportunities for cooperation and mutual input at the various stages of a case. There is also the issue that, while the majority of cases are investigated at the federal level, the responsibility for prosecuting them falls to the provinces, creating an institutional barrier across which cases must pass in order to be successfully resolved. Thus, 'to say it's a mess would be the understatement of the year' (Former OSC #1: 1).

Recognizing these difficulties, the original model for the IMET program included an allowance for an embedded Crown,[17] with the plan being that these individuals would function strictly in an advisory capacity and would not be directly involved in the prosecution of individual cases. There was also a provision that, while the provinces would retain the right to first refusal, should they opt to waive this right IMET cases could then be prosecuted at the federal level, thus maximizing the operational and financial synergies between the investigative and prosecutorial phases of the case. Not unlike the other woes that have befallen the IMET program, these initiatives have encountered a number of practical roadblocks, including difficulties in securing the necessary funding to staff these positions and uncertainty on the part of embedded Crown Attorneys as to their proper role in investigations:

> A perfect example would be participation of Justice at witness interviews ... When I first came the lawyers weren't involved *at all* and I'm not prepared to operate that way. So then it became totally involved, not to the extent that we were leading the interviews, but that we would participate. And then there was a change in policy and just recently a decision was made that the lawyers should be watching the interview but should be able to stop the interview and intervene and maybe go in if it seemed to require it but shouldn't necessarily be there in certain cases. And then in other cases maybe they should be. So what we're dealing with right now is we don't know what we're doing.
>
> (IMET #20: 1–2, emphasis added)

The participation of federal Crown Attorneys in the actual prosecution of these cases has also been limited by the perception amongst the provinces, Ontario and Quebec in particular, that federal involvement represents an unjustified incursion on their territory: 'The AG has a monopoly on these cases and that's why they don't like the IMET setup because, like anyone who owns a monopoly, you never like to give up your monopolistic powers' (OSC #4: 14). The police thus find themselves in the difficult position of the provinces refusing to waive their rights to IMET cases, while imposing very strict standards on those that will be accepted. Although this 'dysfunctional relationship' (IMET #7: 3) between the police and Crown is by no means unique to Canada, it has been exacerbated by forms of institutional conflict and federal-provincial rivalries firmly embedded in Canadian legal and political culture.

Police and securities commissions

Another form of conflict involves relations between the police, and in particular IMET, and the provincial securities commissions, a struggle that reflects fundamental philosophical, procedural and legal differences between regulatory and criminal spheres. As many of the cases with potential criminal overtones originate at the securities commissions, one of the key issues involves the conditions under which cases can, and should, be passed from regulators to the police. Given the historically weak commitments of the police to this area, past practice has been for the securities commissions to retain much of this work even in cases of patently fraudulent activity.[18] However, with the recent reincarnation of the police, other factors have motivated the securities commissions to retain a hold on files regardless of their criminal overtones. Foremost among these are the procedural obligations that saddle the criminal process, slowing investigations and creating legal hazards capable of derailing even the strongest of cases. These include the much higher evidentiary standard of 'beyond a reasonable doubt', the burden to fully disclose all aspects of a case and the strict adherence to constitutional rights. When combined with a commitment by the securities commissions not to proceed with their own actions until the criminal aspects of cases have been resolved, thus leaving them exposed to their own critics,[19] many commissions have been hesitant to hand off cases to the police or at least have become extremely selective about the cases they deem suitable for referral:

> The problem is you never know if they're ultimately going to lay charges so it's hard to sit back on something that looks as though it's got significant wrongdoing that people need to be taken out of the marketplace and say 'we'll just wait and see if there's charges laid'. Because if we've got an investigation that goes on for three years and they say 'we're not charging' then that puts us in the position that either we're not going to do anything or we're going to pick up a case that's several years old already, neither one of which is desirable.
> (OSC #12: 8)

This reluctance has only increased with the move to self-funding and greater sanctioning powers, which have meant that in addition to speed, fewer resources and the ability to proceed on the basis of a less burdensome legal standard, securities regulators are able to impose fairly stiff penalties, thus allowing for the kinds of punitive remedies deemed appropriate even in the most egregious of cases. The result is an incentive on the part of the commissions and SROs to assert a regulatory interest in cases that may be deserving of criminal charges: 'Sometimes because of the need to use those extraordinary powers, securities regulators will go for a regulatory offence rather than a criminal offence knowing that there's a lesser penalty but knowing that they can use their extraordinary powers and the burden of proof is lower' (Former OSC #1: 4).

With case flow dependent on the strategic interests of the regulatory community, another point of mandate-related conflict is a prevailing view that criminal enforcement is best suited to cases involving smaller, more marginal players that have presented difficulties for regulators in the past. These are the cases most congruent with conventional incarnations of criminality, with perpetrators of dubious backgrounds targeting innocent victims through schemes that are patently fraudulent and in which evidence of intent to harm is incontrovertible:[20] 'There are times we're dealing with people who really are criminals and all we can do is slap them with trading bans or fines' (Hyndman in Lewis 2003: A45). With these regulatory needs in mind, it should come as no surprise that one of the most common complaints directed by regulators towards IMET is their unwillingness to take on smaller files with clear criminal overtones: '[The IMETs] don't touch anything unless it involves multi-millions of dollars whereas the small frauds, they don't have time for' (Lawyer #6: 7). In the words of another respondent: 'they want to be able to look at important cases. They don't want to deal with the little ones. And that may be a problem' (Former OSC #1: 6). One senior securities regulator used the example of boiler rooms to drive home this point: 'There's so much [boiler room activity] going on, we just don't have the resources to do it all. It's primarily and fundamentally fraud, and the police should be doing it, but ... that stuff doesn't fall within the mandate of IMETs' (OSC #12: 4).

The desire for the police to pursue the players with shady backgrounds and dubious intentions reveals an interesting duplicity. On the one hand, IMET stakeholders advocate for a strong police response to securities misconduct and fault the RCMP for their past record in this area. On the other hand, the desired police presence is one that can be articulated within a very narrow band, with the police envisaged as the sanitary engineers of the regulatory world tasked with collecting the refuse of the other players and purging it from the system. This effort on the part of regulators to manage the criminal process according to their own interests reveals the unique politics at play in the regulatory system, thus restricting IMET to the cases that make it through the regulatory filter[21] and reinforcing their subordinate position in the enforcement field.

Beyond conflicts around case assignments and the regulatory division of labour, another point of tension between police and the securities commissions involves the flow of information. In most jurisdictions, including the US and the UK, regulators are able to share information regarding ongoing investigations with the police and vice versa with few restrictions, an information flow that is critical to nurturing cases in both spheres. In contrast, the Canadian landscape is defined by a strict separation between the securities commissions and the police, whereby the regulators are prevented from passing on and police are prevented from accepting, information bearing on a criminal case obtained through the course of a regulatory investigation. The crux of this issue hinges on the very different legal regimes in which these players operate, and thus the types of powers to which they have access and the standards with which their investigations must comply. As administrative bodies, securities commissions enjoy extensive investigative powers, including the power to compel witnesses to speak with them. The difficulty is that this violates the constitutional protection against self-incrimination afforded through the Charter of Rights and Freedoms in the criminal sphere, which includes the option not only for suspects but also for witnesses to refuse to speak with the police.[22] As a means of managing this juridical divide, one of the conditions placed on testimony obtained through these regulatory powers is that it cannot be disclosed to the police absent written consent from the respondent or the execution of a search warrant on the regulator.[23]

For their part, the police are hyper-aware of this legal line, approaching it with an 'abundance of caution' (Securities Superconference 2009) and striving to ensure that the integrity of their cases not be compromised by accepting 'tainted evidence': 'the police wouldn't take [a case] if we had used our compulsory powers because they'd be afraid that they would get all the way down to trial and spend millions of dollars and lots of time to have the court throw it out' (Former OSC #1: 4). Police concerns are so great that they are reluctant to accept information obtained from interviews even where witnesses consented to their statements being made available to the police, this on the grounds that even the most mundane exchange of evidence could jeopardize their case. The result is a legal membrane across which information flows freely in one direction, from the police to regulators, yet is effectively blocked from moving in the other: 'What goes one way can't go the other' (IMET #3: 1).

The fact that the criminal process is so clearly differentiated from the regulatory impacts both information sharing and inter-agency referrals (Emerson 1991). Regulators knowingly place themselves in a position where, in order to make use of their powers of compulsion, they close themselves off from the police who, lacking the ability to access key witnesses, are often left in the evidentiary dark without the facts needed to proceed with their investigation. Cooperation is thus a significant problem, particularly in high profile cases with notable stakes for both agencies: '[The OSC has] that compellability power for getting their witnesses so they have a huge advantage that they don't want to compromise. I've gotten more cooperation from the SEC than I have from the OSC' (IMET #12: 3). A similar dynamic plays out in inter-agency referrals as regulators, once they invoke their powers of compulsion, ensure that the case will remain in the regulatory fold, thus shutting the police out entirely. The result of these fears of 'cross-contamination' (OSC #1: 8) is an extremely sterile, yet unproductive regulatory environment.

Taking a step back, what is intriguing is that this legal line between regulators and the police is often made out to be much brighter than is necessarily the case.[24] While restrictions on the transfer of information from the regulatory to the criminal sphere are believed to be quite firm and incontrovertible, they are based more on past practice than judicial decree. The sharing of information with the police is not expressly prohibited by constitutional protections so long as the purpose of the investigation, up to the point of transfer, is to determine regulatory compliance rather than penal liability (Cory and Pilkington 2006).[25] Existing accounts of this issue also fail to recognize the importance of context in determining the validity of Charter claims: 'The entire context of a Charter claim … is crucial in determining the extent of the right asserted … Thus, the question of whether investigators may be pursuing a "truly criminal" or a "regulatory" violation does not in itself define or delimit the nature of Charter rights that may be impacted by state actions' (Reynolds 2006: 3). With Charter principles viewed as 'contextual' and 'contextually driven' rather than absolute (Securities Superconference 2009), there would appear to be untapped opportunities for information sharing.

Granted, things become much more complicated when the powers of compulsion are involved as the restrictions on information sharing are more fully articulated and codified in Charter-based protections against self-incrimination. And yet, even here there would appear to be a measure of ambiguity as this strict prohibition is intended for individuals who would themselves be subject to criminal charges. It is less certain whether this same degree of protection would or should apply to witnesses or third parties provided, once again, that the testimony was compelled by the regulator prior to the formation of penal intent: 'The Charter is for people who are accused of a crime, not witnesses. There is no Charter implication here' (Hannaford in Gray 2007: 3). Citing ambiguities in the landmark *Jarvis* decision, and thus the applicable standard as to the point at which a case crosses the Rubicon from the regulatory to the criminal realm, a prominent defence attorney acknowledged that there is indeed room for pushback by regulators and the police around information sharing:

> Are you familiar with *R v Jarvis*? When you first read it you think that this is a tremendous victory for the defence. But it's not. I see *Jarvis* as a case where if a regulatory body wanted to use those powers and disguise it all until there's no way they could deny that the threshold test had been met, that it could just be so abused. But the commission here won't use compulsory powers if they want to have a criminal investigation. Period. Whether it's for a predominant purpose or not … I think they misread *Jarvis*. What worries me is if somebody says let's test the limits of this case that they'll find it's really easy from a regulators' point of view to just push to the limit. They'll find a judge will accept it.
>
> (Lawyer #1: 8)

Moving beyond these front stage legal debates, the investment of regulators in maintaining a strict separation between themselves and the police may have more to do with the fear that, were this line to be dimmed, they too may be subject to greater constitutional scrutiny, thus compromising their regulatory advantage and providing a potential boon to defence attorneys:[26]

> The stand of the securities commission is that their activities should fall under administrative law so that they have a lot more flexibility. The defence bar sees the securities commission as a big tool of the government. They are really law enforcement. And they would love to find any little excuse to convince the courts that in fact securities regulation should come under the Charter.
>
> (IMET #16: 3)

From this it would appear that both the commissions and legal counsel have a distinct interest in maintaining these barriers to information sharing and thus preserving existing regulatory and criminal silos as this confers advantages to both sides. For commissions it is the ability to operate under a less burdensome legal regime and maintain greater control over its cases, while for defence counsel it is a means of pressuring regulators not to overstep their boundaries, with the police the odd person out. This also reveals one of the great ironies at play in the field of securities enforcement as many members of the legal community are extremely vocal about the failure of securities regulators and the police to take action in high profile cases, while behind the scenes they are busily advocating for the very barriers known to frustrate these investigations.

Securities commissions and SROs

A final form of inter-agency conflict flows from the relationships between the commissions and the SROs, particularly the IDA and RS. Given the degree of overlap in their respective mandates and the possibility that more than one agency will assert an interest in any given case, a frequent complaint voiced by the SROs is that the commissions are prone to stepping on their toes and assuming control over cases that are rightfully theirs: 'We've had cases where we've done the bulk of the work and matters have been announced and our names haven't been on the press release. You would think that there would be some collegiality there. So there's issues with respect to protection of turf' (IDA #4: 7–8). The possibility of the securities commissions stepping in to 'take cases' is also noted by a respondent from RS: 'We've got personal experience with that where very interesting cases come up and we were maybe in the process of doing something and inform them because there's going to be a piece of it that's coming to them, and it's just taken. And nothing's happened' (RS #3: 12).

Exacerbating these tensions is the fact that the SROs, by virtue of their contractually defined authority, are limited to enforcing violations against their own members, in the case of the IDA brokerage firms and their employees and in the case of RS the individuals and firms that trade on the exchanges for which they are the recognized 'regulatory service provider'. This arrangement creates difficulties especially in instances where alleged misconduct extends beyond the contracted membership to include investors and issuing companies, both of whom fall under the jurisdiction of the securities commissions as statutory regulators: 'None of the SROs have any jurisdiction over clients. If you are not a registered trader, if you are not a principal of a brokerage firm, if you are not an investment counselor or portfolio manager, we have absolutely no jurisdiction over them to compel information or to prosecute. So the commissions have to do those' (RS #3: 4). The exclusion of the client in particular from the regulatory purview of RS and the IDA has critical implications for the ability of these agencies to pursue more complex cases as they are dependent on the commissions to substantiate the broader claim of action and proceed against the external market participants:

> Sometimes I think it's a turf war, everybody's protecting their own turf ... And that's a continual source of frustration for us having to rely on other agencies to assist us in doing what we want to do ... The IDA does an investigation and you have a bunch of market participants that fall outside our jurisdiction and then at the end of the day we take disciplinary action against our broker, but the commission has no appetite to chase those guys. Then when we go to our hearing, a natural question for one of the hearing panelists is 'what's happening over here?' 'Nothing.' 'Oh nothing. Well if nothing is happening over here then why is this so serious?' So you're not getting the total picture.
>
> (IDA #2: 5–6)

These limiting effects have been especially acute for RS given its position on the regulatory front-lines and its ability, by virtue of its surveillance technologies, to pick up a wide range of abnormal or questionable activities, most notably forms of market manipulation and insider trading. With regard to the former, in cases where the manipulation is initiated or directed by a client, RS is able to pursue the trader for his part in the scheme but is unable to take action against the end client with the merits and urgency of its own investigation often suffering as a result: 'On a manipulation case, if we think the firm either failed to supervise or one of their employees was actually involved in the manipulation, that would be the jurisdiction of RS. The client who's directing the manipulation, the commission has to deal with that person' (Former RS #2: 5). And yet, many of the commissions are hesitant to take on manipulation cases, given the difficult evidentiary challenges combined with their own competing priorities and caseloads. This catch-22 has resulted in a palpable sense of frustration on the part of RS staff who, on a number of occasions, have been left with the remnants of a much weaker case: 'There are some cases where we end up prosecuting dealers or traders for helping their clients undertake a manipulation, and yet the underlying manipulation never gets prosecuted' (RS #3: 1).

An even more discomforting dilemma arises in cases of insider trading, which typically involve end clients and once again fall outside of RS's purview. One of the complicating factors here is that, while RS lacks the authority to pursue these cases, it not only possesses the capacity to detect insider trading but is mandated to do so by virtue of its agreements with the statutory regulators, with the understanding that detected cases will be referred to the appropriate securities commission for further investigation. This arrangement has fuelled an ongoing tension between RS and the larger commissions in BC and Ontario as it remains unclear at what point suspicions of insider trading must be referred up the regulatory chain:

> There's a boundary issue of when we detect what looks like insider trading at what point do we then refer the case to the Commission for further investigation and enforcement? ... Obviously we prefer to hand it off earlier because the more our people spend chasing down or investigating insider trading cases, the less time they have for doing the things or cases under our rules. Whereas the Commissions prefer to have the case handed to them on a platter with a nice little bow and then take it from there.[27]
>
> (RS #2: 1–2)

This is further complicated by the fact that each commission has different expectations and protocols for case transfer. While some commissions have asked that RS turn over all potential insider trading cases, others have requested only substantiated cases meeting pre-defined thresholds in terms of size and profit: 'If it doesn't meet a certain criteria, they didn't want us forwarding it up there' (RS #5: 9). This same respondent went on to suggest that this may be less a case of maximizing efficiencies and more one of building-in plausible deniability: 'They could do the filtering up there but this way if they never saw a case, no one could ever point a finger at them for dropping the ball ... It's so stupid' (RS #5: 9). If not the specific threshold, it is once again variable and conflicting enforcement priorities that impede case transfer:

> Each one of the securities commissions has a completely different focus and mandate around insider trading. Sometimes it's very important and they've publicly said it, others have said 'It's totally unimportant, we won't do anything.' And yet, we are obligated to continue to do all the work regardless if it never goes anywhere. So it's extremely frustrating.
>
> (RS #3: 3)

With the commissions more interested in generating their own files rather than taking on 'cases that are cast aside by RS' (IMET #18: 7), the result is that few cases of insider trading make it across this organizational divide: 'We may forward a few hundred suspected cases of insider trading a year to the various commissions and very few come out the other end' (RS #5: 9). This reflects the enduring tensions between the SROs and the commissions, as well as their regional character with the inter-agency divide deepened by variable budgets, staffing levels and enforcement priorities across the various commissions.

Jurisdiction and the legal encoding of regulatory space

Enlivening many of these inter-agency conflicts are legally encoded limits on the scope and authority of the enforcement agencies, limits that give rise to conflict through the carving out of distinct powers and obligations, as well as forced alliances and mutual dependencies. The legal roots of these tensions are best understood through the concept of 'jurisdiction'. Defined in terms of the legal encoding of space, or the juridical construction and authorization of spatial differences (see Blomley and Bakan 1992; Blomley 1994; Ford 1999; Lange 2003), jurisdiction is typically conceived in politico-territorial terms as the geographical boundaries or limits on the authority emanating from a particular government entity, whether this be municipal, provincial or federal (Ford 1999). There is no doubt that these kinds of jurisdictional markings play a role in the field of securities enforcement. In fact, a recurring criticism is that regulation continues to be grounded in geographically or territorially-based divisions of labour and authority, whilst the markets are increasingly transnational in nature. This creates a number of logistical challenges including: (1) a limited view of misconduct as regulators in any given jurisdiction may lack the integrated view of the markets required to understand and substantiate more complex violations; (2) coordination difficulties resulting from the need to work with a number of different partners, some of whom may be disinclined to cooperate or whose assistance may not be forthcoming;[28] (3) confusion over which agency should be assigned carriage of the case; and (4) difficulties in identifying offshore accounts and secrecy havens. While each of these factors is challenging in-and-of-itself, the last is especially troublesome, given the invisibility of offshore transactions:

> There's probably a lot more things that [the regulators] could take action on if there were more restrictions placed on how accounts were established ... You'll always have tax havens and offshore jurisdictions that aren't required to cooperate and provide information. And we'll have problems with this. And the OSC will go on and on about that for you. It's a huge barrier.
>
> (Former RS #1: 12)

As predicted, this was identified as a major problem by a senior member of the OSC:

> A problem that's been ongoing for years and continues to be a problem is the use of offshore jurisdictions to hide the identity of people who are conducting transactions. It's not at all unusual still to find a transaction that has gone through five or six different countries in the process of going through a brokerage firm here. The brokerage firm has no idea who the client is and often it's a transaction that started off in Toronto and ends in Toronto and they just move it around the big loop trying to hide who it is. And depending on the countries that it goes through, that can take you an awful long time to find out who it was who was involved, and sometimes we never find out.
>
> (OSC #12: 6)

Of course, in the Canadian context these difficulties are magnified by a regionalism that arguably exerts an even greater effect on enforcement than do national differences, this given the compounding of challenges relating to coverage, coordination and information sharing by provincial politics and the often discordant regional flavourings of the regulatory mix.

While recognizing the significance of jurisdiction cast in the form of territorially-defined 'state' borders, one of the unique features of securities enforcement as a field of multiple agencies and distinct legal tracts is that many of the preceding lines of conflict are informed, not only by geographically encoded and thus more or less incontrovertible limits to their reach and scope, but rather more artificial distinctions between the areas of market activity on which they are legally allowed to tread and the types of market actors over which they are able to exercise their authority. These distinctions reflect a very particular carving up of the regulatory pie, as well as the different legal spheres in which these agencies are obliged or choose to operate. Thus, much of the tension between the police and securities commissions flows from their respective positions in two very different legal universes, one criminal, the other administrative, a positioning that binds them to the fates of distinct powers and obligations despite lingering ambiguities as to the very nature of these boundaries. Similarly, in the case of the commissions and SROs, while inter-provincial distinctions certainly muddy the waters, the essence of inter-agency conflict flows from the contractual roots of SRO authority with the scope of agency activities limited to particular 'member' groups and their authority constrained by the principles of contract law. In each of these respects, it is not simply the existence or materiality of these legal distinctions that is significant, but also their degree of ambiguity and artifice as agencies are positioned somewhat precariously on the borders of a number of different legal domains with the very setting of these jurisdictional markers part of the game play in the enforcement field.

Besides the inter-agency tensions noted above, these jurisdictional dynamics play out in two additional ways that are relevant to the practice of securities enforcement. The first follows from the fact that the contractual roots of SRO authority not only limits their ability to proceed in cases of misconduct extending beyond their own membership, but also effectively removes a number of sites and transaction points from their regulatory purview. This creates added difficulties both in proceeding based on suspicions of misconduct, and detecting problems in the first instance. A perfect example of this is the inability of RS to engage in effective cross-market surveillance as its jurisdictional reach is limited to the oversight of equities-based exchanges with entirely separate agencies tasked with regulating the bond (IDA), derivatives (Montreal Derivatives Exchange) and commodities (Winnipeg Commodities Exchange) markets. This limited view of trading activity is significant given that it prevents RS from detecting cases of cross-market manipulation, a common strategy employed by individuals wishing to engage in illegal conduct while subverting the usual regulatory controls:

> When it comes to market manipulations, very few people are foolish enough to identify themselves clearly by trading in their own accounts, manipulating

> on a single marketplace. Anyone with any sense is going to cross-market manipulate. And so the simple fact that you just look at equities, when the world trades in baskets and commodities, you're only seeing part of the issue. You'll never be able to see the whole manipulation.
>
> (RS #3: 8–9)

Similarly, rather than using inside information to trade directly, investors may instead purchase a derivative whose value is tied to the underlying security but sold on the derivatives exchange:

> The really smart inside traders are ... probably not going to run out and buy and sell a bunch of your company's stock on the TSX. But you may do a bunch of trading in derivatives on the Montreal Exchange. Not covered by us. Or you may go and do trading in fixed income instruments that are tied somehow to the value of your company ... There's information sharing but in terms of what activity we can look at and our process would be to look at the trading around material news releases but only in the markets that we regulate.
>
> (RS #2: 6)

For stocks listed on more than one exchange, this jurisdictional divide is more like a chasm: 'Trading in multiple markets makes it easier to hide things. It's often difficult to identify who is behind the trading and regulators often cannot see the full picture' (Atkinson 2004: 8–9).[29]

A second implication of the jurisdictional confinement of the SROs to their contracted membership is that these agencies have virtually no authority over individuals should they opt to terminate their membership and leave the industry.[30] In the case of the IDA, this has resulted in difficulties in collecting fines as the decisions of its hearings panels are not recognized by the courts, thus precluding the use of civil claims as an avenue of recovery in cases involving former members. A similar jurisdictional bind plagues RS, although here the opportunities for recourse are even more limited as traders found to be in violation of its rules can simply cease trading and move into other areas of the securities business such as selling mutual funds or managing portfolios: 'If you do something wrong and we catch you and we convict you, all we can do is terminate your access to the marketplaces we regulate ... The limits of our jurisdiction means that we really can't get somebody out of the industry the way that the IDA can' (RS #2: 2). As with the IDA, this also means that penalties, such as fines, cannot be enforced against individuals once they leave RS's jurisdiction: 'Our sanctions are not enforceable in that if we levy a fine against somebody, and they just don't pay, there's nothing we can do' (RS #3: 9). Although these 'exit' options may not be available to everyone, with many firms and individuals required to face proceedings and pay fines as a cost of staying in business, these jurisdictional limits inevitably reduce the size and weight of the regulatory stick.

While these limits on the types of actors and forms of activity to which the regulators have access and on which they are able to exercise their authority are the primary manifestation of jurisdiction's effects on the enforcement field, a second dimension involves the investigative and procedural powers of the SROs relative to the securities commissions. Bound to the conventions of contract law and lacking statutory authority, the ability of the SROs to demand document production and subpoena witnesses in the course of hearings is limited to their own membership. They are thus effectively barred from compelling documents or testimony from third parties, powers long enjoyed by the securities commissions:

> We don't have the necessary powers to do what is required of us and we need statutory powers to get third party documents because banks try to hold out giving us documents ... If we had the statutory power to collect documents from third parties we wouldn't have these challenges. If we had the ability to subpoena witnesses we wouldn't have these challenges.
>
> (IDA #4: 7)

These investigative and procedural limits, which also include the absence of statutory immunity from civil liability, have fuelled a long-running campaign by the SROs for the same statutory powers enjoyed by the commissions. Thus far these requests have fallen on deaf ears with opposition not only from the industry, but also from the securities commissions themselves who remain invested in the current order of things:

> I think that as the SRO role develops and as more things are downloaded to SROs the Commissions want to keep a clear distinction between what the securities commissions do and what authority they have, and what the SROs have ... So the commission seems very set on maintaining those boundaries.
>
> (RS #2: 10)

A seemingly technical matter of how authority and responsibility are divided up across different enforcement agencies, jurisdiction instead emerges as part-and-parcel of the politics underlying the field of securities enforcement, as well as one of the key political stakes at play in the field itself. Extending well beyond its more conventional politico-territorial imaginings, the workings of jurisdiction are evident in the positioning of enforcement agencies in very different legal territories with the agencies themselves seeking to preserve and/or challenge these boundaries. For the commissions the concern is primarily with maintaining their privileged position in the enforcement field, shoring up their borders with both the police and SROs and laying claim to a distinct legal space defined by its statutory form and its roots in the administrative tradition. Similarly, the workings of jurisdiction are evident in the limited scope and authority of the SROs relative to the commissions, with the former confined to a rather narrow regulatory orbit and, for those cases that extend beyond the pale, their dependence on the good graces of the higher regulatory authorities to substantiate their claims and/or accept the fruits of their labour on the promise they will be jammed into future regulatory actions. In each of these respects, it is the presumed *technicality* of jurisdiction that actually matters most as what are in fact highly contingent and somewhat ambiguous legal distinctions are seemingly set in stone. The result is a series of artificially bright jurisdictional lines that simultaneously confer and reproduce regulatory advantages, while the gaps in scope and authority are used, often quite strategically, to cherry pick the cases best suited to the interests and agendas of the larger players. How these various jurisdictional lines and associated legal encodings are cast, constituted and depoliticized is thus critical to the organization and politics of this field, with enforcement invariably bearing the stamp of these competing interests and power plays.

Fragmentation and the problem of 'regulatory arbitrage'

Far from the image of a highly integrated regulatory system, with regulators tripping over one another to take on cases and engage in the proverbial 'piling on', the reality of securities enforcement is one of much more limited and tightly circumscribed regulatory territories occupied by agencies each seeking to take on the cases that provide the best returns in terms of both internally recognizable and valued 'hits' and public displays of successful regulatory outcomes. From this it would appear that the more pressing issue to emerge from the distinct tracts of regulatory activity is one of fragmentation rather than overlap, with the latter confined to the minority of high profile cases in which multiple agencies are required to take action. The result of this fragmentation is a limited view of, and engagement with, the markets with regulatory activities lacking coordination and weighed down by inter-agency politicking, and no one agency possessing the degree of scaling or perspective needed to appreciate the larger picture: 'The issue is that jurisdiction is based on who you have jurisdiction over and what portion of their activity you have it over. When it comes to activity, you only get parts of the activity so you never *see* the whole thing' (RS #3: 1, emphasis added). This inability to peer across the markets and move cases across jurisdictional divides represents a critical brake on regulatory efforts.

And yet, the danger of this regulatory fragmentation is not simply that some activities will be missed, but that these gaps will be used strategically to skirt regulatory scrutiny. While many respondents denied that this was a real issue, others acknowledged opportunities for what they referred to as 'regulatory arbitrage'. Following from the well-worn practice of market arbitrage, a trading strategy in which traders exploit small differences in the pricing of equities, currencies and other financial instruments across different exchanges, this involves efforts on the part of market participants and legal counsel to take advantage of gaps between regulatory regimes. This dynamic certainly comes into play in the context of cross-border cases, where market players intentionally organize their activities so as to exploit the differences between international regulators and play the odds that these jurisdictional divides will prevent agencies from grasping the true extent of their misconduct and/or hinder cooperation in the event their activities are discovered. However, a number of respondents pointed to a more subtle yet nefarious form of arbitrage staked on jurisdictional divisions *within* national enforcement fields. This includes the aforementioned practice of spreading trades across different exchanges in order to take advantage of gaps in inter-market surveillance, a routing through market nodes that are functionally integrated yet jurisdictionally distinct. It also encompasses what one respondent referred to as the strategy of playing regulators off of one another:

> What I do is I look for scenes and angles and how to try and play one off against the other for the benefit of my clients … if you know how each of those agencies uses jurisdiction and how it interacts with other agencies you can usually find an approach that works to your benefit.
>
> (Lawyer #12: 3–5)

This 'capacity to pit one [regulator] against the other to achieve a client's needs' (Former OSC #2: 11) is not quite the same as the characters in the old *Dukes of Hazzard* series speeding across the county line to avoid arrest, but it certainly speaks to the tactical advantages provided by jurisdictional distinctions, which are often treated *as though* they were lines on a map.

These opportunities for regulatory arbitrage, and the fact that securities enforcement hinges on these somewhat arbitrary jurisdictional divisions and regulatory territories, are especially troubling when viewed in relation to the increasingly fluid and seamless nature of the markets themselves. While the traditional distinctions between financial sectors or 'pillars' continue to erode, regulation remains distinctly product-centred, hence the aforementioned treatment of securities as a matter of provincial jurisdiction, while banking and insurance are governed at the federal level through an entirely separate regulatory regime. The artificial and anachronistic nature of this regulatory division of labour vis-à-vis the markets is nicely captured by a senior manager at RS using the metaphor of an apple corer:

> It's kind of like an apple corer, one of those things that you can press down on an apple and it takes the core out of the centre and divides all of these little pieces up. That thing is like what our regulatory structure is and the apple is the financial markets. Each one of these little wedges is treated differently, completely artificially. And the thing in the middle, the core, you throw away. You don't even look there. That's kind of it. You have this strange jurisdictional press over top of everything and each piece of the action is treated differently.
>
> (RS #3: 18)

Once again, this raises the question of regulatory gaps, as while individual regulators may not be capable of, or interested in, 'looking over the fence' (RS #2: 11), market actors are able to move across jurisdictional lines with relative ease, using these divisions as covers for their activities and a means of running interference should they run afoul of the law. The difficulties associated with monitoring financial activities in a highly differentiated system of markets and products returns us to the question of space and the notion that the markets and regulators are mapped onto two very different kinds of spatial territories. The first is defined in terms of fluid linkages between players extending across a series of urban financial nodes, while the second entails artificially segregated regulatory fiefdoms fortified by jurisdictional boundaries and staked on the protection of a preconceived regulatory turf. It is within these divergent spaces of finance and regulation that the fault lines underlying the enforcement field are brought most clearly into view.[31]

Conclusion

Despite sharing a common mandate to protect investors and maintain the integrity of the markets, the relationships between the agencies tasked with enforcing securities laws are far from harmonious, with an equal measure of conflict, struggle and rivalry. However, it is not the mere existence of conflict that is significant here, but the fact that these skirmishes are rooted in relative positions of advantage and disadvantage, strength and weakness, and autonomy and dependence, the embedded features of a larger field of play. It is in this respect that the work of Pierre Bourdieu and his concept of a social field have proven valuable, helping to capture the diverse and uneven topography of securities enforcement as a particular kind of field, one inhabited by both regulatory and non-regulatory players and defined by the relative distances between these various actors and the markets themselves. With the mandates of enforcement bound to the legalities of authorization and obligation, these positions are further shaped by differences in legally encoded and strategically enacted authority, scope and powers, which have the effect of limiting the range of motion for some agencies more so than for others. Juxtaposed with the freedom of movement accorded to industry players and intermediaries, these forms of market distance and legal emplacement serve to obstruct the regulators' views of the markets, while at the same time limiting the scope of their interventions. It is these disjunctures that market actors are able to use to their advantage, whether intentionally or not, in managing regulatory risks. Thus, the world of securities enforcement is far from flat, with its depths and textures reflected in the positions, spaces and boundaries that underlie the enforcement enterprise and which engender a uniquely politicized field of play.

One of the benefits of framing securities enforcement in terms of a social field is that it allows for a more richly textured view of the limits encumbering enforcement agencies, linking them to the unique features and localized politics of the field itself, rather than the influence of interests from the financial beyond. For example, the opportunities for insider trading created by the geographical and institutional separation of the equities (Toronto) and derivatives (Montreal) markets[32] are rooted more in regional differences and related jurisdictional divides than industry schemings. Similarly, tensions between police and Crown Attorneys are couched in age-old provincial/federal politics buttressed by distinct organizational priorities. While less manifestly political in nature, much of the force behind these inter-agency tensions and points of regulatory fracture is the treatment of the distinctions between agencies as technical matters that are uninteresting, straightforward and taken-for-granted (Riles 2005; Valverde 2009). Thus, the move from the regulatory to the criminal sphere is viewed by the police as a technical matter of law long settled by the courts. Likewise, differences in the authority and scope of the SROs relative to the commissions are conceived as products of the technical distinctions between contract and statutory law. The point here is that while members of the industry no doubt benefit from the gaps in enforcement, they are not necessarily of their own making. Moving forward, and setting the stage for a more up-close view of the enforcement enterprise, the question that remains is how these distances and distinctions underlying the social and legal spaces of enforcement shape the working practices of regulators. A matter of the interpersonal rather than purely institutional side of enforcement, the issue is how 'distance from the markets' is reflected in the backgrounds, tendencies and performances of the players inhabiting the enforcement field.

Notes

1 These include legal pluralism, systems theory, governance theory and the work of Foucault and the governmentality tradition, although the incorporation of the latter is quite selective and overlooks other aspects of the perspective that are in some ways inconsistent with the networked governance framework (see Williams 2006).

2 For example, many of Valverde's criticisms stem from Bourdieu's 1987 article on the juridical field, understandably so given her interest in law. However, this article is written specifically for a legal audience and is thus not the best representation of his work. In particular, very little insight is provided, other than through the translators' introduction, into the concepts of field, capital and habitus, with the full complexity and colour of these concepts only emerging from his larger body of work. There is also the issue that, for Bourdieu, law exists in an especially intimate relationship with the field of class relations and is thus thought to possess a more limited autonomy relative to many of the other social fields examined in his writings. The problem may thus be more with his particular understanding of, or approach to, law specifically rather than his larger framework, which is arguably far more appreciative of autonomy, struggle and slippage.

3 While Bourdieu often conceives of fields in terms of relations between individuals, he does recognize, particularly in his later work, that fields may also be understood in terms of relations between organizations (Bourdieu 2005).

4 Foremost among these was the passage of the Charter of Rights and Freedoms and the ensuing body of Charter-based case law, which significantly altered the field of play for the police, creating new barriers to information sharing with the regulatory community, imposing additional procedural requirements and severely restricting the use of investigative tools such as wiretaps.

5 Notable cases include Bre-X, Livent, Phillips Services and YBM Magnex.

6 One of the main drafters of the IMET initiative commented that part of his strategy in selling the plan was to shift the problem of financial crime from bikers and terrorists,

the folk devils of the recent past, to the newly discovered 'enemy within': 'Instead of pointing at evil bikers, instead of pointing the threat at Bin Laden saying it's terrorism, we called it the enemy within. It's the enemy within the corporate boardroom' (IMET #19: 2). This suggests that IMET was not simply a reaction to scandals south of the border but represented an active attempt on the part of key entrepreneurs within the RCMP to reclaim lost territory.

7 Charges were laid in June 2008 in two of its most high profile cases. However, with one of these cases ending in an acquittal and minimal observable progress in the other, these charges have done little to dull criticisms of the IMET program.

8 Similar criticisms and charges of ineffectiveness have been directed towards the Serious Fraud Office in the UK (Levi 1993; Fooks 2002). Even the FBI and the Department of Justice, for many the gold standard for criminal prosecutions in this area, have been challenged over the lack of criminal charges stemming from the sub-prime crisis (eg Taibbi 2011).

9 These include: (1) new offences for fraud and market manipulation; (2) increases in maximum fines to $5 million and terms of imprisonment to five years less a day; (3) administrative penalties of up to $1 million; (4) orders to disgorge profits; and (5) a regime of civil liability for secondary market disclosure (Cory and Pilkington 2006: 199).

10 The OSC for one became self-funding in 1997 allowing it to retain levied fines and penalties, as well as the fees charged for administrative and regulatory services. This not only increased the budget of the agency but also provided for much greater control over its finances and operations.

11 Interestingly, this arrangement is not so much a matter of constitutional or legal design but ad hoc delegation as responsibility was acceded to the provinces and territories under the 'property and civil rights' clause, section 92(13), of the Constitution Act 1867 (Grafstein 2006: 5). The legalities of this arrangement have since emerged as a key area of controversy in discussions to establish a national securities commission, with the federal government asserting its right to regulate the markets based on its constitutional powers over 'national trade and commerce', the grounds for its jurisdiction over banking and insurance. These issues were brought before the Supreme Court of Canada in April 2011, with the verdict pending at the time of writing.

12 All indications from the jurisdictions that do possess a national securities commission are that regionalism and regional conflicts endure, a point which applies to both the US (Scribner 1986; Underhill 2001; Smith and Walter 2006) and the UK (Board et al. 2002). For example, a lack of cooperation between the regional offices of the SEC was cited as a key impediment in the *Madoff* case (SEC 2009; Markopolos 2010).

13 This is true of all provinces with the exception of Alberta where the IDA has been granted statutory authority by the Alberta Securities Commission, yet another indication of the bizarre patchwork that defines the Canadian regulatory landscape.

14 The advantage over the IDA is that this is a 'no-cost option' with a cap of $350,000 rather than $100,000. However, on the downside, the agency is unable to enforce its recommendations and, as a condition of having their cases accepted, complainants must surrender their rights to civil litigation.

15 In reality, this may be a bit of a spurious argument as Condon et al. (2005) estimate the number of cases pursued concurrently by more than one regulator to be less than 5 per cent of the total. Puri (2005) also points to the rarity of concurrent investigations, noting that only 2 per cent of RS investigations are concurrent with the IDA and less than 7 per cent are concurrent with the OSC. Both authors argue that overlap is most common in high profile cases.

16 In some Canadian jurisdictions the police are responsible for laying charges but it is then up to the Crowns whether to move these cases forward for prosecution, while in others, such as BC, the police must first seek approval from the Crown Attorney's office before charges can be laid.

17 These Crowns were to be recruited from the federal prosecution service, which is responsible for handling complex drug, tax and fraud cases and which offers the added benefit, relative to provincial Crown Attorneys, of maintaining federal control over all IMET expenditures.

18 This persisted despite the commissions not having the tools to properly deal with these cases as was evident in the fact that, up until 2002, the Ontario Securities Act did not have a fraud provision. The result was that for many years the OSC had to 'struggle with how to characterize charges', often requiring that staff 'pigeon hole' or 'shoe horn' cases that were 'out-and-out scams' into ill-fitting Securities Act provisions (Crime and the Corporation 2006).

19 Given the intense scrutiny of regulators in recent years, they have become less inclined to accord the police this privilege, or at least have been much more vocal in signalling their own regulatory interest, especially in high profile cases.

20 The perfect example would be a worthless stock sold to senior citizens through a boiler room operation.

21 Not only are the commissions often the first to detect cases of misconduct, they also possess an institutionalized right of influence over which files are passed on to IMET, this given their positions on the Joint Management Teams that oversee IMET caseloads and decide which files are best suited to criminal investigations.

22 Canada is one of the few jurisdictions where police forces lack this power of compulsion. In the US, it is afforded through the grand jury process based on Fifth Amendment protections, while in the UK not only witnesses but also suspects are required to answer questions, even if those answers may incriminate them (see Levi 1995).

23 In most provinces, the prohibition against turning compelled information over to the police is a matter of regulatory convention. However, in the case of Ontario, this has been formally codified in provincial securities legislation (ie Ontario Securities Act).

24 This is reinforced by the use of such geographically inspired terms, such as 'crossing the Rubicon', to refer to the movement of cases from the regulatory to the criminal realm.

25 The two seminal cases on this question are *R v Jarvis* and *R v Ling*, both of which involve tax rather than securities matters and have been characterized as 'unclear and complicated legal precedents' open to 'differing interpretations' (Capital Markets Institute 2008: 21–2). The issue of the applicability of these cases to the securities context was raised by the following respondent: 'In terms of how that kind of a case would apply to a securities act investigation, I don't know if it's been tested yet by the courts. *Jarvis* was a tax case and the facts are a little bit different. Whether the same strict test of whether or not once you have enough evidence that you cross the Rubicon and you have to do everything according to a criminal investigation, I don't know if that would apply here or not' (OSC #2: 6–7).

26 There have already been cases where defence counsel have argued, thus far unsuccessfully, that the Charter should apply to securities commissions, given their status as state agencies whose proceedings are increasingly punitive in nature (see, for example, *BC Securities Commission v Branch*).

27 Interestingly, RS is able to investigate possible instances of insider trading, this by contacting issuers and making inquiries concerning the disclosure or non-disclosure of material information, only by virtue of the fact that responsibility for enforcing timely disclosure rules has been delegated to the agency by the Toronto Stock Exchange: 'We have a contractual relationship with the issuer through the exchange's timely disclosure policy. So we can contact the issuer through that jurisdictional link and have them give us a chronology and who knew what when' (RS #5: 1–3). However, in the future this link may no longer be available to RS. There have already been rumblings from the TSX that it would like to reclaim responsibility for continuous disclosure, primarily in the interests of cost-savings.

28 For the police this includes trudging through the notoriously cumbersome Mutual Legal Assistance Treaty (MLAT) process.

29 This was borne out in the case of Livent which, just prior to the public announcement of its impending bankruptcy, experienced a sudden spike in trading on the NASDAQ exchange but not the TSX, the latter the more obvious platform for these trades given the Canadian roots of both the company and the majority of its investors. This represented a clear indication that 'something unusual was going on' (Consultant #3: 2).

30 In a seminal case on the ability of the SROs to pursue former members, a split panel of the Ontario Divisional Court ruled that there is no specific language in the Ontario Securities Act that entitles the IDA (IIROC) to regulate former members. This decision was subsequently overturned at the Ontario Court of Appeal, with lawyers seeking leave to appeal to the Supreme Court of Canada (Harman 2009).

31 These fault lines are readily apparent in the proposed merger of the Toronto Stock Exchange (TSX) and the London Stock Exchange (LSE) which, if consummated, would raise difficult questions as to the division of jurisdictional authority between Canadian and UK regulators.

32 This separation remains, despite the 2007 purchase of the Montreal Derivatives Exchange by the TSX group, the parent company of the Toronto Stock Exchange.

Chapter 4

Symbolic capital, experience and expertise

Introduction

One of the challenges confronting the agents of securities enforcement in their daily work is not only accessing the informational networks through which signs or symptoms of securities misconduct may be discerned, but also shaping the views of those with whom they are required to engage, and on whom they must rely, in the course of their investigations. This includes members of the industry and their professional counsel as well as judges, mediators and other participants in the regulatory system broadly defined. Rather than the strict application of legal rules, the enforcement process hinges on the ability to mobilize arguments that will be deemed reasonable and credible by other players in this same regulatory space, powers of persuasion that are fundamentally social in nature. Informed by Bourdieu's concepts of social and symbolic capital, this chapter examines the social competencies required for successful regulatory performances, and the extent to which their possession varies across the different positions in the enforcement field. This has important implications for the role of expertise in the regulatory process, which clearly matters, but not in the way we are often led to believe.

The problem of expertise

From the vantage point of the unschooled outsider, the financial markets are an exceedingly strange land defined by abstract and highly specialized concepts imported from mathematics, law, accounting and finance. This is the world of options, puts, upticks and private placements, home to accountants, lawyers, traders and consultants who have devoted their entire careers to understanding the markets and finding new ways to make money by tapping into the transactional flow. Given this degree of expertization, it should come as no surprise that one of the recurring criticisms of regulators is that they lack the knowledge and expertise to properly oversee the markets. While no agency has been immune from this criticism, it has been levied with particular force and frequency against the securities commissions and the police, serving as one of the 'go to' explanations for the failures of securities enforcement: 'Many provincial regulators and most local law enforcement authorities lack expertise in investigation and prosecution of securities offences, and have few opportunities to acquire such expertise' (Canadian Bankers' Association 2008: 7). In the blunt assessment of a senior litigator:

> Unless things have improved remarkably, and it sounds like they've gotten worse, in my day the RCMP couldn't do anything. They were police officers who had no sophisticated understanding of financial markets. I don't want the securities commission to investigate murder. I don't want the RCMP at the same time to investigate insider trading. Most of the RCMP that were involved had a long history as police officers with very limited knowledge of the market. They were often given six week courses or six month courses in accounting and law and expect them to become experts. It's a joke.
>
> (Lawyer #22: 4)

On one level, there are shades of merit to these complaints. Those in the regulatory world tend to be more junior and to possess less market-related experience than their counterparts in the private sector. Moreover, as soon as they accrue a degree of knowledge and understanding of the markets, including the practices of the regulators themselves, they become very valuable to the industry and are thus highly susceptible to poaching. Lured by sizeable salaries, bonuses and opportunities for advancement, this informs the high rates of turnover experienced throughout the regulatory system, and the difficulties in attracting and retaining professional staff below the senior management level. Nowhere is this attrition more evident than the police, who are notorious for their inability to recruit and retain qualified investigators. While the majority of the more talented investigators tend to avoid this area altogether, this given their preference for 'catching the bad guys' rather than risking obscurity toiling away in financial crime units, those who do enter the fray often spend a number of years accumulating expertise and contacts, only to defect either to other units in the RCMP or to more desirable and better paying positions in the regulatory or private sector.[1] These factors have contributed to rates of turnover estimated by one report to be as high as 33 per cent over a four year period (Le Pan 2007: 39), a constant drain on the police knowledge base and a recurring source of concern for the IMET program.

And yet, despite there being a kernel of truth to these complaints, in reading between the lines what appears on its face to be an indictment on the grounds of technical knowledge is in fact rooted in a much more amorphous set of personal attributions. More often than not what regulators and the police are seen to be lacking are the intangibles of sound judgment and a proper attitude: 'It's *attitudes*, not just legal attitudes, attitudes. It's the *sophistication* of our enforcement people' (Lawyer #5: 2, emphasis added). A common refrain of enforcement's critics is thus the failure of the police and regulators to 'attract the *right* people' (Lawyer #28: 12–13, emphasis added). One example of this non-technical side of regulatory expertise is revealed in a recommendation from a major policy report, strongly endorsed and widely cited by stakeholder groups, that the police establish a 'Senior Independent Review Officer' (SIRO) position (Cory and Pilkington 2006). The vision for this position is that it would be occupied by a senior and well respected member of the private bar who would be responsible for guiding investigations and would possess the 'ultimate authority to limit or curtail or to eventually terminate the investigation, or to refer the matter to the appropriate prosecution service' (Cory and Pilkington 2006: 213). What is interesting about this recommendation, ostensibly the parachuting of a member of the private sector into a key managerial post, is that it is couched in attributions of status and judgment. As Cory and Pilkington (2006) note in their rationale for the position: 'Consideration should be given to processes for focusing and expediting investigations, and ensuring quality control and the exercise of *good judgment*. What is needed, in each IMET locale and each securities regulator, is an experienced lawyer with the *seniority*, *status* and *confidence* to exercise independent and sound *judgment*' (121, emphasis added). The importance of status and credibility is also evident in comments from the police and regulators themselves. For example, one IMET member referred to credibility, and the need to appear credible, as a key concern and consideration underlying their work: 'When you're sitting across the table from a subject of interest, your largest fear is that you don't come across as credible. So you spend an inordinate amount of time making sure you *appear* credible' (IMET #10: 2, emphasis added).

These allusions to the social side of expertise resonate nicely with work on the conversational features of the markets (Preda 2001) and regulation (Black 2002), that is, their roots in interpersonal interactions and situated exchanges. Preda (2001) has argued that finance hinges on a credibility gained through skills in the art of conversation: 'credibility is shaped by habitual conversational features: voice, demeanour, phrasing, and the like' (300). This broader view also dovetails with the insights of the cultural economists and the conception of markets as social spaces rooted in interpretive communities, and interpersonal contacts and connections. It is thus not necessarily a textbook knowledge that is needed, but rather a more informal working knowledge of the social world of the markets:

> Some of the case data that we're looking at, invariably the game sounds familiar, the players don't. So when the players sound familiar that means I know the background and I can fill the void, or fill some of the void that people have in terms of what is this person's relationship to that person? What does this person do? What are they like? Do they have any regulatory history? Now these goodies are something you only get by spending time on the Street.
> (IMET #9: 6)

In this respect, it is not simply 'what' one knows that is critical to the success of enforcement. Of equal if not greater importance is a more subtle social knowledge combined with a certain communicative comportment, an embodied confidence, credibility and sense of judgment that stem from one's position in, and perspective on, the field of securities enforcement. This suggests that in order to understand the relevance of 'expertise' to regulation we need to engage more fully with its social side, a task that returns us to the work of Pierre Bourdieu.

Social and symbolic capital: the social side of expertise

In the previous chapter, it was noted that the notion of social space, and the distinctions or differences between the relative positions within this space, is central to Bourdieu's theoretical corpus and is expressed, by way of an inherently relational logic, in his concept of social field. Positioned closely alongside the concept of field is that of 'capital', which represents the logic or principle according to which these differences are constituted and manifested in terms of a hierarchy of positions. Put somewhat differently, it is the unequal distribution of a particular form of capital that determines the relative positions in a given social field, and thus the underlying principle of hierarchy or division operative in this social universe. For Bourdieu, capital can take an infinite variety of forms depending on the field in question, although these are typically variations on a number of more generic types, including economic or financial capital, cultural capital and social or informational capital. While economic capital involves the possession of money and property, cultural and social capital refer to more intangible qualities such as educational qualifications and connections, acquaintances and network ties (Bourdieu 1986). Bourdieu and Wacquant (1992) thus define social capital as 'the sum of the resources, actual or virtual, that accrue to an individual or a group by virtue of possessing a durable network of more or less institutionalized relationships of mutual acquaintance and recognition' (119). These forms of capital are not mutually exclusive but can be converted from one to the other. Thus, the cultural capital of credentials and qualifications can be parlayed into the financial capital of employment. Similarly, the possession of social contacts and connections may provide access to cultural capital in the form of university admissions and prized educational credentials. Bourdieu also makes the critical point that these individual forms of capital are especially valuable in their symbolic form, what he refers to as symbolic capital. This is a type of attributed authority or status that comes from having one's connections and competencies recognized and respected by other players in the field. A form of 'recognized power' (Bourdieu 1991: 72), symbolic capital is thus the 'form that the various species of capital assume when they are perceived and recognized as legitimate' (Bourdieu 1989: 17).

One final point regarding the links between capital and social practice is worth noting. For Bourdieu, social and cultural capital are not simply *possessed* in a manner akin to a credential or degree; they also assume a distinctly embodied form as the interactional competencies associated with particular skills and forms of status or expertise depend on modes of communication and posturing rooted in the body itself, including comportment, gestures and clarity and sophistication of speech (Bourdieu 1984, 1991). As Bourdieu (1991) himself notes: 'Ways of looking, sitting, standing, keeping silent, or even of speaking ("reproachful looks" or "tones", "disapproving glances" and so on) are full of injunctions that are powerful and hard to resist precisely because they are silent and insidious, insistent and insinuating' (51). It is these forms of embodied capital that are captured through his concept of 'habitus' as a manner of viewing and engaging with the world that is unconscious, distinctly embodied and rooted in one's relative position in social space (Bourdieu 1989), what Bourdieu refers to as 'the durable and transposable systems of schemata of perception, appreciation and action that result from the institution of the social in the body' (Bourdieu and Wacquant 1992: 127). The body is thus itself critical to effective social performances, and the communication and reproduction of the differences in status and prestige that lie at the heart of social fields.[2]

While these concepts are no doubt laden with abstraction and may on their surface appear to have little bearing on the practicalities of securities enforcement, they are essential in revealing the social origins of the status differences that underlie social fields, enforcement among them, and the dependence of these status differences on recognized attributions of authority and credibility. These are the symbolic roots of social authority which represent not only an essential resource in interactional exchanges, but also a necessary condition of effective social performances. In order to make a claim or advance a position, one must possess the requisite social and institutional authority *and be recognized as so doing* by the relevant social audience(s). Reflecting Bourdieu's interest in how the structural properties of fields inform social practice, this concern with the effectiveness of social performances speaks to the ultimate value of the various forms of capital as they provide the authority needed to be successful in social interactions, reflecting and reproducing divisions in the field itself in the process.

When applied more directly to the world of securities enforcement, a number of interesting implications emerge from this perspective. First, as with the other fields of practice examined by Bourdieu, securities enforcement is rooted in a series of social performances the stakes of which are the ability to successfully advance a particular understanding or framing of an alleged offence, and to have this interpretation accepted, whether grudgingly or not, by other players. As noted by Bourdieu (1987) in the context of the juridical field, this involves 'a confrontation among actors possessing technical competence which is inevitably social and which consists essentially in the socially recognized capacity to interpret a corpus of texts sanctifying a correct or legitimized vision of the social world' (817). Police officers, regulators and legal counsel are regularly engaged in this very struggle.

Second, this ability, and thus the success of these performances, hinges on the ascribed status of the players involved and its communication through projections of confidence and assertiveness as well as recognized signs of credibility. It is here that the trappings of professionalism enjoyed by lawyers and accountants are brought to bear on the field of enforcement as they are able to signal, as well as *perform*, a superior standing relative to the police and other more modestly trained regulatory actors. This unfolds through the invocation of insider networks and prized contacts, a 'capital of relations and inside knowledge' (Dezalay and Garth 1997: 113; see also Dezalay and Garth 1996), as well as appeals to specialized knowledge in the form of 'numbers, arcane terms, and of debates and arguments that only insiders can understand' (Clarke 1999: 134). Modes of speech are likewise critical to these powers of persuasion as professionals benefit from a 'mastery of eloquence' (Bourdieu 1991: 194) and an 'access to legitimate language' (Bourdieu and Wacquant 1992: 146) that distinguishes the capacity to speak from the likelihood of being listened to:

> The competence adequate to produce sentences that are likely to be understood may be quite inadequate to produce sentences that are likely to be listened to ... Speakers lacking the legitimate competences are de facto excluded from the social domains in which this competence is required, or are condemned to silence.
>
> (Bourdieu 1991: 55)

Not necessarily known for their eloquence, police and regulators may indeed find themselves so silenced, despite their vocal protestations to the contrary.

The notion that securities enforcement, like other professionalized fields, is rooted in social and communicative performances designed to assert, argue and convince, with the success of these performances dependent on the relative possession of social and symbolic capital as an embodied competence and recognized form of social authority, offers a very different way of engaging with the alleged problem of 'expertise'. Rather than simply *what* regulators know in terms of a specialized knowledge of the markets, of equal if not greater importance is *how* they know it, that is, the ways in which the knowledge associated with degrees, credentials and experience is expressed and brought to bear on situated interactions. There is the use of specialized language and embodied modes of enunciation that signal competence and confidence, and which are supplemented by non-verbal displays such as comportment and posture. There is also the knowledge of contacts and connections that flows from one's position in a larger professional network (Canan and Reichman 2002) or interpretive community. It is these differences in how knowledge is performed that distinguishes players in the enforcement field, and which are masked or misunderstood as differences in expertise.

This brings us to a third implication of Bourdieu's work and a transition point to a more focused discussion of how these dynamics actually play out in the enforcement field. Following from his interests in social space as an expression of the relative positions of social actors, what is critical is the extent to which the aforementioned *differences* in social and symbolic capital are expressed in and through the *distances* between police, regulators, lawyers and the markets mapped not only in social and cultural, but also physical space.[3] These relative positionings, first intimated in Chapter 3, may be articulated along three core dimensions that reflect the embeddedness of enforcement in the social, cultural and geographical features of the markets, and which provide for the translation of social distance into various forms of interactional (dis)advantage. These include: (1) biographical; (2) geographical/architectural; and (3) social.

Biographical

The first point of differentiation involves variations in personal biographies framed in terms of social and economic background, educational credentials, training and work experience.[4] Here the most stark contrast can be drawn between the police, occupying the outer limits of the enforcement field and the lawyers, accountants and industry players operating at its centre and with whom the police are regularly brought into contact in the course of their investigations. Many of the police officers attached to the IMET units come from working-class or middle-class backgrounds, and generally lack professional training, having been recruited into the RCMP soon after graduating from high school:

> The norm is you've got officers who may have come out onto the force when they were eighteen, maybe had taken a law or accounting course or something like that, who have maybe done regional policing, who finally sees a posting with an IMET group, and says 'oh, this sounds really interesting'. Well, that's great, but at the end of the day, how effective is that going to be? How capable is that officer going to be without climbing a very, very high learning curve to be *comfortable* to take the steps that may be required to be capable.
>
> (Former OSC #2: 9–10, emphasis added)

This background and experience stands in direct contrast with their legal counterparts, many of whom boast a more privileged upbringing along with extensive professional training, which they have parlayed into positions at some of the most prestigious law firms in the country.

Following Bourdieu, what is especially noteworthy about these distinct biographical profiles is the extent to which they are translated into, and expressed through, distinctions in language, posture and even dress.[5] This fits the observation by McDowell (1994) that work in the financial services sector and by extension other professional services, is rooted in embodied performances informed by physique, mannerisms and the ability to project an air of confidence: 'Selling financial advice to a large extent depends upon radiating an air of confidence, of selling one's self-image as part of the product' (663; see also, McDowell 1997). The existence of confidence as a key marker of interactional advantage is evident in the comments of one relatively junior IMET member: '[Legal counsel] make more money than I do and they know that. And I make reference to the dollar value because money makes people confident. If you have money you're more confident than somebody who's scraping paycheck to paycheck' (IMET #2: 2). Another IMET respondent offered a similar reference to the cachet of high powered defence counsel: 'Here you're dealing with the Downtown lawyers who are making incredible amounts of money with big law firms … [Counsel X] is involved in our investigation. Just the name alone and you can be sure you're going to be running into a lot of argument' (IMET #12: 4–5). Language serves as a further interactional marker as lawyers are gifted in the linguistic presentation of self and are able to reproduce their social authority through their use of sophisticated language and complex modes of enunciation (ie manners and style of speech), as well as more aggressive posturing. Lacking this same degree of polish, the police often come across as less competent and credible. Here the real disadvantage for the police is that these forms of embodied authority and linguistic competence are not easily transferred, embedded as they are in a particular background as well as a distinct occupational worldview. Unlike the definitions of derivatives and options, these are exceedingly difficult 'to learn'.[6]

While it may be true that these biographical differences are not nearly as stark at the level of the securities commissions and SROs, with these agencies staffed by lawyers, accountants and other professionals with experience in the private sector and possessing similar social and educational roots, key differences remain. For example, the professionals occupying these positions in the regulatory world tend to be much more junior, thus lacking both the insider's view and the degree of polish, sophistication and confidence enjoyed by their counterparts in the private sector. The high rates of turnover amongst regulators are a barometer of this gap and figure as a constant drain on the confidence and credibility needed to function effectively in this role. This very point was made by a member of RS's surveillance unit who explained that part of the job of surveillance officers is to contact traders, some of whom are quite aggressive and interpret any call from the agency as an accusation of wrongdoing, as well as directors and officers of public companies to inquire about noted irregularities in trading activity. This task requires a degree of confidence that may only be accrued over time and which is quickly eroded by defections to the private sector. A similar concern was raised by another respondent, albeit in the context of the ability of surveillance officers to detect misconduct in the first instance: 'They've had a lot of turnover there in the last few years and that was beginning to show … When you have more junior people they were quite concerned as to whether or not everything out there was being picked up' (Former RS #2: 5). Another indicator of enduring differences between regulators and the private sector is the fact that many of the enforcement units at the commissions and SROs are populated by former police officers and Crown Attorneys,[7] a source of dismay for critics who see in this a reincarnation of many of the same problems that plague the police. This suggests that the aforementioned biographical distinctions may be more evident and play out with greater force in enforcement units than in other divisions (eg compliance) which are more closely tied to the markets in terms of both personnel and perspective.

Geographical and architectural

These forms of biographical distance are accompanied by distinctions rooted in the physicality of geographical and even architectural space. Framed through the insights of the urban and cultural geographers examined in Chapter 1, and their understanding of the markets as rooted in the spaces of urban financial centres, one of the defining features of the enforcement field are the physical distances between the respective regulatory players and the financial core. In this respect, the concentric circles representing the positions of the various agencies and extending outwards from the core of the markets can be interpreted not only in social and cultural, but also in geographical terms. While these forms of physical distance are evident in a number of financial centres, they are especially stark in the case of Toronto, the recognized financial capital of Canada. As noted earlier, the downtown financial district of the city is defined by a fairly narrow corridor consisting of a four block area bisected by Bay Street, Canada's Wall Street. This space is inhabited by the major financial players, including the banks, brokerage houses, insurance companies, institutional investors and the major professional service firms, all of whom are centrally located and, perched on the upper floors of the massive office towers that are iconic of the downtown core, boast sweeping views of the city below. Extending outwards from this core, the three self-regulatory agencies are positioned close by either in the very same office buildings, albeit on lower floors and with more limited views, or on surrounding streets. In contrast, the offices of the Ontario Securities Commission are located several blocks to the north next to an urban shopping centre and on the outskirts of the financial district, while the police are stationed even further afield in a low rise office building more than 20 kilometers from the financial district and on the boundary of the City of Toronto itself.

While it is important not to read too much into these geographical differences,[8] they do speak to the variations in status, stature and prestige that define the players in the enforcement field. In the same way that dress, bodily comportment and modes of enunciation are constitutive of interactional advantages and signal differences in symbolic capital, the ability to lay claim to a prestigious location in the downtown core also conveys a certain air of authority. This extends to the architectural design and aesthetics of the firms themselves, many of which boast central staircases and are decked out in wood panelling, expensive works of art and other trappings of moneyed professionalism. By contrast, up until the formation of IMET, the RCMP offices responsible for securities investigations were located in nondescript buildings in distant suburbs, a reflection of the cachet of the financial district and the prohibitive costs of downtown office space. This locational disadvantage has long been a source of embarrassment for the RCMP and a testament to the agency's ailing commitment to white-collar crime.[9] Commercial real estate markets are thus one of the technicalities of enforcement that have exerted a tremendous effect, both symbolic and practical, on the effectiveness of the police in this area with the marginal locational improvement of IMET offices doing little to offset this deficit.

The police case also reveals another key implication of these relative forms of physical and geographical distance. This involves different degrees and forms of access to the social and interactional networks that lie at the heart of the markets and which permeate the downtown core. As noted in Chapter 1, a key insight of the economic geographers is that international financial centres remain relevant because of the interpersonal connections and opportunities for information sharing that these centres, as socio-spatial agglomerations, provide. Here Bay Street lawyers and other professionals, and to a lesser extent the SROs, benefit from their close physical proximity to the markets working directly with companies, investment bankers and other market players on a daily basis, and operating in a common social universe superimposed on the physical features of the financial core. Lawyers work out of the same glass office towers and frequent the same food courts as their clients, providing opportunities for networking and getting in on the action. Removed from the financial front-lines, the securities commissions and in particular the police are disadvantaged as they lack the close proximity so essential to 'insider' knowledge and information: 'Proximity produces information, bit by bit' (Schmidt 2005: 35). They thus not only have fewer contacts but less ability to acquire intelligence, spot trends and tap into the localized 'centres of interpretation' (Thrift 2000: 695) and forms of 'social connectivity' (Sassen 2005: 27) that underlie the markets. Instead, they must rely on other agencies to supply them with intelligence potentially two or three times removed from its source:

> We are only as good as what is reported to us. We're not out there. We're not sitting in a brokerage firm seeing what's going on. We're not at a reporting issuer looking at what's happening in the accounting. We don't have undercover people sitting in various companies. So you can't expect us to uncover everything because we only really look at what comes to us.
>
> (OSC #5: 17–18)

The costs associated with these degrees of estrangement from the social world of the markets are another testament to the fact that, when it comes to enforcement, *place* really does matter.[10]

Social

Underlying these biographical differences and distinct locations in the urban geography of finance is also a form of *social* distance revealed in the travels of police investigators, regulators and lawyers and their clients in very different social circles and their immersion in distinct social networks. These take the form of the relationships, connections and forms of interpersonal knowledge that flow from a similar social and professional background, common work experiences and histories, and the seemingly mundane yet essential participation in social gatherings, retreats and other such engagements. These kinds of interactions help to forge contacts, build familiarity and accord players the benefits of an immersion in the kinds of dense social networks that confer status and recognition. Here the police are further distinguished by the very tenuous nature of their ties to the social world of the markets. One of their few opportunities to come into contact with legal counsel and members of the industry, outside of formal investigations, is industry-sponsored conferences, a potentially useful yet ultimately quite artificial form of social contact. This sense of social separation is certainly less stark for those in the regulatory community, as they work with the regulated and their legal counsel on a more regular basis, and may themselves have been recruited from the private sector thus possessing some degree of experience from the other side of the table. Nevertheless, critical differences remain, particularly for those in the investigative ranks who tend to be much more 'police-like' in terms of their social background, experiences and travels.

In contrast with both regulators and the police, legal counsel enjoy the benefits of a close connection to the social world of finance, along with long-standing relationships with those in the regulatory sphere. For example, many of the self-described practice leaders in this area boast past secondments with the regulators and are thus able to move in both regulatory and industry circles enjoying the social as well as informational advantages that such mobility affords, not the least of which is the ability to use these personal contacts and connections to build credibility in the eyes of their counterparts. The problem for many regulators and the police is that they lack this very capacity and thus forego the benefits of being a known quantity: 'To go beyond the network is to step outside the loop of information, knowledge, and interpretation; it is to take a step into the unknown' (Leyshon 2000: 441).

There may be a tendency to see in these kinds of social connections an even more blatant set of advantages for counsel and their clients. Where relationships with regulators are the strongest, particularly at the upper levels of regulatory agencies, which tend to be filled by 'Bay Street people who have essentially worked for financial institutions or law firms' (Lawyer #22: 8), there may be opportunities to influence regulators and the types of issues or cases that they pursue. This highlights the difficulties associated with simply moving individuals from the private sector into key regulatory positions. The impact of social proximity is also intimated by an IMET investigator, this time in the context of the courts: 'Lawyers, judges, prosecutors, executives all float in the same circles … It may even be a subconscious trait but the same judge that sits on the bench might be dining with the same executive that will one day pass through his courtroom' (IMET #10: 5). While not denying the possibility of these types of influences, they are more likely to assume a less nefarious form. This would include commonalities in perspective, orientation and worldview that contribute to the framing of regulatory problems in particular ways[11] and which feed into determinations of risk, the selection of strategic priorities and a sense of sympathy or willingness to give the benefit of the doubt to acquaintances from their previous professional lives. Here again the social capital of connections and relationships, and the distinct social topography of the markets, remain critical not only as a source of information but also various shades of mutual influence and recognition.

Through the perspective provided by Bourdieu, it would seem that the deficits in expertise cited by enforcement's critics are rooted less in differences in the technical knowledge of the markets, and more in gaps in symbolic capital understood as a form of recognized authority, status and credibility. Possessing very different backgrounds, credentials and experiences, and moving in distinct social circles, those on the regulatory side of the fence lack the informational advantages familiarity and closeness afford along with the social intangibles that are manifested in displays of confidence and which engender attributions of credibility. In a field where 'ability', 'status' and 'success' are determined 'as much by how tasks are done as by what is done' (Power 1995: 329), the biographical, geographical and social distances separating regulators from the markets are translated into informational deficits and interactional disadvantages that are bound to undermine regulatory performances. That securities enforcement, as with most forms of regulation, relies heavily on constructions of legality that are themselves rooted in contests over relevant case details and strategies of bargaining and bluffing around 'desired' case outcomes (Reichman 1992; McBarnet 2005), speaks to the importance of these deficits in social and symbolic capital and highlights the distinct power relations at play in the enforcement field. This is a first glimpse of sorts into the social and performative undertones of the enforcement enterprise, a dimension that is rarely mentioned in official reports yet which emerged as a key theme of this study.

Risk aversion, narrow perfectionism and regulatory unreasonableness

One of the benefits of framing enforcement in terms of differences in social and symbolic capital is that it sheds light on a number of tendencies that constrain the regulatory process from within. While these play out primarily on an interpersonal level, they also assume a distinctly organizational form. As noted in Chapter 2, organizations are symbolic creatures that seek to manage their reputations and preserve their legitimacy, hence their adoption of standards, benchmarks and expectations that filter down to the more micro-contexts of daily work routines and thus shape the workplace identities, motives and considerations of front-line staff. It is in this respect that symbolic capital can be conceived not only as a matter of individual difference and disadvantage but also an organizational asset that is carefully managed and whose repercussions extend throughout the organization. The intersections between these individual and institutional forms of capital contribute to three self-limiting features of the enforcement process.

Risk aversion

The first of these tendencies is the emergence of a working culture that is decidedly risk averse, an attribute that has been noted in a number of other regulatory contexts (Gunningham 1987; Hawkins 2002; Braithwaite 2005). This is evident in the approaches, attitudes and judgments of individual investigators who operate in an organizational culture more inclined to punish individuals for their failures than to reward them for their successes, and who often lack the confidence, critical sensibilities and symbolic authority to adopt riskier case strategies and courses of investigative action. The fact that investigators are 'motivated more by fear of criticism than by aspiration for commendation' (Gunningham 1987: 89), part-and-parcel of a regulatory culture where 'the rewards for successfully experimenting with a high-risk solution to a large problem are low and the punishments for failure high' (Braithwaite 2005: 173), is expressed in the conservative mindset of police and regulators, and their tendency to set exceedingly high standards for case viability and merit while carefully plotting their investigations according to the safest and most secure paths possible. This sense of conservatism was evident in the comments of a litigator and former member of the OSC, who recounted the following exchange with a member of the litigation staff:

> I remember one time where I wanted to bring an insider trading case and he came up and tried to convince me that I shouldn't bring it because we could lose because of this and this. I basically said 'bring the case we're gonna win it'. And the people pleaded guilty shortly after the charges were brought.
>
> (Lawyer #22: 7)

Another respondent referenced what he saw as a problem of 'regulatory inertia, the just plain we're afraid to lose mentality at the commissions. They only take things they think they can win' (Lawyer #21: 2). While risk aversion was noted throughout the regulatory establishment, it was seen as especially prevalent among the police and in particular Crown Attorneys:

> The big problem with risk aversion is the Crown. I don't think anyone wants to take half-assed cases to court ... but at the same time there's no sure wins. And I think the Crown wants what I think is a sure win before it will even take on a case.
>
> (IMET #13: 5)

This sense of caution, and lingering fear of failure and embarrassment, was also mentioned by regulators themselves as a reality of their job and a reflection of the exceedingly high personal stakes of investigations. In the words of one respondent:

> You have to be very conservative ... I've always taken the stance that it's not the person you're investigating that's on trial. It's the investigator that's on trial. And that's how I approach my investigations. And because of that it causes you to be very cautious.
>
> (IMET #12: 5)

Not surprisingly, this 'tread carefully' message was driven home by a Crown Attorney with experience prosecuting securities cases:

> You tend to want to take a conservative approach to these things because the cost of getting it wrong is pretty high ... Your case could be thrown out unless you can find another way of proving it. You don't want to embark upon a three, four, five year investigation based on information obtained from the securities commission as your cornerstone. So you want to be conservative.
>
> (Crown #2: 1)

One of the unrecognized byproducts of this institutional and personal aversion to risk, and its expression in exceedingly high evidentiary and case thresholds, is a hesitation to take on more difficult or complex cases: 'The risks of losing encourage [regulators] to search for and act on violations which are less problematic in legal terms: they look for cases that are easier to prosecute, can be prepared quickly, and are unlikely to be defended' (Hawkins 2002: 403). Here complexity is reflected in features such as: (1) the size and scale of the case, including the number of players involved and the scope of the transactions; (2) the involvement of professionals and areas of professional judgment; (3) the absence of a clear definition of illegal activity and the reliance on less than air-tight circumstantial evidence; and (4) the dependence on undeveloped or untested areas of case law. Regulators are likewise fearful of taking cases to court, given not only the possibility that they will lose, but also the risk that, even if they win, tighter rules or more narrow precedents will follow: 'There is concern about losing in court. Indeed, there is concern about winning in court if the win would nonetheless lead to tighter definitions of what is not allowable and by implication what is' (McBarnet 2005: 216; see also Hutter 1997). Collectively, these complexities are undesirable to the extent that they disrupt normal case flow, threaten the comfort level of investigators used to handling files defined by certain parameters, and distract from the pursuit of the winnable cases that provide opportunities for symbolic messaging while minimizing the risks to both the organization and individual investigators. The result is a skew in the regulatory caseload, with the emphasis placed on cases that meet specific processing criteria, rather than necessarily those bearing on larger policy issues:

> Their preoccupation with the risks posed by the legal process to a successful prosecution leads in turn to legal control being more readily applied to certain kinds of case ... This can produce perverse effects. One is to skew the distribution of prosecuted cases towards straightforward matters at the expense of those which may be more complicated.
>
> (Hawkins 2002: 404)

These concerns with organizational and personal jeopardy are also evident in the adoption of well-worn investigative and legal tracts in the cases that are pursued. The police are especially guilty of this pursuit of the safer course. For example, in deciding on charges, investigators tend to rely on the general fraud section in the Criminal Code rather than specific market-based provisions such as market manipulation, issuing a false prospectus or insider trading. From their perspective, this makes eminent sense as the fraud offence is simpler, easier to prove and comes with a wealth of case law.[12] And yet, the failure to use these newer and more specialized provisions simply reproduces the paucity of securities-specific case law, while failing to signal the seriousness of market misconduct relative to the more generic fraud offence.[13]

Similarly, aversions to risk are evident in the adoption of less aggressive enforcement approaches and the tendency to tread softly on controversial areas such as information sharing, privilege and disclosure. As noted in Chapter 3, this applies to the superabundance of caution exercised by police and Crown Attorneys in refusing to accept evidence from regulators, even where it is within permissible limits:

> To the extent that one may be convinced that any cross-pollination between regulator and criminal law enforcement could give rise to constitutional implications resulting in a flaw, the preferred course would be 'well, don't take on that risk'. Well, that decision, which is often a correct decision from a purely financial point of view, the effect of that is you immediately create a wall . . . I think that there's a real resistance to taking on any risk.
>
> (Former OSC #2: 7–8)

This sense of reticence is also noted by a former RCMP and current OSC investigator:

> The police are loathe to take anything from us that we got under our compulsion powers. They're like we don't want to spend three years and millions of dollars on this investigation. 'We don't want to ruin it by getting something from you where we could have gone to the third party and gotten it ourselves'. So they are more likely to be very, very cautious and go that route . . . IMETs look at it every time and say no thanks. I don't know if that's right. If I was sitting in that chair I may be saying that's going to save us three months.
>
> (OSC #8: 9–10)

As this same respondent went on to argue, one of the problems with this hard-line approach is not only the failure to take advantage of organizational synergies, but also lost opportunities to challenge or, at the very least, clarify case law around issues such as information sharing: 'If this gets fought through the Supreme Court then we'll have a decision on it' (OSC #8: 9–10). The preference for clear winners thus mitigates against the adoption of more aggressive strategies and interpretations of case law that could deliver long-term benefits.

While the rational calculation of costs and benefits certainly comes into play in the adoption of these more conservative strategies, of even greater significance are the aforementioned deficits in symbolic capital. Interactional confidence is essential to advancing more creative arguments and courses of action, as is the symbolic authority which renders these moves credible and legitimate in the eyes of legal counsel and the courts. The fact that the police and regulators lack these forms of symbolic capital breeds an individual and institutional insecurity, and contributes to the construction of these more aggressive tactics as unacceptable risks which can then be rationalized through appeals to cost or other organizationally relevant criteria. These deficits in symbolic capital also translate into a tendency to be overly accepting of the authority of opposing counsel, as well as the naturalness and incontrovertibility of the larger legal environment. This is part of the ontological force of legal technicalities, which are seen as unquestionable and beyond reproach, a product of rational legal decision-making that renders them off-limits and results in a narrowing of 'beliefs about what is thinkable or possible within the regulatory domain' (Scott 2001: 333). This way of thinking is ingrained in the occupational vision of the police in particular, who are taught the importance of adhering to the rule of law, and who tend to approach these kinds of questions from a bureaucratic stance that is uncomfortable with creativity. Here again the police and regulators are affected by high rates of turnover which sap institutional confidence and erode the institutional memory of 'what works', including creative strategies that may be used to deal with problems outside of the normal framework of formal policies and procedures.

'Narrow perfectionism'

Faced with these deficits in symbolic capital, and immersed in an organizational culture that is not only risk averse but also extremely sensitive to the reputational costs of gaffes, failures and missteps no matter how minor, one of the corollaries of this abiding sense of regulatory conservatism is the embrace of formality and technical compliance as a means of diffusing criticism and protecting one's reputation. A perfect example of this 'narrow perfectionism' (Sparrow 2000) is the fate of production orders. These are court orders that were initially built into the IMET start-up as a simpler, less onerous and more expedient alternative to the search warrant process, given the lower standard of 'reasonable suspicion'. In practice, however, these have been treated no differently than search warrants, with investigators falling back on the higher and more familiar watermark of 'reasonable and probable grounds':

> Unfortunately what's happened is that people are still sticking to reasonable and probable grounds and the vision of reasonable suspicion didn't happen because they just cut and paste the reasonable and probable grounds from search warrants or from other work. They are just as complex a document as the search warrant was.
>
> (IMET #19: 4–5)

This assessment is reiterated by an IMET investigator, who admitted to this creeping formalism, while noting its roots in legal uncertainties and a desire to avoid the criticisms that could result from venturing into untested waters:

> The reason why we're not very keen in resorting to them is they haven't been tried in court. And we're taking the stance that a production order and getting a search warrant we're going to put to the same standard ... why open ourselves up to criticisms with production orders? Let's get everything we need for the search warrant.
>
> (IMET #12: 5)

A slightly different manifestation of the formalism imposed on the enforcement process, and its role in limiting the flow of information, is the hesitation on the part of police and regulators to deal with cases on a more informal basis. This would include providing opportunities for potential or actual witnesses to come in and speak with them 'off the record':

> The biggest thing on my mind right now is the willingness of the regulator and the police to speak to people with no pen in their hand and no court reporter. I think that would make a big impact ... Even IMET has been doing their interviews having the witness sworn. So it's sworn testimony. And I understand why they're doing it, so that they can nail down the statement. But do that later. Get a sense of where this witness is coming from ... So I think there needs to be a better system for managing these cases and thinking about how to get more honey from the bees.
>
> (Lawyer #3: 14–15)

Collectively, these examples represent lost opportunities to skirt or at least play at the edges of the formalities of the enforcement system, strategic moves that, while potentially subjecting them to scrutiny and producing a less than airtight case, could yield significant returns to the police and regulators in the form of better information flow.

The inclination towards narrow perfectionism is also evident in an overriding concern with defensibility, that is, the construction of defensible positions that will help to protect police and regulators against charges of failing to take action, or to take the right kind of action. On a larger organizational level, this is revealed in the aforementioned use of risk-based metrics to justify decisions and buttress the agency against claims of over- or under-reaction. On an individual level, this takes the form of an excessive attention to detail (see Markopolos 2009b) and a preoccupation with 'leaving no stone unturned' (Lawyer #17: 4): 'You're always worried about someone coming along later saying, why didn't you look at that?' (Consultant #1: 8–9). For a former senior manager at the OSC this was a key source of frustration:

> The way they had been trained is that they had to follow up every single lead to the very, very end to prove that there couldn't be a case. I didn't want them to prove that there wasn't a case, I wanted them to bring cases. So when it was obvious to me that this was going to be a dead end, I did not

> want them spending the next year proving that it was a dead end. I didn't want my limited resources proving that it was not going anywhere. I already knew that.
>
> (Lawyer #22: 5)

As noted by this same respondent, this is a strategy that in the eyes of regulators and the police is best served through the creation of document trails potentially leading nowhere yet providing a clear account of the journey: 'It's all about paper work. *It's about papering everything* as opposed to actually showing results' (Lawyer #22: 5, emphasis added).

Regulatory unreasonableness

A third consideration to emerge from the deficits in symbolic capital and the associated postures of risk aversion, perfectionism and defensibility is the widely held view that regulators and the police are unreasonable in their approach to cases and their dealings with legal counsel and members of the industry. This takes a variety of different forms, one of which is the aforementioned resistance to more informal means of accruing information and building insight into cases, an unfortunate strategic move that for legal counsel signals a lack of understanding of what it takes to move cases forward. The sentiment is thus one of disrespect rather than simply regret for a lost opportunity.

Another charge of regulatory unreasonableness stems from the view that police and regulators fail to understand the importance of narrowing their cases. Rather than mining for as many charges as possible, they are exhorted to adopt a surgical approach targeting a handful of responsible parties and producing a narrow, yet easily digestible, band of evidence in support of the 'best charges'. The corollary of this failure to narrow investigations is the assertion that, in over-reaching and extending their investigations beyond their reasonable bounds, regulators lack the requisite sensitivity to the interests of those who are, or who may be, touched by their investigations.[14] With respect to the police, there are 'widely-held concerns that some investigations and prosecutions that have been undertaken have been unjustified. They resulted in unfair damage to individuals' careers and should not have been pursued' (Cory and Pilkington 2006: 213). Respondents also chided regulators and the police for their inattentiveness to the collateral damage caused by their investigations, including the possibility of further shareholder losses precipitated by the very fact that a company has been placed under a cloud of suspicion.

Perhaps the most common, yet least well articulated, charge of unreasonableness is the view that regulators and the police adopt a 'black and white' approach, while failing to appreciate the ambiguity of finance: '[Enforcement people] perceive themselves as the great protectors of the marketplace. I'm the white knight and everybody else is a bad guy. And black and white. It's not the way the world works. It's shaded grey' (Lawyer #21: 7–8). This sentiment is echoed by a private litigator who attributes this bifurcated view of the world to the personalities and backgrounds of those in positions of regulatory authority:

> In recent years there's been a perception that the OSC enforcement branch has gone overboard and has more of a tendency to look at things as being black and white and having more difficulty seeing the shades of grey. I think it's partly a function of the personalities at the enforcement branch. In particular the head of enforcement is a former prosecutor and there are at least a few former prosecutors who are working in the enforcement branch, and that's more of a Crown mentality. I'm not saying it's wrong but it's very different.
>
> (Lawyer #10: 1)

The mere fact that 'police mentality' (Lawyer #22: 5) carries such a derogatory connotation in legal and industry circles suggests it is more error than difference that is being implied here.

Unlike risk aversion and narrow perfectionism, these and other charges of regulatory unreasonableness are not so much a by-product of deficits in symbolic capital and associated strategies of self-preservation. Rather, they reflect the differences between police, regulators and the markets, of their relative location in a social and organizational universe that affords a very different understanding of, and perspective on, the world of finance. Revealed in Bourdieu's use of the term 'habitus', the biographical and social distinctions between police, regulators and the markets are reflected in particular habits, tendencies and performances, as well as ways of seeing and engaging with the world that breed conflict, disrespect and derision from those otherwise predisposed. And yet, one of the implications of this distance and sense of unreasonableness is a further erosion of an already limited store of symbolic capital, as their actions and approaches are deemed unprofessional, inappropriate and out-of-place (Williams 2008b). Here regulators are caught in a critical double bind, as the symbolic capital needed to undertake more creative or aggressive regulatory moves is itself undermined by the very perception of these moves as being unjustified, illegitimate or over-the-top; another testament to the precariousness of their position and the impossibility of their mandate.

Conclusion

There is no doubt that securities professionals possess a vastly superior knowledge of, and experience with, the markets, placing them at a distinct advantage over their regulatory counterparts. However, if this were simply a matter of a 'knowledge gap', an obvious solution would be greater training for regulatory staff. The fact that this receives nary a mention in reports and inquiries, which tend to place all of their eggs in the recruitment of players, logics and practices from the private sector, suggests that something else is afoot. This chapter has argued that when it comes to enforcement it is not the deficits in technical knowhow that matter most, but rather *how expertise matters* in the course of regulatory encounters. Defined in terms of an embodied form of social authority instead of an easily transferable bit of information, the place of expertise in enforcement highlights the social and performative features of the regulatory enterprise and the critical role played by attributions of competence and credibility. On this count, not all players are equally well endowed nor equally capable of engaging in these performances, a reflection of their distinct positions in the spaces of enforcement and their distance from the markets expressed in biographical, geographical and social terms.[15] Relative to market insiders, police and regulators are disadvantaged by their lack of contacts and connections, by their isolation from the interpretive communities of finance, by their inability to signal their competence and demonstrate the strength of their arguments through the requisite posturings and linguistic displays, and by a perspective and approach bound to be unreasonable and out-of-touch. When combined with an immersion in organizations that are themselves lacking in confidence and preoccupied with the management of their own reputational reserves, it is no wonder that these gaps in 'expertise' are manifested in an overriding sense of conservatism that mitigates against more aggressive and imaginative regulatory moves.

As a window into the enforcement enterprise, expertise represents a kind of rallying point for many of the themes addressed in the book thus far, and a bridge to the chapters to follow. Possessing its own inherently relational logic, and interpreted using the lens of symbolic capital, expertise is an expression and embodiment of the different positions occupied by regulatory agencies in the field of securities enforcement relative to each other, to non-regulatory players and to the social world of the markets. As a mark of distinction, it highlights the conflicts between these various players, framed less as battles over knowledge and more as contests over the quality and compellability of regulatory performances. It also speaks to the points of tension and slippage in the mandates of regulators, with these performances bound to be somewhat schizophrenic given the multiple audiences to which they are directed, and the contradictory metrics that allow police and regulators to be faulted both for a lack of risk-taking and their unreasonableness when more aggressive poses are struck. In light of these intersections between markets, mandates, fields and competencies, the question moving forward is how these relative positions and deficits are reflected in the actual practice of securities enforcement. The next two chapters address this very issue, engaging more directly with the enforcement process itself. This includes the criteria and considerations brought to bear in detecting and selecting cases, the subject of the next chapter, and the interactions between regulators, counsel and clients as suspicions morph into active files, the subject of Chapter 6. In each case, an underlying concern is with how the various features of this social field, and the relative distances between regulators and the markets, are translated into particular courses and causes of regulatory action.

Notes

1 Besides the attraction of greater pay scales, these departures also stem from the arcane human resource policies of the RCMP. For example, the agency allows a police officer to retire with a full pension after 25 years of service, thus allowing IMET investigators to complete their required tenure and retire to the regulatory or private sector where they can receive a substantial supplementary salary. Typically in their mid-40s, many of these seasoned investigators are in their prime and represent a significant loss to the force.

2 This point about embodied social performances often elicits debates as to whether knowledge operates through bodies or networks, and the criticism that Bourdieu's understanding of capital and habitus is actor-centric (Valverde 2005). While there is certainly a tendency in his work to overlook the agency of non-human actors, as well as the specificities of legal knowledge as it extends through networks rather than embodied agents, it is arguable that for Bourdieu the body is itself a kind of technicality. This follows from its existence as both a subject and an object, a point of transition or intermediation between human and non-human actors defined by the materiality of its postures, movements and enunciations. As noted by McDowell (1997) in reference to the role of embodied performances in the financial services sector: 'Clearly, corporeality has a materiality that matters' (188). There is also an interesting resonance here with the work of Latour and his assertion that legal objectivity is effected to a large degree through bodily habits: 'The strange thing about legal objectivity is that it quite literally is *object-less*, and is sustained entirely by the production of a mental state, a bodily *hexis* ... It therefore depends entirely on a quality of speech, deportment, dress and on a form of enunciation, and therefore on all of those external appearances that have been derided since Pascal' (Latour 2010: 236–7, original emphasis see also Valverde 2008: 907). In this respect, Bourdieu's concepts of capital and habitus are not entirely inconsistent with the ANT framework.

3 Lange (2003) for one has argued that Bourdieu's predominantly 'cultural' approach to space might be supplemented by a more 'geographical' perspective, a position that dovetails nicely with the work of the cultural economists.

4 These are presented as general trends only with exceptions likely in individual instances.

5 One of the more intriguing observations to emerge from my attendance at the various regulatory conferences is that the police are invariably dressed more formally than lawyers, regulators and other attendees. This formal dress inadvertently serves as a reputational and status marker as the police appear somewhat out-of-place and desperate to obtain a legitimacy granted to lawyers by virtue of who they are, and what they know, instead of how they are dressed. Informality, in this respect, is itself a sign of status and authority.

6 Returning to Latour, the difficulties encountered by the police and other regulators with the enunciative modalities of law, and thus their inability to speak or at least to speak competently, is similar to the sense of frustration he himself experienced as an ethnographer at the Conseil d'Etat: 'The ethnographer noticed this many times, by becoming aware for example of his own stuttering, of the extent to which it was impossible for him, even after several years of familiarization, to get gradually closer to the legal utterance. To speak of the law he lacked not only words and concepts, but everything, *absolutely everything*' (Latour 2010: 255, emphasis added).

7 It used to be that this was exclusively the case with former police officers dominating the investigative ranks of the regulators. However, it would appear that a shift may be underway with more specialists and non-police investigators recruited to enforcement units.

8 These distinctions are much less stark in other financial centres, such as Vancouver, Calgary and Montreal, where the securities commissions and IMET units are positioned much closer to the downtown core. However, the fact that Toronto is home to the most

high profile investigations means that the geographical positioning of this single unit has a significant bearing on the IMET program as a whole.

9 For many years the RCMP's commercial crime unit did have its main offices close to Toronto's financial district but pulled out in the early 1990s owing to budgetary cutbacks.

10 One of the key recommendations offered by Harry Markopolos during his testimony on the SEC's handling of the Madoff affair is that the agency move its offices from Washington DC to a location closer to the financial centres of New York and Boston 'because Washington is a political center not a financial center, so you won't find the most qualified people there for the job at hand' (Markopolos 2009a: 51). This further highlights the importance of 'place' to the social organization of expertise, and reinforces the locational contingencies of enforcement.

11 For example, it is noteworthy that the recently appointed Director of Enforcement at the OSC once commented during his tenure as the CEO of RS that: 'enforcement is probably the least effective form of enhancing market integrity' (Atkinson in Condon 2004: 430).

12 As noted by the following respondent, one of the challenges in making use of the specialized market provisions in the Criminal Code is not only the absence of cases but also the unworkability of the provisions themselves, 'from the point of view of being able to find guidance in case law, it's very hard ... some of these stock market sections are unworkable and so they haven't been used' (IMET #20: 12).

13 There is also the possibility that proceeding under the more specialized, market-centred provisions would yield longer sentences, notwithstanding lower maximum penalties. However, whether or not this would actually be the case is likely to remain an open question, given the police preference for more certain legal routings.

14 The fact that one of the most high profile IMET investigations netted a high ranking member of provincial parliament, who was later exonerated, has done little to soften these perceptions of regulatory overzealousness.

15 The fact that these social biographies, backgrounds and networks become more similar the closer one moves to the centre of the enforcement field, reflecting not only commonalities in background but also the frequent movement between regulators and the private sector, suggests that the distances between positions in the field are not as stark as one might imagine following a strict interpretation of Bourdieu.

Chapter 5

Technologies, narratives and morality plays

Introduction

To the extent that securities enforcement is viewed as a machine, generating cases out of the raw materials of financial and human resources, the focus invariably remains on the nature of its products. It is the number, profile and disposition of cases that matter most. While this may be fair on one level, as we are all judged by what we produce, it scants the complexities of the machine itself, offering a decidedly narrow window into the enforcement enterprise. Informed by the insights from the first four chapters of this book, which have themselves sought to expand the terrain according to which securities enforcement is framed and evaluated, this chapter takes a major step inside the 'black box' of enforcement, exploring the dynamics through which instances of troublesome activity are first identified and then subsequently processed into viable cases. This is the world of reporting channels and detection technologies, worksheets and data trails, and evidentiary standards and narrative frames, all of which play a key role in determining whether or not instances of misconduct qualify as 'good cases'. In examining in greater detail the 'how' of enforcement, this chapter focuses on the technical as well as moral undertones of the enforcement process as a kind of investigative craft, rather than a mere assembly line.

Detecting misconduct: reporting channels and regulatory technologies

In their bid to uphold the integrity of the markets, one of the main challenges faced by enforcement agencies is how to monitor the vast and densely populated terrain of market activities and extract signs of abnormal or questionable conduct. This is a task made especially difficult given the abstract, virtual and electronically mediated nature of the markets, and their embeddedness in situated transactions, epistemic communities and interpersonal relationships, with these seemingly contradictory features creating challenges with respect to both access and intelligibility. In terms of the former, despite the widespread availability of stock indicators of market activity, including data feeds provided by the exchanges themselves, regulators are far removed from the daily goings-on of the markets, forced to rely instead on a series of discrete reporting channels and detection technologies. The practice of securities enforcement is thus invariably shaped by the fodder yielded by these avenues, itself a reflection of their underlying logics, triggers and assumptions. Following the insights of Callon, Latour and the social studies of finance, a key question is the degree to which these devices do not simply reflect or capture market activities, but instead produce an extracted, second-order view of the markets, which then serves as the principal stand-in for regulatory scrutiny.

Besides difficulties in accessing relevant market information, enforcement agents are also confronted by challenges in processing the sheer volume of data yielded by these various devices and channels, of sifting the 'real cases' from the surrounding financial noise, and of discerning the motivations and connections behind transactions that inspire allegations of misconduct yet are not readily apparent from the data available to regulators. The reality is that enforcement agencies possess a fairly expansive view of the superficialities of the markets, yet limited insight into the depths of transactions embedded as they are in patterns of activity unfolding across time and space. The influences exerted by these dynamics of detection and interpretation are accompanied by other, more managerial concerns, such as the need to select the right types and correct volume of cases given organizational priorities, budgetary constraints and capacity limits. Securities enforcement is thus constituted, as with most forms of policing and governance, in the tensions between a vast and decidedly amorphous 'dark figure of crime'[1] and a series of rather limited detection devices, interpretive capabilities and carrying capacities. It is these tensions that must be borne in mind in examining the production of enforcement cases.

Case origins

Despite variations in their quality and yield, the caseload of enforcement agencies is drawn from a series of distinct channels which combine post-hoc reporting with more proactive scanning for various signs of trouble. These include: (1) public complaints; (2) internal referrals; (3) self-reports; (4) media reports; and (5) detection technologies.

Public complaints

One of the largest channels through which potential cases are brought to the attention of regulators is public complaints. This includes individual investors and, in some cases, members of the industry contacting regulators either with specific allegations of misconduct or more general inquiries regarding an investment, an investment dealer or a set of transactions. These complaints are handled by call centres in each of the major agencies which record, vet and, where appropriate, refer the complaints to other units for a more thorough review. As with most policing agencies in the business of handling public complaints, the majority of these calls take the form of general inquiries, requests for assistance and allegations of misconduct that turn out to be unfounded. For example, investors will often contact regulators after having suffered investment losses easily chalked up to normal fluctuations in the markets, rather than malfeasance on the part of their brokers. After a brief conversation, most calls will be put to rest with no further action. Alternatively, while there may be some merit to their complaints, investors often turn to the regulators as a last resort presenting cases weakened by deteriorating memories and incomplete documentary records: 'We're here to protect the public but often they're not our best source of investigative material. They'll come to us late and as a last resort . . . Sometimes the document records have been tattered by the passage of time' (BCSC #1: 9).

Another issue affecting the handling of complaints is the fact that many of these reported cases appear as isolated incidents which, while significant to the individual, may not have the scale of losses or victims to merit sustained regulatory attention. While prepared to take on individual cases if the circumstances warrant it, regulators are more interested in pursuing what they consider to be more systemic and ostensibly more serious forms of misconduct. As revealed by the following respondent in reference to suitability complaints, individual cases are more likely to attract sustained regulatory attention if they can play the role of 'pathfinders':

> Suitability is the number one complaint that comes from clients and we use those as pathfinders. Where we identify that a suitability case is in fact valid, we might look further into that broker's portfolios to see if this is just this particular client that got put into a particular issue or type of equity, or is it more widespread across all of his clients. We had one example [where] the initial complaint was about suitability. We looked at the broker, and yes it was unsuitable. We looked across his portfolio and yes, he had all his clients in this particular equity. We looked more broadly. It was the branch manager that was actually getting a secret commission to park stock, and he was the one who was encouraging all his brokers to park the stock in their clients' portfolios. So we went from a suitability, to a secret commission, to basically a market manipulation.
>
> (IDA #5: 9)

And yet, the pursuit of these larger cases would appear to be at odds with the designated SRO mandate of dealing with individual cases of concern to retail investors:

> The division of that work ought to be with the SROs focusing on the smaller cases. I'm not sure the IDA has the mindset that that's what they want to do . . . They're trying to demonstrate that they're an effective regulator by finding substantive wrongdoing and dealing with it. I'm not sure that's necessarily in the best interests of individual investors.
>
> (OSC #12: 10–11)

This preference for patterns of misconduct with multiple offenders and victims helps to shed light on investor frustrations with the handling of their cases which are, more often than not, treated as regulatory one-offs deserving of a sympathetic ear but not a fully fledged response.

Besides these considerations of merit and sustainability, another significant source of attrition is the referral of complaints, whether substantiated or not, to other agencies. This is especially true of the securities commissions which, as the agencies with the broadest mandate and highest public profile, receive the lion's share of complaints. As many of these calls relate to areas of regulatory concern that have been delegated to the SROs, most notably dealer-related service or quality issues, the bulk are simply forwarded to the IDA or MFDA, with the commissions handling only the most serious of complaints. Similarly, the commissions may refer cases with criminal overtones to the police, with tax implications to the tax authorities, or with the complicity of lawyers or accountants to the appropriate professional body. There is also the possibility of referrals to other branches within the commissions themselves.

When one adds calls resolved through informal warnings, the outflow of complaints is indeed significant, with one member of the OSC's enforcement division estimating that out of 400 to 500 files a year, 80 per cent to 90 per cent will be screened out; that is, closed with no action, referred to other agencies, or dealt with through either a warning letter or an undertaking in which the firm or individual agrees to a specified remedial action. In contrast, only 10 per cent to 20 per cent will be passed on to investigations (OSC #4: 27). The fact that so many reports are screened out supports the assertion by a number of respondents that the investing public, despite the volume of calls, is a poor source of actual enforcement cases. Many of these complaints, by virtue of their seeming isolation, dependence on the memories of individual investors, and often weak evidentiary grounds, fail to satisfy organizational criteria for both seriousness and deservedness.

Beyond the low quality or questionable merit of the cases which are reported, another significant limitation of public reporting channels is chronic underreporting, a reflection of the invisibility of these offences and the failure of investors to recognize that they have indeed been victimized. There is also a prevailing disinclination even for those who are aware of their victimization to report their concerns, this given an interest in recovering their losses which is best served through either direct negotiations with responsible parties or civil remedies. Unfortunately for regulators, these options result in outcomes (eg settlements) that remain private and thus do not appear in the complainant pool. This tendency to steer clear of regulators, and thus public reporting channels, is noted by a senior member of the plaintiff's bar who regularly advises clients on the pitfalls associated with the regulatory course:

> Strategically going to a regulator is probably a bad idea. It works against your interests because if you go to any regulator one of two things will happen. They will either take your complaint seriously or they won't. If they don't and

> they tell you we don't really see that there is any wrongdoing here, that will give the false impression that there's no liability and the optics are really bad if the regulator rejects the complaint. So that's strategically a bad thing. Alternatively, they will take the complaint seriously. They may decide to prosecute. And in that instance look at the dynamics on the other side. If you're the dealer or the dealer's rep you're suddenly faced with a potentially career ending prosecution. They fundamentally have to decide are they going to roll over and potentially lose their career or are they going to fight. So all of a sudden this may turn into a fight to the death in a case that probably could have been settled if it was kept simply within the civil realm.
>
> (Lawyer #13: 2–3)

In addition, those most likely to report their cases are smaller investors who lack the financial means to pursue these other forms of recourse. The larger, more sophisticated, and better-heeled investors, who are typically facing issues that are proportionately larger and of much greater significance to the markets as a whole, will often resort to the threat of legal action or other more subtle means of dealing with problems in the marketplace (Gunningham 1991). The result is not only chronic under-reporting, but also a degree of selectivity in the cases passed on to regulators.

A final constraint on public reporting channels is what some have described as an unwillingness on the part of regulators to accept tips from third parties and industry insiders. In fact, up until recently, it was the policy of the IDA not to accept complaints from members of the industry (see SIPA 2004: 87).[2] While a whistleblower hotline has since been established under the auspices of IIROC, it is unclear whether or to what degree this has helped to overcome this institutional bias. The tendency to be suspicious and to discount tips from outsiders (Markopolos 2010) is significant not only in limiting the number of cases reported to regulators, but also depriving them of access to the kinds of 'insider' knowledge and informant testimony that are essential to more complex cases. Examples would include market manipulation and insider trading, which hinge on circumstantial evidence and are much more difficult to detect and unravel through the normal regulatory channels (Reichman 1993; Goldwasser 1999). Thus, the nature of public reporting channels and the way they are used and received by regulators offer a somewhat selective and decidedly narrow view of the 'dark figure' of securities misconduct.

Internal referrals

Moving inside the enforcement agencies, a second source of cases is internal referrals from other units or divisions. Compliance units in particular are a common feeder of cases as they are in regular contact with regulated communities collecting information through audits and other mandatory reporting channels on a range of practices and procedures. Questionable activities are often unearthed through this compliance function and may be passed on to enforcement units if the conduct in question is sufficiently egregious or if more compliance-oriented approaches have been found to be ineffective, requiring a stronger regulatory stick. Here questions of solvency often come into play, as the cases bound to be deemed the most serious and deserving of an enforcement response are those where firms are facing a serious capital deficiency or are in danger of collapse. It is also the case that incidents of suspected wrongdoing may be transferred from other divisions if they require the exercise of powers only available to enforcement staff. These kinds of internal referrals are especially meaningful in that they come pre-screened for relevance and are already coded in terms of organizational designations of risk and priority. They are also 'more real time, they are fresher, and they have the benefit of additional analysis by somebody in a position with the knowledge and expertise', thus yielding a 'better platform of evidence' (BCSC #1: 9). The fact that they are passed on by colleagues no doubt provides an added sense of obligation, making them difficult to dismiss. What this reporting channel lacks in volume, it thus more than makes up for in quality and compellability. To these internal referrals, we can also add external referrals from other agencies working in the same national jurisdiction, or from international bodies such as the SEC which provide a steady stream of cases for Canadian regulators.

Self-reports

A third, far more dubious source of cases, is industry self-reporting. This is distinct from the allegations of former insiders or whistleblowers as it involves firms who have detected misconduct usually on the part of their employees and who are eager to report these breaches lest they themselves fall prey to regulatory scrutiny. In fact, this self-reporting is, if not required, actively encouraged by the regulators as part of their 'credit for cooperation' policies, which offer the carrot of more favourable treatment in return for open communication and the confession of one's sins or, as is more often the case, the sins of lower level employees and poor producers.

This self-reporting function has been formalized by agencies such as the IDA, which imposes on member firms an obligation to report a range of incidents to the agency including: (1) written client complaints about trading in their accounts; (2) client allegations of criminal activity; (3) domestic or international investigations or convictions of a firm or registrant by a regulator or criminal authority; (4) civil suits alleging impropriety in trading or client accounts; (5) internal investigations; and (6) denial of registration. This data, bearing the traces of various signs of trouble, is collected and stored in the IDA's 'ComSet' database, where it is subject to further analysis using proprietary mathematical algorithms which identify firms, branches and even individuals trending upwards in these reports, a potential sign of an emerging or evolving regulatory risk. These relative risk scores are then used to direct attention to the firms and/or individuals that are thereby classified as 'risky' and deserving of a closer look.

Despite offering a valuable 'window into the industry that we didn't have before' (IDA #2: 17), these forms of self-reporting are subject to a number of practical limitations. The most obvious is that the integrity of the system is entirely dependent on the willingness of firms to accurately self-report problems or misdeeds that may not otherwise come to light. This is not simply a matter of bald refusals to report as required, but the ability to take advantage of ambiguities and loopholes in the reporting requirements themselves. For example, firms may disabuse clients of the validity of their complaints and/or encourage them not to file a complaint in writing, thus avoiding two key reporting triggers. They may also game the system by playing on the distinction between complaints that are service versus non-service related: 'With ComSet you're supposed to file any internal investigation, any client complaint that is not service related and they've never really given a definition of what's 'service related'. So I think a lot of firms just say 'well it's service related we don't have to file it' (Former RS #2: 6). These ambiguities allow for a degree of discretion that challenges the integrity of the reporting system and fuels the suspicion that dealers 'systematically under-report' incidents (Investor Advocate #2): 'Often the dealers will turn a blind eye to their responsibilities, they'll be informed in writing so that the rep is covered, but they will choose to not report to the IDA, on I guess a discretionary basis' (Lawyer #11: 1). Moreover, the fact that over 90 per cent of reported complaints are resolved by the firms themselves without the involvement of the IDA (Oliver 2006) points to the low likelihood of significant enforcement action, even for those cases which are passed on.

Beyond the integrity of the reporting system, another potential concern is the sensitivity of these kinds of risk profiling tools to audit markers and other signs of due diligence that may have the effect of privileging some firms over others. Firms seen to have robust systems in place for managing risks and dealing with complaints may be deemed lower risk than those whose systems are less well developed or less resonant with regulatory sensitivities. In this way, certain firms, individuals and practices may be *performed* as 'high' versus 'low' risk, largely on the basis of their superficial compliance with '"auditized" representations of business processes' (Power 2009: 853). This further limits the usefulness of these devices in identifying less obvious signs of risk and has the effect of grounding the regulatory process in more normatively informed judgments about firms, their activities and the deservedness of regulatory attention. In each of these respects, self-reporting is unlikely to uncover more systemic violations and is thus another high volume but relatively low quality reporting channel.

Media reports

Rather than simply responding to cases found on their doorstep, there are two additional 'pipes' used by regulators to more proactively identify cases of misconduct. The first of these is the media and, in particular, reports from the financial press. Regulators and the police regularly scan newspapers and financial publications for potential cases, with the media both supplying their own exposés of problems in the marketplace and reporting on incidents discovered through other, often legal, channels:

> So you'll often see matters that don't come to the attention of the regulator until some stuff has been taken by a civil lawyer, whether to place a company into bankruptcy, whether it be to file a notice of an intent to commence an action for false disclosure. And then what you'll see is the regulator stepping up to the plate because the pressure will be too big to do nothing.
>
> (Former OSC #2: 12)

These forms of media reporting offer not only an assortment of possible cases that might otherwise escape regulatory attention, and thus a means of staving off potentially embarrassing oversights, but also a preliminary framing of the incidents in question, including their likely profile and the type of intervention required. Moreover, given the interest of regulators in demonstrating their effectiveness to a larger public audience, the ability to select from cases that already possess a certain public profile and are in a sense pre-coded in terms of their significance to the markets is a key benefit making these cases especially ripe for the picking.

As noted in Chapter 2, the downside to this pursuit of media-relevant cases is the criticism that regulators are overly influenced by the media and are tempted to take on cases that may not otherwise be deserving solely on the grounds of their notoriety: 'There have been cases historically which have been media driven from start to finish' (Lawyer #28: 2). In the words of another senior litigator: 'The minute you have a client that has profile the thirst for that client is palpable. You can see it … even though the evidence is kind of weak, they think they're going to make a splash, which they inevitably do' (Lawyer #6: 7). Arguing in a similar vein, one legal counsel questioned whether 'the regulators are being driven by media attention into areas they otherwise wouldn't explore or care about' (Regulatory Investigations 2007).

While this concern may no doubt be overblown, it does speak to the sensitivities on the part of the police and regulators to the actual or potential profile of cases, as well as their often unrecognized dependence on the media's own standards of newsworthiness. What makes for a 'good story' may not mesh with the issues of greatest concern to the investing public, with the media more likely to pursue the compelling storylines offered by high-profile players engaging in clearly egregious misconduct rather than more systemic problems in the markets. The narrowness of the media frame is also linked to format constraints that prevent the kind of reporting needed to unravel more complex cases. As noted by a seasoned financial reporter:

> The pressure for us is time. I live in the age of the web, newspaper, and television, and I work for all three of them. So for me it's just time. My ability in this environment, where I have many media masters, to go deep on a story is harder.
>
> (Journalist #1: 9)

A handful of respondents further attributed this inability to 'go deep' and report on more systemic issues to financial and editorial pressures, citing examples where reporters had been prevented from publishing stories that were critical of the industry. Accordingly, there was a suggestion by at least one respondent that it is competition over advertising dollars that drives the media's view of the securities world: '[The media] are all in favour of getting advertising. So if you're saying, "This is garbage don't buy it. Run away from it," you're a bitter enemy because it's going to affect advertising dollars' (Accountant #2: 8). The reliance on the media, then, is a bit of a double-edged sword, yielding cases that are not necessarily representative of industry troubles while instituting a case barometer that is impossible, or at least too risky, to ignore.

Regulatory technologies: monitoring and surveillance

A second form of more proactive case detection, and a final major source of files, involves the use of detection technologies and surveillance devices to identify trouble spots in the markets as they are occurring and before they gel into more serious problems. These range from low tech strategies, such as reviewing promotional materials for unsubstantiated promises or unrealistic claims and eavesdropping on online chat rooms for evidence of overly aggressive stock promotion, to more technologically advanced initiatives, including the use of artificial intelligence programs to scan the internet for online rumours and changes in 'market sentiment' that may signal efforts to manipulate the markets or trade on insider information.

Perhaps the most sophisticated of these regulatory technologies, or forms of 'financial surveillance' (Williams 2009), is employed by RS, which makes use of advanced computing technology and complex mathematical algorithms to monitor equities trading in real-time with a view to detecting changes in stock price and trading volume that exceed the designated normal range, thus triggering suspicions of manipulative or insider trading. These abnormal movements are then translated into computer-based alerts that appear on-screen for surveillance officers to review and assess. Based on the data contained within these alerts, along with other sources of information and a suite of visualization and graphing tools, surveillance staff assess whether these anomalies represent true indicators of trading violations requiring a more in-depth look by specialized investigations units, or whether they can be chalked up to such innocuous explanations as the issuance of a news release or the normal vicissitudes of the markets. The use of these kinds of technologies has grown rapidly in recent years, a trend that reflects the aforementioned shifts in the markets from open-outcry to electronic exchanges as well as developments in technology and computing power. Given their ability to tap into these new visibilities of the markets and detect otherwise hidden abnormalities, these technologies no doubt represent an important part of the regulatory arsenal.

And yet, despite their promise, market surveillance technologies are not without their limitations, most notably the assumptions and frames of reference built into the programs themselves. For example, given the logic of statistical deviation that informs the mathematical algorithms used by agencies such as RS, the design and production of alerts invariably hinges on the statistical norms and time periods according to which market activities are adjudged. Here surveillance staff run into a host of problems or challenges as the 'nature of normal' will vary not only across different stocks, with extremely liquid, heavily traded stocks being much more volatile than illiquid stocks that are thinly traded, but also time periods. Considerations of time and timing especially come into play with respect to the 30-day time frame according to which all statistical averages are calculated and normal trading ascertained. One implication of this rather narrow window into the markets is that the surveillance system is geared towards fairly sudden and sharp bursts of abnormal activity executed over relatively short time periods: 'That [trade triggered an alert] because the stock never traded. And on the day before the news, the firm bought everything they could. So they were the biggest buyer that day, caused the price to move, the only activity of the week. And then the takeover was announced the next day' (Former RS #1: 12). In contrast, patterns that emerge gradually, over much longer time horizons, and with a more discrete arc may be missed. As noted by a former trader who is now in the business of market surveillance: 'RS focuses on how is today different from yesterday. And they are looking for inter-day sudden bursts of activity. And they're not looking at something which might have built up over time' (Consultant #3: 2).

These surveillance systems also rely on a limited range of market indicators, namely volume, price, trade rate and order rate, identifiers that provide a rather superficial and overly simplified view of the market. In this respect, real-time market surveillance is rooted in a socio-technology of simplification, a 'summary form of visibility' through which 'much is being turned into rather a little' (Law 2002: 28; see also Knorr Cetina and Bruegger 2000). From this it would appear that surveillance officers are engaged in a task of monitoring, not the markets themselves, but rather particular recreations of the markets. These are mapped out according to a finite range of indicators or by-products of financial activity with a limited view of the actual texture and significance of the transactions themselves. Given this partial window into the markets, the challenge facing surveillance staff is that, even if abnormal activities are somehow picked up, it may not be clear what they mean or how they are significant, leading to their abandonment as enforceable cases. It would thus appear that these regulatory technologies hold great promise but yield more modest results.

The logics and fortunes of case discovery

In her extensive study of the SEC, one of the conclusions offered by Susan Shapiro is that the forms of misconduct detected by enforcement agencies will vary depending on the social organization of offending, and its attending vulnerabilities, combined with the types of detection channels and technologies available to enforcement staff. In her words, 'different intelligence strategies, sensitized to different vulnerabilities, intercept different kinds of offenses at different points in their development' (Shapiro 1984: 99). The challenge facing regulators is that market misconduct, by its very nature, tends to be organized in such a way as to limit these exposures:

> It is usually located in private places; it is frequently consummated in faceless computer or market transactions rather than direct interactions; it is rarely 'situationally specific' but develops across a patchwork of meetings, decisions, and transactions often years in the making; it is easily masked in the trappings of licit routines and readily camouflaged in noise.
>
> (Shapiro 1984: 81)

Moreover, bearing in mind the reporting channels and detection technologies available to most enforcement agencies, the opportunities for discovery are limited to a small handful of regulatory triggers which, somewhat ironically, are most sensitive to the least typical of activities and circumstances. These include the availability of a victim who is aware of and motivated to report the incident, the willingness of insiders to blow the whistle, the bubbling up of aspects of the transaction in public fora such as the internet or the news media and/or discernible and readily interpretable abnormalities in size, scale and profitability. To the extent that trades or transactions are not vulnerable to, or do not trigger these pressure points, it is unlikely that they will be targeted by enforcement agencies. The limited occasions for detection relative to the private and embedded nature of misconduct also points to the fortuitousness of enforcement, which often 'depends upon the curiosity or imagination of investigators perhaps with extra time on their hands or the anger, vengefulness, good citizenship, conscientiousness, or persistence of outsiders' (Shapiro 1984: 69). This fits nicely with the observation by Reichman (1993) that, despite the use of sophisticated surveillance systems, 'accidental discovery continues to play an important role in regulation' (84).

From these various points of discovery, incidents are further subject to different rates and forms of attrition depending, at least in part, on the channels through which they were uncovered. With agencies desperately seeking positive public exposure while remaining suspicious of 'outsiders', a group that includes investors, the industry and in many cases even other regulators, the incidents that stand the greatest chance not only of detection but of serious consideration are those that originate through either the media or internal forms of referral or self-discovery. These tend to make up the bulk of enforcement cases, with reports from the investing public and members of the industry playing a surprisingly limited role: 'I'd say a good portion of our work is self-generated' (IDA #2: 3–4). And yet, it is not merely the detectability of incidents that determines their regulatory fate, but also the extent to which they satisfy a series of additional criteria and thus the ease with which they can run the regulatory gamut.

Making cases: regulatory narratives and morality plays

Following an initial screening and with a basket of substantiated incidents in hand, the next key decision point in the enforcement process involves determining whether these allegedly abnormal or questionable activities are deserving of conversion into an active file. These evaluations are usually carried out by members of a case assessment or intake unit,[3] who probe the merits of reported or detected incidents based on a variety of criteria including: (1) the nature and impact of the activities in question including the number of investors affected and the size of the losses; (2) the degree of urgency as indicated by whether the activity is ongoing, assets remain at risk, or there is a possibility that evidence will be destroyed; (3) investigative value determined by the duration of the activity, whether it involves multiple parties, its ranking according to agency priorities, the resource requirements, and whether the 'offenders' were previously warned or sanctioned; and (4) 'other considerations' such as the case's media profile. Using these criteria, cases are then assigned a numerical value:

> We have a weighted point system that adds the points up for the type of case. Then it's how much harm. Over $100,000? Over $1 million? How much money is involved or how much harm has been done to the public? How many people have been hurt? What kind of activity is it? Is it conspiratorial? Is it egregious or was it just misinterpretation of the rules, nobody was really hurt so it doesn't really matter? How many people have been involved in the activity?
>
> (OSC #8: 7)

The reference to the weighted point system is especially significant as the assessments of both police and regulators are informed by detailed worksheets and calculations. These set out the various criteria, and their relative weighting, providing staff with the ability to score and rank incoming files: 'They have a risk assessment worksheet that they go through. And there's a range where it can go either way and they can discuss it. There may be some overriding factors that don't fit on the sheet. But that's sort of the initial thing. See what comes out' (Former RS #1: 10–11). Based on these worksheets, assessment staff produce initial work-ups of cases, which inform decisions whether they should: (1) close the file and not take any further action; (2) refer the case to another agency; or (3) proceed with the investigation, in which case the file is transferred from case assessment to investigations where it is further classified as an A, B or C file:[4]

> What we do then is we assess what priority to give the file. We make it an A file, a B file, or a C file. If it's an A file that is a very significant file and we devote resources to it and try to conduct the investigation as quickly as possible. If it's a B file, then there may be a clear indication of a breach of securities law. And C file then there's some suspicion. And then there's different procedures that are applied to each of the different categories of files. If it's an A file, we would devote maximum resources to it and try to investigate and complete as quickly as possible. Most of the files are B files. Then there's the C files where there's just a suspicion. And those files we don't require the drafting of an investigation. We say you have sixty days to either look at it,

> analyze it, and decide if it's a B file, or close it. Those are the cases where the evidence is less strong coming into investigations.
>
> (OSC #2: 3)

Despite its seemingly rational nature and roots in objective determinations of harm and seriousness, a closer look at the assessment process reveals not only an element of subjectivity but also a number of additional considerations that extend beyond the substantive features and manifest legalities of a case. First, the criteria are themselves quite vague, referring to a multitude of different factors and case attributes, while providing little obvious direction as to how these criteria should be applied in any given situation. When asked about these scoring systems, a number of respondents commented that they found them to be of limited practical utility, largely reflecting pre-existing but less formally articulated organizational criteria. One respondent was particularly sceptical about the value of these assessment tools, tolerating them largely on the grounds of their flexibility and ability to accommodate staff discretion and gut instinct:

> We have a scoring system in our department, a file screening template that we use, that in my view provides us with no additional value. The template is designed in such a way that it tries to put a numerical value on a particular issue. There's a fair degree of flexibility in the scoring scheme so you can manipulate that score a fair bit. But I dare say that we don't need a scoring template or a scoring sheet to tell us whether a matter is serious or not.
>
> (IDA #2: 4–5)

Second, given that the pool of potential cases is infinite and vastly exceeds the investigative capacities of agencies,[5] case assessments are invariably informed by more managerially-driven concerns, not the least of which is the balancing of costs with the production of an appropriate number and variety of cases relative to agency priorities: 'Just by virtue of resources, we're forced to prioritize. There are more complaints and more referrals than what we can do. So we try to take the best ones forward where we can maximize our impact as to the likelihood of success and addressing the underlying problem' (BCSC #1: 10). Often this involves selecting cases where 'We haven't done anything in this area for a while. Maybe we got to get out there, or we haven't been successful so we want to take one until we are' (OSC #8: 7). A senior member of the OSC's enforcement team described this as 'an exercise in making sure that we are keeping an eye on the kinds of categories that are important for enforcement activity fitting with the commission's priorities' (OSC #11: 5). Compounding the problem of limited resources, enforcement staff also face significant time-related pressures:

> We have really tight timelines here to get things done. In the surveillance team, our goals are to close 40 per cent of them within 45 days, 80 per cent within 90 days, and the remainder within five months. Close or transfer. So

> the maximum that a file can stay with us is five months. When it goes to the investigations team, their goal is to have it done in nine months. So that's 14 months before it goes to litigation … And when it officially goes from the investigative stage to the litigation stage, they should issue the notice of hearing in six weeks. So if all things work out, we should be issuing our notices at the outside by 16 months from the time that we become aware of it.
>
> (OSC #8: 6)

These tight timelines were confirmed by another respondent who expressed frustration with having to close some cases prematurely, often owing to delays in document production, particularly for those borderline 'C' files that 'smell so bad that there has to be something wrong but we haven't figured out what it is' (OSC #6: 3). Thus, the deliberations undertaken in case assessment hinge on whether or how incidents fit into the larger portfolio of active files, as well as their resource demands and evidentiary hurdles, although cases of sufficiently high profile will usually trump all other considerations and jump to the front of the queue.

Third, despite their co-articulation with notions of risk and the risk-based logics noted in Chapter 2, very few of the aforementioned criteria are actually risk-based, that is, rooted in the risks or threats posed by different activities and actors. Rather, they are informed by more normative judgments regarding the deservedness of the case with considerations such as the intentionality of the conduct, the status of respondents, the credibility and degree of complicity on the part of complainants, and opportunities for sending a 'strong message' figuring prominently in these more informal determinations of case worth.[6] That these notions of value, blame and just deserts are essential ingredients of a 'good case' suggests that what actually drives the enforcement process is not the operationalization of technically derived risk metrics, but rather the ability to construct a strong narrative. In other words, regulatory agencies are engaged in the pursuit of compelling stories, with assessment staff keenly aware of the criteria brought to bear at future junctures in determining strong case narratives:

> Storytelling is what I try and train the lawyers to do because even in smaller cases it's just as important. But in the big cases it does inform some of the cases that we take and how many people we will charge, for sure … if you have stories with intrigue that's an easy story … but stories that dovetail motive with evidence and with deception, when you can combine that in a clear comprehensive way then the story is a compellable one. Stories that have sub-plots and sub-sub-plots and gaps that just can't be explained with no motive, *then forget it.*
>
> (IDA #4: 12–13, emphasis added)

A closer examination of these regulatory narratives, their structures, formats and parameters, is thus essential for a deeper appreciation of what drives the enforcement process.

Regulatory narratives

The notion that securities enforcement can be framed in terms of the construction and constraints of regulatory narratives builds upon work in two traditions. The first is a stream in the socio-legal literature concerned with the narrative undertones of the legal process and the importance of storytelling to case construction and disposition (Bennett and Feldman 1981; White 1987; Bruner 1991). The relevance of narrative to the processing of disputes follows from the unique formatting demands of the legal sphere, which include clear attributions of motive and the identifiability of 'offenders' relative to 'victims', as well as questions of timing, sequencing, coherence and causality. Whether a case is likely to be successful depends on effectively linking the actions of an offender to the harms perpetrated on a victim in a way that satisfies basic evidentiary standards and formatting demands, all the while producing an account that is coherent and free of internal inconsistencies. Narrative provides this very structure, allowing for the selective appropriation of past events and characters while imposing on these events a kind of temporal ordering (eg a beginning, middle and an end), as well as an overarching structure or theme (Ewick and Silbey 1995: 200). It is in this respect that the legal process is fundamentally shaped by, and responsive to, the demands of emplotment, a reflection of the thoroughly conventionalized character of adjudication and an indication of the structures, elements and format constraints that must be satisfied if a case is to have a high likelihood of success. These demands are especially challenging as they relate to the financial sphere where forms of victimization are often ambiguous and the ground on which enforcement staff must plot their case is decidedly abstract, lacking discrete arcs of conduct and action.

A second literature bearing on legal narratives and regulatory storytelling follows from the interpretive tradition in regulatory studies and, in particular, the work of authors such as Keith Hawkins which deals with the moral and symbolic versus purely technical or strategic dimensions of the decision-making process in enforcement agencies. In his extensive study of OSHA, the US's health and safety regulator, Hawkins (2002) argues that the decision to prosecute breaches of workplace health and safety legislation is reserved for a minority of cases, hence the use of law 'as a last resort', and that this determination hinges on normative judgments regarding the status and motives of alleged violators (see also Hawkins and Thomas 1984; Ewick 1985; Shapiro 1984). Constructions of blameworthiness figure prominently in this moral calculus: 'The existence of blame is virtually a prerequisite to a decision to go to criminal trial, and often one that is so powerful it can smother any potentially mitigating features' (Hawkins 2002: 335). These attributions of blame hinge not only on questions of intentionality and incorrigibility but also on the imagined or imputed character of both the offender and the victim:

> Blame is frequently attributed or abandoned in response to the perceived personal character and attributes of those involved in the accident or hazard,

> whether as victim or offender, rather than by virtue of what they have done or failed to do ... Character and reputation can be powerful framing devices both to enhance and mitigate blame.
>
> (Hawkins 2002: 367)

It is in this context that the true value of risk management and due diligence programs is most evident, as the ability to point to internal controls and procedures may signal an earnest intention to avoid trouble and thus save the firm, if not the individual, from attributions of a deeper moral culpability. Also at issue is the responsiveness of the accused to regulatory inquiries and the need at least to appear cooperative; attempts to throw up roadblocks may be construed as another sign of 'poor character'. From this it would seem that what is most critical in determining the decision whether or not to invoke the law is not necessarily the legally relevant aspects of a case, but rather attributions of moral character rendered in the form of a compelling story: 'In the creation and re-creation of reality in formal legal processes fundamental models of human character and motive are central. The legal process is a morality play' (Hawkins 2002: 444).

It is not surprising that these kinds of considerations are central to the criminal process whose moral register and 'unique theatricality' (Coffee 1981: 425) beg for narratives of blame and moral fault (see also Levi 2009). In fact, it is the absence of these very elements, particularly when juxtaposed with the standard criminal fare of murders, assaults and drug busts, that accounts for the difficulties faced by investigators in moving their cases forward for prosecution. However, these attributions are not reserved for the criminal process. Similar considerations are brought to bear on the daily mill of regulatory cases which must also pass a certain moral muster to be deemed worthy of enforcement action with signals of moral culpability, and attributions of character, intent and credibility, figuring prominently in the separation of deserving cases from the chaff of more mundane regulatory violations. Set in relation to the formatting demands of the legal process, including the ability to disambiguate or to render a complex set of events into a singular narrative arc, these dynamics of blame and retribution point to four factors as central considerations in the construction of enforcement narratives and thus decisions regarding both the initial problematization of cases and their subsequent regulatory disposition: (1) profile and publicity; (2) offender status, character and motive; (3) victim status and credibility; and (4) case features and evidentiary barriers. While the first three speak to the moral and dramatic features of regulatory narratives, the fourth captures the structural and formatting constraints that set the story in motion and provide it with the necessary coherence, cogency and compellability.

Profile and publicity

Much has been said about the influence of the media, and the degree of publicity attached to events and actors, in driving the enforcement enterprise. Indeed, this is one of the primary considerations differentiating 'A' from 'B' files: 'The amount of media attention that the case may have attracted and if it's something where everyone is talking about this, then it becomes a matter of priority. That's a factor that goes into whether or not it's an A file or a B file' (OSC #2: 4–5). Not to revisit ground already covered in this and other chapters, what is most critical in the context of case assessment and investigations is not simply the opportunity to send a strong deterrent message to market actors through cases 'which will, in one way or another, have the most impact on the marketplace' (OSC #12: 2), but the fact that higher profile targets provide the necessary ingredients for a strong regulatory narrative including compelling characters and plot lines and morality tales of the tragic fall (eg Conrad Black). This certainly does not mean that enforcement agencies do not take on lower profile cases; however, the notoriety of events and individuals remains germane to the allocation of investigative energies. In weighing cases of high versus low profile, the former will invariably win out.

'Offender' status, character and motives

While high profile players may make for the most attractive targets, these cases are not only rare but very often lack the features of blameworthiness and clear culpability so essential to the moral narratives of enforcement. The most obvious manifestation of this emphasis on character, status and motive is the fact that many of the more serious enforcement cases are directed towards fairly marginal actors who have repeatedly engaged in clear breaches of regulatory, and often, criminal laws. These are the 'wayward capitalists' (Shapiro 1984) or, more pejoratively, the 'committed sociopaths' (Lawyer #7: 2), 'evil people' (Lawyer #24: 3) or 'really bad, consistent offenders' (Former BCSC #2: 12). They range from individuals who are clearly operating outside of the regulatory fold (eg unregistered investment advisers or products), to those whose activities are clearly manipulative or fraudulent in nature (eg boiler rooms), to those who have failed to heed past warnings and are thus deemed incorrigible and deserving of a more punitive regulatory response: 'The real objective of the regulatory framework is the fringe people, the market manipulators, the poker dealers, the people who cheat little old ladies out of their savings, who take companies and engage in fraudulent activity, those people need to be prosecuted' (Lawyer #12: 9).

Following from this, respondents from both regulatory and legal communities articulated what was in their minds a clear and incontrovertible distinction between the majority of market participants who have good intentions, are generally good citizens and have an abiding interest in playing by the rules, albeit while engaging in the occasional 'technical' transgression, and the minority of much more questionable market players with dubious reputations and an absence of both good intentions and ties to the financial core: 'You're going to have the legitimate, honest people that you don't have to worry about, then you're going to have this band that is either lacking in intention or prone to looking after themselves at the expense of the law, and then you're going to have the *decidedly rotten scoundrels*'

(Lawyer #6: 7, emphasis added). A similar language of 'good guys' versus 'bad guys' is invoked by the following respondent, with 'intent' providing the necessary point of juxtaposition: 'There are places where people messed up and did something they shouldn't have and then maybe those aren't bad guys but they are people who've done something wrong. In most cases we're talking about people who knew what they were doing and did wrong. Those are the bad guys' (Lawyer #5: 5).

While these stark invocations of criminality versus deviance clearly inform the enforcement process, and all but guarantee that cases involving shady characters and truly fraudulent activities will be subject to enforcement action, the use of these moralized narratives are by no means limited to the most egregious cases. Given the need to produce compelling narratives, they also inform the assessment of cases involving the so-called mainstream or legitimate players, where a clean record and the ability to convey both a lack of intent and an appearance of contriteness is likely to limit or at least mitigate the degree of regulatory scrutiny (Lange 2002). Reporting one's misdeeds immediately to the regulator is also likely to curry favour, as is open and ongoing cooperation in the production of documents and responding to queries. Better yet, truly contrite firms will produce an internal report at their own expense to be passed on to regulators and used as a roadmap for their investigations. In contrast, more formal enforcement actions are reserved for those whose conduct is clearly intentional and who have acted in bad faith while providing limited cooperation. This is further supported by the belief amongst the regulated that it is inappropriate to pursue inadvertent transgressions or instances where respondents have made a 'wrong judgment call' that only becomes clear with the 'benefit of hindsight'; hence the need to apply 'good faith discretion' in these kinds of 'grey' or 'purely regulatory' areas (Lawyer #7). Not surprisingly, this same element of intentionality figures prominently in the sanctioning principles of the regulators themselves. For example, RS's sanctioning guidelines state that the cases most deserving of sanction are those where the misconduct was 'intentional or willfully blind to regulatory requirements' and which 'involved deliberate planning' (Market Regulation Services 2006: 4).

Heavily moralized narratives of character and blameworthiness thus permeate the enforcement process. Operating as a moral calculus built into worksheets and risk metrics, these stories are key considerations, first, in selecting cases and then separating those dealt with through informal actions (eg warning letters), if they are dealt with at all, from files subject to formal proceedings. These are the 'normal case categories' that 'frame the terms within which processing decisions are approached, and inform and justify the decisions ultimately made' (Emerson 1992: 18). As noted by a former regulator: 'When we sit around the table and we're looking at a complaint or information that's come to our attention, it's usually pretty clear in which category people fall' (OSC #11: 6). And yet, enforcement caseloads are not limited to the marginalized rogues, the hapless outsiders who affront legitimate business interests, or the high profile, publicity-driven cases, but include a diverse assortment of cases and circumstances that fall somewhere between these two extremes while nevertheless satisfying similar narrative (and normative) criteria. There is thus a much wider arc of impugned and sanctioned conduct. The difference is that, as one moves through this spectrum of impropriety, transgressions are attributed less to the *essential character* of individuals and firms and more to the *circumstantial aspects* of the conduct in question, a feature that continues to separate the misguided transgressors from the truly recalcitrant.

'Victim' status and credibility

In conventional narratives of crime and criminal justice, constructions of not only the offender but also the victim stand front-and-centre. The ability to juxtapose the moral failings and evil intentions of an offender with an image of the victim as undeserving, free of any degree of complicity and playing no discernible role in their victimization, is essential to attracting the sympathies of lawyers, judges and juries. Besides their emotive value, these constructions of the victim remove shadings of doubt and ambiguity from cases, establish clear lines of causality and responsibility, and provide the form or manner of vilification so essential to the very narratives of good versus evil on which the criminal justice process depends. While less dramatic, similar dynamics come into play in the regulatory world, where questions of case strength and likelihood of success hinge on the imputed innocence as well as credibility of the victim. As noted by Hawkins (2002): 'Characteristics of victims also help inspectors understand how blameworthy a rule-breaker may be. A victim accorded socially valued attributes, thereby generating particular sympathy, often adds to an inspector's sense that the employer is to blame' (373). In the realm of securities enforcement, a number of specific considerations are brought to bear on the construction of the victim and thus the further assessment of a case's regulatory merits.

The first is the nature of the underlying harm: 'In a world of limited resources and too many cases to do, we make assessments based on things like the nature and the extent of the harm . . . harm is a huge factor from a protecting investors/public interest perspective' (OSC #11: 5). The harmfulness of misconduct is usually straightforward in cases such as misappropriation, where investors have lost their life savings suffering financially and physically. These are the *real* victims. They may not show the injuries, but they are psychological victims, they're financially broken (IMET #5: 10, emphasis added). Yet, for cases where the victim is either the markets as a whole or an anonymous class of investors, not only are clear signs of harm absent but conceivable harms must be articulated according to abstract and inherently nebulous frames such as 'market integrity': 'If it's a harm to the client scenario it's easy . . . The harder cases are sort of understanding theoretically the harm to the markets stuff' (OSC #9: 8). Cases such as insider trading would clearly fall into this category, 'so an insider trading case, unless it's a really noteworthy individual or a huge amount of money that's involved, would not normally make that grade', especially 'where there's no particular individual who can be identified and the market as a whole is a loser' (OSC #2: 4–5). The same goes for market manipulations which either fail to affect the stock in the way intended, or which actually boost its value to the benefit of all. In the case of accounting misstatements, it is the difficulties in quantifying alleged harms that seriously complicate the lives of enforcement staff: 'You've got a misstatement in your financial results and investors are buying your shares and relying on that. How do you characterize and quantify that as harm? There is a real, measurable harm to investors although it's hard to put a dollar value on it' (OSC #11: 7–8). While troublesome in a regulatory context, the absence of clear and incontrovertible forms of victimization are often the death knell in the criminal realm, which demands the narrativity provided by live victims: 'I've spoken with the Crowns on the investigation ... and to them it's "well where is the victim?" "Well the victim is the shareholder." To them that's not a tangible face or person. It's almost like a ghost' (IMET #12: 3).[7] Returning to the regulatory fold, there is also the issue of whether the harm is ongoing: 'Current scams where somebody may be calling more investors and taking their money tomorrow would get resources and priority over something where it's an historical disclosure issue' (OSC #11: 5). The reference here to 'scams' is telling, as is the implication that offences which, by their very nature, are bound to be uncovered only after the fact will be accorded a lower priority and thus quickly moved to the back burner of active enforcement files.

A second consideration is the credibility of the victim, and other cooperating witnesses,[8] and their willingness to remain engaged throughout the enforcement process. Compelling case narratives depend not only on the presence of a 'live' victim, but a victim that comes across as credible, with these determinations resting on their background, their actions and motives, and their ability to recollect and clearly recount the details of alleged improprieties. Regulators may experience difficulties where 'complainants may not be really good witnesses, and although you can see that there's wrongdoing by the individual, there might be issues of delay, memories fail' (IDA #5: 15). There are also instances where motives are drawn into question, for example, where complainants only raise concerns about investments that lose money: 'Those clients have no credibility and even if you had to build some kind of a prima facie case initially, you've got a client that is not credible and that's what you're going to be relying on for your case' (IDA #2: 9–10). Judgments of character thus impact the fates of victims and offenders alike. Those with shady backgrounds, who have a history of making complaints, or whose accounts are riddled with inconsistencies, make less compelling witnesses and may give regulators pause about their stories. Victims also have their own interests at heart, which may include seeking financial compensation through the civil courts, rather than pursuing 'justice' through regulatory or criminal channels: 'The victims have a lot of money at stake typically. And they are usually at the same time themselves trying to recoup the money. So there's a reluctance to deal with us because they're still hoping they can recover their money' (IMET #16: 5). One of the more troubling implications of this from a regulatory point of view is that victims may, after laying an initial complaint, receive a settlement offer and withdraw from the enforcement process entirely: 'Once they've been satisfied, they have no interest in pursuing the regulatory prosecution' (IDA #5: 6). This breeds the suspicion amongst regulators that investors simply use the complaints process to leverage their own private settlements.

A third factor impacting the strength of regulatory narratives is the complicity versus innocence of the victim. The strongest cases will feature victims who are 'truly innocent', that is, who cannot be construed to have played any contributing role to the events in question. Investors whose motives are conceived as impure, acting out of greed rather than a prudent effort to save for their future, or who fail to properly understand or take action upon discovery of misconduct, will be less likely to trigger regulatory sympathies, producing accounts in which lines of responsibility are obscured along with the very distinction between 'victim' and 'offender':

> You have two groups of clients. You have clients who are greedy and common sense would suggest that they should know better than to do what they did and the only reason they got into it was they got blinded by the greed. And they're smart and they're educated and there are lots of red flags that they didn't pick up on or refused to recognize. The other type of client is the typical widower, pensioner, not very sophisticated ... those are very sad cases.
>
> (IDA #2: 9)

These considerations of innocence and complicity frequently come into play in broker/client disputes, where there is invariably a degree of complicity on the part of the investor, and where the interactions in question unfold in private spaces absent third party witnesses (Langevoort 1996: 629; Condon and Puri 2006: 33). In these scenarios, in which it is often the client's word against the broker's and where the standards governing consent and 'suitability'[9] are themselves unclear, allegations of complicity are often made by defendants in an effort to displace blame and undermine the credibility of the client, notwithstanding the appropriateness of the complaint. This extends from allegations that the complainant consented to the activity, to their failure to take action to stop the misconduct or remedy the situation, to their naiveté and failure to monitor their accounts. In fact, the industry and their legal counsel have gone to great lengths, and with a remarkable degree of success, to build these very narratives of blameworthiness into case law,[10] with the result being that 'many judges have mistakenly gotten too skeptical of the average investor's vulnerability. And I think that vulnerability is still there in many cases. It's become problematic that the courts are not sufficiently attentive to that' (Lawyer #13: 12). Even more critically, it would appear that these interpretive frames have percolated into the regulatory community, particularly at the SRO level, as enforcement staff have been known to invoke a similar logic of complicity in assessing the merit of complaints:[11]

> They believe this theory in a lot of cases that it's the client re-writing history because they don't like the end result. And in not enough cases do they really take an objective look at what happened. Maybe the client is stretching the

> truth. But I don't even have to go there to be critical of the quality of the advice that was provided.
>
> (Former BCSC #1: 8–9)

Given this view of investing as a risk to be managed by responsible and prudent investor-subjects, to be successful complainants must overcome this institutionalized proclivity towards 'blaming the victim' with the difficulties in establishing one's 'innocence' to a standard sufficient for a strong regulatory narrative accounting for the high degree of attrition for complainant-based cases. As noted by Spalek (2001), 'regulators thus function according to the claim that individual investors should be aware of the risks that they are exposing themselves to, and moreover, that investors have some choice of those risks' (81). Thus, the framing of the victim plays a critical role in the narrative construction of incidents as legitimate and bona fide cases or, alternatively, in their normalization and thus rejection as the risks invariably borne by individuals in playing the markets. A certain morality of investing ultimately informs each of these positions with significant implications for the enforcement project.

Case features and evidentiary formats

While publicity and profile set the stage for an enforcement case, according it a certain degree of profile and notoriety, and the construction of the offender and victim furnish the basics of the plot, a fourth and final consideration involves the formal requirements needed to sustain enforcement narratives, that is, to provide them with a juridically recognizable coherence and cogency. Notwithstanding their compellability on other grounds, regulators must satisfy the basic standards of legal evidence and associated forms of 'proof', a requirement that hinges on another kind of reformatting as lived events and clusters of embedded transactions are transformed into the legal framing of a case (Hawkins 2002; Black 2004). According to Black (2004), the decision to pursue regulatory objectives through the invocation of law not only transforms these incidents, extracting them from their lived contexts, but also imposes a different set of evaluative criteria:

> The decision to prosecute transforms the whole case. The events which surround the breach and which prompt the recourse to prosecution have to be reframed to fit the requirements of the law. As a result, events have to be substantially recast. Cases or incidents are taken out of their complex social context, facts selected, and interwoven events and causes transformed into individualistic criminal law conceptions of causation, responsibility, and sanctioning. This has a significant and systematic impact on the enforcement activities of regulators (51).

This is what Bourdieu (1987) refers to as a process of translation, a key feature of legal work: 'Since juridical facts are the products of juridical construction, and not vice versa, a complete retranslation of all of the aspects of the controversy is necessary in order . . . to institute the controversy as a lawsuit, as a juridical problem that can become the object of juridically regulated debate' (832). The basic dilemma facing enforcement staff is thus as follows:

> We may agree that the investor's been harmed. We may agree that something was wrong. But can we prove it? If we can't prove it, then we can't go to a hearing. Or, if we do go to a hearing and the panel is not convinced, then that's as far as we can go.
>
> (IDA #5: 15)

And yet, while the law is clearly central to this process, imposing the requisite evidentiary standards and frameworks, these formalities are underlain by the implicit narrativity of cases. Events must be situated in time and space and imbued with particular forms and relations of connection and causality. Seemingly abstract, virtual and anonymous transactions must likewise be personalized and linked to specific identities and social connections. These considerations are central to the formatting of cases and further shape assessments of the odds of winning.

Faced with these evidentiary requirements, the enforcement process hinges on a number of specific challenges and potential pitfalls. One of the first of these is the ability to access records, documents and data bearing on the identities of transactors and the details of transactions. Examples include tapes, emails and messages from trading desks, with some firms deleting their tapes as early as 10 days after recordings are made. With frequent gaps in records and audit trails, regulators are often unable 'precisely to reconstruct the market' (Scribner 1986: 24). Here the police in particular are placed at a disadvantage, as they frequently lack access to brokerage records and trading data and thus cannot ascertain the identities of those behind key trades: 'They have no tools available to them to find out who traded. Without knowing who traded you can't even start an investigation' (Dialogue with the OSC 2006).[12] As noted in Chapter 3, the police are also impaired by their inability to compel witnesses to cooperate with investigators, thus depriving them not only of critical evidence but also evidence rendered in the form of more compelling testimonial narratives.

Second, regulators and police face significant hurdles in establishing, with sufficient clarity and evidentiary robustness, the intent of the accused. The mindset of traders, investors and other market participants cannot simply be read from available records or trade flow data and, in the absence of cooperating witnesses or informants, must be inferred from the piecing together of different bits of data framed in such a way as to support the underlying theory of the case. The result is that many of these cases hinge on circumstantial evidence that may not be strong enough to sustain a regulatory or criminal action. These challenges are especially difficult, and noteworthy, given the absence of a clear separation between legal and illegal activities, with intent representing the sole marker of the wrongfulness of conduct and thus means of differentiating, for example, aggressive from manipulative forms of trading:

> Under the market manipulation prohibitions, regulators must show an intention to affect prices for the purpose of inducing others to buy or sell … The fact is that inquiries as to motive are problematic and unusual behaviour is often simply aggressive but legitimate trading. This makes the task of the regulators in proving manipulative intent extremely difficult.
>
> (Goldwasser 1999: 494)

Investigators are thus confronted with the ambiguous ontology of securities offences (see Katz 1979: 446), where 'the dividing line between what's appropriate and inappropriate can be a fine line' (Lawyer #13: 10) and 'everything is in a grey zone' (OSC #1: 4). This was conveyed by one respondent through the juxtaposition of financial with more conventional forms of crime:

> In the drug world, drugs are drugs. If you get caught with drugs, we've got the evidence against you. Murder is murder. It's a matter of finding the evidence and finding out who did it. Whereas in the white-collar world, we are looking at transactions and pretty well every transaction we look at can be a legitimate transaction or can be an illegitimate transaction. And how can we demonstrate the difference and prove that there is a regulatory or criminal culpability there. And even a trade with three parties that act in concert may not necessarily be a manipulative trade. There may be a legitimate purpose for it. So our job is not just to investigate a transaction but to demonstrate through analysis the criminal or regulatory wrongdoing of that transaction.
>
> (IMET #13: 7)

The boundary between legal and illegal activities thus hinges not on the superficial aspects of the activities themselves, which on their face may be perfectly legal, but rather on questions of intent, causality and effect (ie profit or loss) that lie beneath. In this respect, it is the seeming normality of aggressive strategies and tactics, and the close resemblance between legitimate and illegitimate transactions, that represents a significant challenge for regulators.

Another evidentiary hurdle is the handling and formatting of evidence. Given that the markets, notwithstanding their electronic form, are largely document-driven universes, enforcement cases hinge on the ability to process, sift through and organize thousands upon thousands of pages of documents and then to select those that are most germane to the case. The management of documents and the preparation of files is thus itself a significant stumbling block, regardless of the evidentiary viability of a case. This dovetails with the observation by Latour (2010) that file preparation is critical to the legal process and to the materiality of law, with files assembled through a series of detailed practices and assuming a life of their own as key 'actants' in legal networks. Similarly, in the enforcement context, much of the life of a case is rooted in the production of a documentary record, a record that is itself shaped by technological logics and capabilities, the presence or absence of technical support staff and the knowledge base of investigators, many of whom have been trained in a more conventional investigative mould and may be unsure about how to extract meaningful data from the documentary trail. This is what one respondent referred to as the importance of 'systems capabilities':

> The other thing to add about expertise is systems capabilities ... sometimes you have to extract data and look at how trading has been done. And I don't mean e-mail searches and stuff like that, but really the IT specialist skills figuring that out. We are finding more and more when we do files we often have a couple of people so that they can actually go and extract the *right* data.
>
> (Accountant #1: 7–8, emphasis added)

Relative to private sector firms, regulators are at a clear disadvantage in terms of these technological and analytical capabilities, an often overlooked aspect of the enforcement process: 'What they have available [in forensic accounting firms such as KPMG and Ernst and Young] is extraordinary. And the OSC doesn't have anything' (Journalist #1: 7). In fact, these very technological and capacity limits were cited by a number of respondents as one of the great challenges confronting the IMET program, as the administrative and technological support required for these cases was 'under-resourced' and 'grossly under-estimated', resulting in bottlenecks at three key junctures: (1) search warrants for document retrieval; (2) computer forensics for mining relevant data; and (3) major case management for processing accumulated evidence (IMET #3: 2). Without these supports, investigators are 'flying blind' (IMET #3: 2). For agencies such as RS, the challenge extends beyond the processing of massive volumes of data to include the even more basic question of storage capabilities:

> The other thing that RS is dealing with is just the exponential growth in trading volume. And that's just a technology issue. How do you do real time surveillance and keep up, and how long do you store the information ... when it's just like terabytes of massive, massive trades and bids and offers and how do you deal with that? You have to preserve it for enforcement purposes but you also have to be able to do real time surveillance that you're being asked to do and you don't want your systems to be bogged down. There's constant technology issues for RS to deal with.
>
> (OSC #9: 6)

There is also the challenge of presenting these documents, in combination with available witness testimony and other forms of evidence, in a way that supports the dominant narrative of the case such that its core features are easily digestible by the adjudicative audience, whether this be the senior management of enforcement units, the members of hearing panels or Crown counsel, judges and juries. This is the challenge of '[knowing] how to package the issues in a proper, simple, organized way and . . . to make advocacy understandable' (OSC #11: 10). Investigators were quick to point out that incorporating documents into case narratives is much more difficult than non-documentary forms of evidence, such as witness testimony. This accounts for the reliance on forensic accountants skilled not only in the digestion of complex financial data, but also its visualization through 'inscription devices' (Latour 1987, 2010), such as graphs, tables and timelines. Here again the police face the most daunting challenge, given their lack of experience in these matters along with the fact that they must package their cases for relatively unsophisticated audiences (eg Crown Attorneys, judges and juries) while satisfying strict disclosure requirements, to say nothing of the document-intensive nature of judicial authorizations: 'The process of securing judicial authorizations, whether it be warrants, wiretaps, gathering orders, is a very paper-intensive and can be a very time-consuming process' (Former OSC #2: 5–7).

While shaping the organizational futures and regulatory fates of all cases, respondents were quick to point out that these evidentiary challenges and formatting constraints affect the enforceability of some forms of misconduct more so than others, one obvious example being insider trading (see also Reichman 1993; Szockyj 1993; Condon et al. 2005). This is an offence that is notoriously difficult to investigate, given that it transpires in private settings, is embedded in 'sophisticated inter-organizational networks that lie beyond traditional means of surveillance and information access' (Reichman 1993: 87) and yields data trails that are often incomplete, misleading and provide little meaningful insight into either the identities of traders or the transaction points through which questionable trades were effected. The difficulty here is 'how do you insert yourself into the process so that you can tell the difference between an insider trade and a regular trade?' (Former BCSC #1: 1). The problems of access, and the reliance on alternative but much less convincing sources or forms of evidence, are noted by a senior regulator using the example of a CFO trading on inside information:

> In an insider trading case, you're looking at the CFO for trading with knowledge of a material fact. The people who are under him who are still working for him are not likely to say 'well I knew that he had information'. So then you have to try and gather information. And that may come from e-mails or sources within the company. They're obviously not going to try to leave a smoking gun and they will be reluctant to cough up any inculpatory evidence. (OSC #2: 5)

Things become even more complicated given the need to distill from these spotty documentary records evidence of foreknowledge or intent suitable to withstand adjudicative scrutiny, with the added difficulty being that the offence of insider trading hinges on a number of legal technicalities which are themselves ambiguous and subject to interpretation. This includes the requirement that trading be based on information that was 'material' and known to be so. The person charged with the offence 'has to appreciate that he's in possession of material information. "Yes, I knew that next quarter's results were going to be bad and I sold my stock, but I didn't think they were going to be that bad." And then it becomes a question of opinion' (IMET #18: 10). These evidentiary hurdles are most daunting in the criminal context, where intent must be proven beyond a reasonable doubt,[13] in response to which a former regulator offered the following rosy appraisal:

> Good luck proving most of these cases beyond a reasonable doubt. Because either you've got a bad guy who's rolled over on his colleagues, which most judges find a little less than shall we say believable, or you've got circumstantial evidence. And circumstantial evidence doesn't very often rise to the level of, you know, there's no CSI in securities law. There's no DNA.
>
> (Lawyer #21: 3–4)

From the vantage point of another respondent, these cases come down to the matter of whether: 'Somebody said something to somebody in the hall or didn't they? And by the time you prove all of the elements of your case beyond a reasonable doubt, it can be rather unclear' (Lawyer #8: 8). The cumulative effect of these barriers is that: 'It's very difficult, almost impossible to prove an insider trading case and the vast majority of them get away' (RS #5: 1–3).

These investigative and evidentiary challenges are by no means limited to insider trading. In fact, it may be the case that they are simply more recognizable and better understood. With surveillance capabilities guaranteeing a steady supply of suspected cases, and insider trading figuring prominently in the regulatory brand (Langevoort 2002), regulators have been pressed to try their hand in at least a nominal number of insider trading cases, thus allowing them to test the investigative and legal terrain and accrue insights into potential hurdles. While less well developed, this given their resistance to available reporting channels and detection technologies among other factors, similar challenges are brought to bear on instances of market manipulation and accounting misstatements, the latter being among the most difficult cases to bring to a successful resolution given: (1) the ambiguity of accounting treatments; (2) the reliance on often convoluted documentary evidence; and (3) the absence of clear forms of offending and victimization, both of which jeopardize the narrativity of these cases. Accounting cases thus embody the challenges of detection, assessment and formatting addressed in this chapter. No wonder they infrequently appear in the caseloads of enforcement agencies.

Conclusion

In a 2009 speech then OSC chair David Wilson offered the following advice to assembled members of the regulatory community: 'The most important recommendation is the need to focus more on less. All parties should concentrate on those charges that are most strongly supported by the evidence and that are most likely to deliver a conviction' (Wilson 2009). This expediency is king mantra of focusing on 'the best charges' (IMET #6: 3) and 'sure hits' (IMET #3: 1) is a frequent refrain amongst the policy set, one that has been driven into the investigative consciousness of police and regulators alike. Besides revealing the outward politicization of the regulatory function, this raises the question of the types of criteria that are brought to bear on this search for the 'best' cases. While the seriousness of the activities and the sustainability of the charges would appear to be good bets, this chapter has drawn attention to a number of intervening factors that exert an equal if not greater effect above and beyond the substantive merits of a case. These include: (1) the limits and forms of self-exclusion built into existing reporting channels; (2) the parameters underlying available detection technologies; (3) opportunities for publicity and susceptibility to reputational risks; and (4) the narrative and formatting demands of the regulatory process which require, particularly for more serious cases, clearly discernible forms of offending and victimization, as well as easily digestible attributions of responsibility and blameworthiness, all the while satisfying the distinct formatting requirements of securities cases. The detection of misconduct thus depends on the surfacing of questionable dealings in a way that sets off regulatory triggers, while the decision on which cases to pursue from the available pool hinges on their subsequent reconcilability with heavily moralized frameworks of harm and blameworthiness. It is this moral frame, along with the features of plot, sequencing and causality, that reveal one of the primary considerations at stake in the handling and narrowing of cases: '[having] a nice story to wrap around the offenses' (IMET #18: 2).

A number of implications emerge from this account of the enforcement process that bear directly on the remaining chapters. First, the logics and parameters that are built into the reporting channels, detection technologies and assessment worksheets used by regulatory staff invariably produce particular types or patterns of cases. There is thus a kind of built-in selectivity to the enforcement process to be fleshed out in the chapters to follow. Second, the fact that enforcement turns on these contingencies, decision points and degrees of reconcilability with dominant moral frameworks and narrative schemes further unsettles the truism that agencies focus almost exclusively on the marginal players. While size does indeed matter in the processing of cases, this is not simply a product of overt politicking or a clear consideration of interests to be avoided or protected, but rather the influence of variables that may be correlated with size, yet which impact the regulatory process from within, as it were. The fact that enforcement caseloads boast a diverse assortment of players, rather than simply the usual suspects, further highlights the importance of these materialities of enforcement. One of the remaining tasks is to trace the connections between these influences and the production of a distinct regulatory vision, while avoiding simplistic attributions of capture or accommodation.

Before making this final step, there is one other critical yet often misrecognized set of influences on the enforcement process. This involves the matter of legal defensibility. From the preceding discussion, it is clear that regulators prefer to take on cases that are simpler, more straightforward and easier to prove. An additional factor that informs these determinations, beyond relevant case details and their reconcilability with applicable formats and storylines, is the imagined legal futures of cases and the likelihood that they will be met by a vigorous defence (Emerson and Paley 1992; Hutter 1997; Hawkins 2002; Black 2004). As noted by Hawkins (2002), 'enforcement is channeled into particular types of case. The complex, the costly, and the *legally defensible* are less likely to be prosecuted' (440, emphasis added; see also Hutter 1997: 234). This element of legal defensibility suggests that the enforcement process is further shaped by the position of legal professionals in the enforcement field, and the forms of legal gamesmanship and entrepreneurialism that are brought to bear on their encounters with regulators. It is these connections and scrimmages, with law herein conceived not as a straitjacket but rather part of the field of play, that are the subject of the penultimate chapter.

Notes

1 This concept is used in the criminological literature to denote crimes that do not appear as part of the official police record, thus serving as an indicator of the limited scope of police engagements relative to the total 'volume' of criminal activity.

2 This actually triggered a lawsuit in one case in which a member of the industry contacted the IDA regarding a professional issue, only to have the agency follow-up directly with the individual's employer, a seemingly clear breach of confidentiality.

3 At the OSC, there are two points of entry for potential cases: (1) a surveillance unit that both handles trading files referred from external agencies such as RS and generates its own line-up of cases; and (2) a case assessment unit that 'deals with everything else' (OSC #4: 27).

4 These particular designations were used to describe the OSC's enforcement process, although other agencies employ very similar categorizations to prioritize their files.

5 According to one respondent, the ideal carrying capacity for the OSC's enforcement branch is 30 to 35 cases; however, over the last several years, the actual caseload has swelled to closer to 50 cases (OSC #2).

6 Despite the seemingly technical language in which risk-based metrics are couched, when asked about what would qualify as a 'high risk activity', the following respondent cited an entirely conventional form of misconduct: 'High risk matters? Where we have an illegal distribution being done by a multiplicity of brokers through some sort of a syndication. A fraudulent pump and dump scheme for example where the broker's facilitating the pump and dumps' (IDA #5: 7).

7 A respondent offered the following example of a case which, despite its regulatory merits, did not make the grade in the criminal realm: 'Because it was a failed attempt to manipulate the market, this is a stock that did not [increase in value] but not for lack of effort and intent on the part of the people we were looking at. So because (a) it was not successful and (b) they didn't make any money in the process we were advised by Crown counsel that this was somebody who probably wouldn't have a reasonable likelihood of success in court' (IMET #18: 1–2).

8 The downfall of one of the more high profile cases undertaken by the OSC in recent years, a case of tipping, was contradictory evidence and a lack of credibility on the part of a key cooperating witness, together with the fact that the individual charged with the offence did not directly benefit from the transactions in question.

9 That is, whether the products purchased and/or sold on behalf of the client are consistent with the client's financial position, investment objectives and risk tolerance.

10 Legal precedents remain decidedly ambiguous, as investors have been held to a higher standard for mitigating losses in some cases and a lower standard in others. This ambiguity raises the stakes of these proceedings and represents a potential deterrent for plaintiffs who may be unable to assume this kind of risk for financial or other reasons.

11 Some investor advocates have alleged that these industry logics so permeate the regulatory world that many of the letters received by complainants mirror industry rationales in disputing the legitimacy of their grievances (ie a lack of knowledge or a failure to monitor their accounts). Thus, complainants 'find that their problems are "officially" de-legalized, defined as unsuited for legal solutions' (Merry 1990: 132).

12 The Supreme Court reaffirmed this limited access while revealing its problematic logic in *BC Securities Commission v Branch*, in which the court found that brokerage records are matters for which there is a low expectation of privacy, but then introduced a key contextual distinction arguing that there is a low expectation of privacy if they are being used for a regulatory but not a criminal purpose: 'So they've hamstrung the police in doing these investigations' (Dialogue with the OSC 2006).

13 The technicalities of legal language and their existence as a key barrier to investigations is especially evident in the new Canadian Criminal Code provision dealing with insider trading, which is rooted in a 'knowing use' standard. This has been widely criticized as an overly high standard and as being unworkable in practice, an 'insurmountable evidentiary obstacle' in the assessment of one report (Insider Trading Taskforce 2003: 39). In fact, during testimony before the Senate Banking Committee in June 2003, the OSC made this very point noting that, in order to meet the test, the police and Crown would be required to prove that the informant knew the information had not been disclosed to the public and that he/she specifically sought to take advantage of this fact. As an alternative they recommended that the test of 'knowing use' be changed to 'trading with knowledge of' inside information. However, this effort was 'rebuffed and labeled by federal government lawyers as unconstitutional' (Twelve Minute Securities Lawyer 2005). Interestingly, in the European context, there appears to be a move away from the use of intent as the reigning standard for insider trading cases (see Dorn 2011).

Chapter 6

Legal couplings and regulatory encounters

Introduction

It is perhaps somewhat ironic, in a study devoted to 'offences', 'breaches' and 'violations', that law has thus far played a relatively minor and in many ways supporting role, notwithstanding references to mandates, jurisdictions and evidentiary requirements. This is neither by oversight, nor by accident, but reflects the complex relationships between the practice of securities enforcement and questions of legality. On the one hand, securities enforcement is saturated with law. Legal principles, regulations and statutes furnish the grounds for the authority, powers and obligations of agencies, as well as the menu of rules whose violation is fodder for the enforcement enterprise. Indeed, financial products owe their very existence to legal and regulatory codifications (Moran 1991; Picciotto and Haines 1999). And yet, much of what actually passes for enforcement on a daily basis unfolds in the *relative* absence of law, consisting instead of informal negotiations and forms of strategic posturing between enforcement staff and legal counsel. This chapter examines the place of law in securities enforcement, while paying particular attention to the role of lawyers in shaping the regulatory process by virtue, not only of their advocacy work in specific cases, but also their efforts to shape the larger policy environment in which they work. Revisiting questions of conflict and struggle addressed in Chapter 3, and those of expertise and symbolic authority explored in Chapter 4, the chapter reflects on how different competencies, struggles and forms of social authority shape the enforcement process as it moves from detection, to allegation, to resolution.

Regulation and the question of 'law'

While a great deal has been written on the legal dimensions of regulatory practice, much of this is informed by a 'formalist' (Lange 1999) or 'exogenous' (Reichman 1998; Edelman 2002) view of law as an external and repressive force imposed on corporations from without and countered through various forms of resistance and circumvention from within: 'In this view, law is determinate, coercive, and defining; the implementation of law is seen as a top-down regulatory process, which begins with legislation and proceeds through judicial interpretation and administrative enforcement. The role of organizations is limited to reacting to laws that have been imposed from above' (Edelman 2002: 192). In contrast with this approach, which yields an overly static view not only of law but also of the regulatory process itself, this chapter is informed by three distinct yet interrelated literatures, which challenge the formalist view and offer a more nuanced perspective on the role of law in securities enforcement.

Drawn from what is variously referred to as the interpretive, naturalist or endogenous approach (Edelman and Suchman 1997; Reichman 1998; Edelman 2002; Hawkins 2002), the first of these literatures conceives of law as a product of the substantive contexts and interactional encounters underlying the regulatory project. Rather than a pre-packaged set of directives, with circumvention or acquiescence the only available moves, law and the meaning of compliance itself are seen as underlain by a degree of ambiguity and uncertainty (Parker and Nielsen 2009), a reflection of the 'spectrum of greys at the boundaries of legality and criminality' (McBarnet 2004: 158). It is this ambiguity that allows for and in fact requires situated negotiations over the meaning of law, and problematizes the drive in much of the regulatory literature to document and account for the problem of non-compliance as an overt legal transgression. The result is a shift in focus from circumvention to interpretation, that is, from why enforcement fails to how the regulated are able to take advantage of legal ambiguities and slippages in legal meanings to challenge claims that they have violated the law (Reichman 1992; McCahery and Picciotto 1995; Lange 1999; Picciotto 2002, 2007; McBarnet 2004). This is what Doreen McBarnet has referred to as the problem of 'creative compliance' (McBarnet 2004; McBarnet and Whelan 1992, 1999), in which individuals seek to abide by law's technical requirements while nevertheless violating its spirit:

> Creative compliance means resisting regulation not by flagrantly breaking the law, but by using it. Faced with regulations they do not like, companies find imaginative ways to package deals or interpret rules such that their activities can be claimed to comply with regulations at the same time as avoiding any disadvantageous impact they would otherwise have had. Creative compliance involves advantageous interpretations of grey areas, seeking out loopholes in specific rules, complying with letter not spirit, with form not substance, or dreaming up devices which regulators have not even thought of, let alone regulated.
>
> (McBarnet and Whelan 1999: 68)

It is this interpretive ambiguity and legal gamesmanship that inform regulatory encounters and set the stage for struggles over the meaning of law and the parameters of 'legal' violations.

A second insight follows from the notion advanced by a number of socio-legal scholars that much of what actually passes for regulation unfolds through forms of ordering that are coupled with, yet which operate somewhat independently of, law.

This is a key premise of the 'decentred regulation' or 'networked governance' literature alluded to in Chapter 3, which decentres not only regulation but also law itself, acknowledging various other forms or sources of ordering such as 'issuing warnings, writing letters, publicizing details of infractions and so on' (Scott 2001: 345). Law thus represents only one of the available options in the regulatory arsenal (Black 2001, 2004; Scott 2001, 2004; Parker and Braithwaite 2003; Schmidt 2004). Socio-legal scholars have further argued that much of the impact of law follows less from its formal invocation and more from its role in setting the terms or parameters for regulatory negotiations, signalling the range of future legal moves available to the parties involved. Here law may be seen to function in terms of a much broader and far more diffuse horizon of possibilities, a constellation of logics, aspirations, threats and innuendos through which incidents are accorded a primordial legal intelligibility and located within various paths of legal consumption. This is what socio-legal scholars have referred to as bargaining in the 'shadow of the law' (Mnookin and Kornhauser 1978; Galanter 1981; Rose and Valverde 1998), a reference to the indirect role of formal legal rules and procedures in shaping informal negotiations largely by endowing players with different types of leverage, what Mnookin and Kornhauser (1978) refer to as 'bargaining endowments', as well as risks and liabilities. This is indicative of yet another form of creative lawyering, the stakes of which are not simply the interpretation of legal rules relative to case details but also opportunities for delay, which can suffocate the regulatory process regardless of the strength and/or merits of a case (Macaulay 1993).

The notion that the regulatory process hinges on these kinds of negotiations and the enactment of shared definitions of 'legality' points to a third insight, namely the role of professionals, most obviously lawyers, but also accountants, consultants, technicians and other professional intermediaries, in managing and mediating the regulatory process (Reichman 1992; McBarnet 2004; Schmidt 2005; McCahery and Picciotto 1995; Dezalay and Garth 1996; Williams 2006). This follows Reichman's (1992) argument that we must 'look beyond the relationship between regulator and regulated, and locate regulatory policy and practice within the complex networks of clients, legal and accounting personnel, and market competitors that offer authority and legitimacy for business activity' (245). These are the groups that do battle with regulators, controlling information, engaging in strategic exchanges to advance their clients' interests and shape the regulator's view of a case, supplying the creative energies needed to work at the edges of law and yielding interpretations not only of law but also of assembled facts and bits of evidence. The value of legal professionals in this 'incessant negotiation over competing claims, for which assertions about what the law is and should be have particular currency' (Schmidt 2005: 211), stems from their ability to draw from the very forms of symbolic capital noted in Chapter 4. It is through these attributions of credibility and symbolic authority that the interpretations of professionals are accorded an aura of objectivity and technical sophistication, notwithstanding their roots in subjective judgments and particular interest positions (Reichman 1992;

Dezalay and Garth 1996). In other words, it is the ability of the regulated to access what Reichman (1992) refers to as 'professional capital' that accounts for their influence over the regulatory process: 'Business organizations that can embed their compliance activities within the legitimation structures of other professional groups are more likely to exercise authority over the regulatory process than business organizations that cannot situate their activities within a professional network' (Reichman 1992: 257–8).

While it is important to acknowledge the role of professionals, as bearers of symbolic authority, in the enactment of regulatory arrangements favouring the regulated, this cannot be reduced to the straightforward pursuit of client interests. Far from mere courtesans, lawyers are 'double agents serving their own interests as lawyers and those of the merchants who retain their services' (Dezalay and Garth 1996: 119). Attention must thus be paid to the 'professional stakes in the construction of devices of regulation' (Dezalay 1995: 8) and 'how professionals' narrow self-interests in their own market projects cross over to structure market institutions, the state, and substantive law' (Carruthers and Halliday 1998: 7). As noted by Dezalay and Garth (1996), this professional mediation includes the intra-professional struggles that underlie most areas of legal and regulatory practice as different groups and sub-groups of professionals each seek to expand their jurisdiction, solidify their authority and define these fields of practice in a way that best suits their own distinct brand of expertise. Thus, the creative contributions of lawyers to the regulatory process must be framed not only in terms of the mobilization of symbolic capital in the pursuit of favourable interpretations of law, but also the extent to which these engagements are shaped by forms of professional self-interest, internal politicking and the conditions under which their labour is produced and supplied to the regulated. These professional interventions are a further testament to the uncertainties within 'the law' as it is constituted and enacted in specific regulatory contexts. It is in this respect that law serves as an 'absent presence', shaping informal interactions from a distance in the spaces provided by the slippages and ambiguities in legal meanings, and is subject to mediations and forms of labour that are both professional *and* entrepreneurial in nature. It is these very complexities that must be borne in mind in exploring the legal contours of securities enforcement.

Laws, legalities and practices of securities enforcement

As a form of legal regulation, securities enforcement shares many of the aforementioned features, including the ambiguity of core concepts, the reliance on informal negotiations unfolding in the shadow of the law and the mediation of legal professionals. And yet, the tensions between law and the markets remain distinct and, from an enforcement perspective more difficult to reconcile, given the unique features of financial space and the very particular nature of this regulatory project. This is reflected in the tethering of legal regulations to such infirm guideposts as 'investor confidence' and 'market integrity'. There are also challenges in translating financial concepts and principles into law (Reichman 1991, 1993; Hertz and Lepinay 2003),[1] a task made even more difficult given the abstract and virtual form of financial space and the highly contextualized nature of wrongdoing. As noted in the previous chapter, it is within this space that the line between legality and illegality hinges not on the materialities of financial practices, but rather diffuse and much more subjective attributions of motive and determinations of circumstance, thus creating 'room for subjectivity and debate as to standards and interpretation' (OSC #9: 15–16). In the assessment of one respondent, it is the technicalities residing in legal definitions that breed this precariousness, eating away at the certainties of law: 'All of our rules have little technicalities about them that sometimes we miss out on certain things. Use of "knowingly", or someone will add in "or ought to have known". But how do you prove that somebody "ought to have known?"' (RS #5: 15). The result is that the 'penumbra of uncertainty' (Braithwaite 2005: 146) surrounding securities laws is more extensive than for other regulatory domains, a fact made evident in the tensions within agencies themselves between advocates for more specific rules and proponents of more flexible principles to better accommodate the particularities of individual cases and fact patterns:

> There's always this internal tension between our policy people and our enforcement lawyers who want us to write things very specific. But what happens is when you write it specific the actual fact pattern that comes up might vary a little bit and then the guy gets away. You know he's up to no good, you know he's done something wrong, but the rule doesn't actually say that.
>
> (RS #5: 15)

Thus, it is certainly the case that 'the basic building blocks of securities law are characterized by significant ambiguity and open-endedness' (Condon et al. 2005: 183).

However, this uncertainty extends beyond the evidentiary challenges noted in Chapter 5 to include more fundamental ambiguities in the very scope and meaning of legal provisions. For example, in reference to market manipulation, one respondent asked rhetorically: 'If I put an ad in the newspaper about my company, promoting the company, and it has the effect of encouraging people to invest in the company, is that an act in the furtherance of a trade or is it just an ad in the newspaper promoting a company?' (Lawyer #10: 11–12). Similarly, in connection with insider trading, the evidentiary hurdles noted in the previous chapter pale in comparison with the much more intractable problem of what constitutes 'inside' information in the first instance. This is relatively clear-cut for trades executed by true company insiders using non-public information obtained by virtue of their corporate position; however, things become far murkier when the information underlying a trade consists of a leak or rumour:

> It's very difficult to prosecute insider trading when it comes to leakage because they're not insiders and you have to actually prove that they knew that what they were getting was inside and they intentionally used it ... It doesn't cover people in brokerage firms who have some ideas about a potential financing and use that to trade on. That's not inside information. But is it? So the concept of what insider trading is has moved a lot further than the rules allow. (RS #3: 5)

As implied by one senior counsel, there is also the issue that what qualifies as 'information' is not limited to the more conventional notion of an inappropriate *disclosure*, but extends to the textures and innuendos of the interpersonal networks that underlie the markets, possessing their own discrete clues as the direction in which the winds are blowing: 'The fact that I can make three phone calls looking for friends to go and have lunch with and they're not available and I make the fourth telephone call to confirm, I can probably tell you who's doing the deal. Is that inside information?' (Lawyer #21: 8). Insider trading laws are thus both vague in terms of their core concepts and overly narrow with respect to their scope, a testament to the challenges underlying the legal encoding of market activities and the immiscibility of certain forms of trading with available legal frames. The result is that members of the industry possess considerable latitude to 'work their way around the rules' (Lawyer #13), with these slippages acknowledged by lawyers themselves who picture finance as a world of multiple shades of grey, of 'judgment calls' (Lawyer #7), rather than the monochromes of black and white.

Beyond this element of ambiguity, there are three additional features of the field of securities enforcement that are relevant to the legalities of these cases and the contributions of legal counsel. First, ambiguities linger not only in the formal statutory definitions of market misconduct, but also a host of ancillary provisions, policies and instruments. Rather than a single legal regime, market activities are governed by a variety of sites and sources including: statutes; regulations and rules; national and multilateral instruments; policy statements; staff notices; judicial decisions; and regulatory decisions, orders and rulings (Condon et al. 2005). This results in multiple sources of uncertainty, as well as the possibility of tensions in the way that core concepts are used and defined across different legal or regulatory fora. Second, this legal diversity is further magnified by the multiple avenues for recourse and recovery, including enforcement proceedings, arbitration and various civil actions. This ratchets up the stakes of proceedings as legal counsel must remain aware of the possibility that actions undertaken in one realm will influence or even trigger those in another. Finally, as with most other forms of regulation, much of what passes for securities enforcement is informal in nature and unfolds in the shadow of the law as revealed by the heavy reliance on warnings or settlements to resolve the majority of cases. Ultimately, it is through these elements of ambiguity, diversity and informality that legal professionals come to play a critical role in the enforcement process. To understand this role, and further flush out enforcement's legal footings, it is necessary to situate these engagements in terms of a particular market in legal services.

'Securities and enforcement litigation' as a professional market

While terms such as 'network', 'community' and 'field' are often invoked to describe the activities of professionals, including lawyers, a more appropriate concept is that of 'professional market' (Williams 2006). This captures a number of distinct features and influences underlying the production of legal labour. As noted above, the most obvious of these is the dual nature of professions as both sources of legitimate authority wedded to claims of professionalism, and commercial markets geared to the satisfaction of client interests and the maximization of firm revenue; hence the tensions between professionalism and commercialism that define fields such as law and accounting (Dezalay and Garth 1996; Abel 2003). The financial logics underlying professional markets are especially noteworthy, as they introduce a degree of self-interest to legal tactics, with lawyers seeking to define the interests of their clients, and thus the nature and scope of their legal problems, in ways that allow for the maximization of billable hours. Rather than mere actualizers of client interests, there is thus a degree of autonomy and unpredictability to the legal field. And yet, while incentivizing lawyers to pursue courses of action potentially incommensurate with client interests, the fee-based structure of the market also introduces a degree of constraint. The fact that legal labour is so closely tied to the ability and willingness of clients to pay for services rendered means that lawyers may be unable to pursue arguments or causes of action that could yield long-term professional benefits and make things easier for them down the road.

Besides financial incentives and constraints, professional markets are further shaped by the vicissitudes of supply and demand. This is by no means limited to a mere responsiveness to fluctuations in client demand, but includes efforts to actively intervene in and shape these very market forces. This includes strategies such as restricting supply through educational and certification requirements and other entry barriers, as well as creating demand through the identification of new forms and areas of legal risk and opportunities for realizing the strategic advantages that come from gaming the law. There is also the issue of competition between different groups of professionals, each seeking to stimulate demand for the particular services that they offer, a point recognized by Bourdieu (1987): 'The juridical field is the basis of the supply of legal services arising from professional competition; demand is always partially conditioned by the effect of this supply' (841). The existence of professional markets as both epistemic communities *and* competitive spaces (Dezalay and Garth 1996), bound to the incentives and constraints of financial logics and the forces of supply and demand, is helpful in capturing a number of unique features that define the area of practice most relevant to securities enforcement, what can loosely be described as 'securities and enforcement litigation'.

The demand and supply of legal services

By the mere fact of their existence, and obligation to produce at least a nominal stable of enforcement cases, the police and regulatory agencies invariably create a certain level of demand for legal representation and thus the services of legal counsel. Given the modesty of these efforts, including the minimal presence of criminal enforcement, as well as their unpredictable ebb and flow, for many years this demand was met by a small group of securities lawyers specializing in the more arcane aspects of securities law and simply moonlighting in enforcement-type work on behalf of preferred clients. However, with greater funding and new-found powers, in combination with the ever increasing profile and politicization of securities regulation, enforcement agencies have become much more active of late, significantly increasing the financial and reputational stakes for those ensnared in regulatory proceedings: 'What they're laying on people now, what they have the power to lay on people is extremely onerous' (Lawyer #8: 7). Combined with the return of the police and the increasing 'potential for civil litigation' (Lawyer #19: 3), this surging demand for representation has contributed to the need for counsel with different backgrounds and skill sets, including experience in regulatory, criminal and civil domains.

The result of these developments has been a notable diversification of this practice area,[2] as securities lawyers have given way to civil litigators and criminal defence attorneys:

> Originally back twenty-five years if there was an OSC enforcement investigation of a dealer, the securities lawyers went up for the interviews and everything. That changed over time. They started to bring litigation lawyers with them and then the litigation lawyers decided to do it alone. So what generally you would see in front of the OSC are either commercial litigation lawyers or criminal defence lawyers.
>
> (Lawyer #28: 14–15)

For civil litigators well versed in the arts of negotiation and settlement, this was a natural extension of their work in other areas, a migration that also made eminent sense given the need to protect clients from the civil liabilities potentially emanating from regulatory actions. Ironically, it was the securities commissions that helped pave the way for the entry of civil litigators, largely through their participation in secondment programs with the large Bay Street firms. This allowed lawyers with an interest in expanding their knowledge base, and no doubt their marketability, to work as members of agencies such as the OSC for a period of one to two years, in almost all cases returning to their firms at the end of the designated term. The benefits of these arrangements were not only an insider's view of the regulatory process and an ability to 'understand where staff are coming from', but also valuable contacts and connections and thus 'instant credibility' (Lawyer #24: 4) with regulatory staff.[3] In the words of one respondent seconded for a time to the

OSC, this experience was invaluable in providing insight into 'how they go about investigating cases, what powers they have, and the kinds of things that they'll consider when deciding whether or not to proceed' (Lawyer #10: 2).

In contrast, for criminal defence attorneys, the attraction was more financial. Enforcement work allowed them to broaden the horizons of their practices and to tap into a pool of clients that were financially more well endowed and thus better able to afford their services: 'You do see more criminal lawyers trying to do this kind of work now and I think it's partly financial ... looking for clients with deeper pockets' (Lawyer #10: 3). Once again, this movement from the criminal to the regulatory realm was facilitated by the greater stakes of the regulatory process and the 'increased exposure to significant liability' (OSC #12: 6). Thus, considerations of both demand and supply have come into play in the emergence of 'securities and enforcement litigation' as a professional market that is both diverse and shaped by the confluence of various legal backgrounds, skill sets and forms of expertise.

Returning to the question of the links between the structure and composition of professional markets and the practice of securities enforcement, one of the unintended consequences flowing from the entry of civil litigators and criminal defence attorneys has been the importation of principles, standards and practices from the civil and criminal realms into regulatory proceedings. Examples include: (1) demands for the disclosure of information in support of commission orders;[4] (2) arguments around due process; (3) concerns with procedural proprieties; and (4) Charter-based challenges to the authority of the commissions and SROs packaged in terms of a rights-based discourse: 'The rights of the accused are paramount ... I'm not saying that they are not, but that's exploited in a way and I think that we have counsel within our environment who are also in the criminal courts and they often try to apply the same standard' (OSC #5: 15). Playing on the differences between legal regimes is thus about gaining a leg up on the competition: 'A lot of counsel ... are looking more and more to procedures that are being followed in a criminal context, as well as a civil context, as *useful analogies* that we can rely upon in arguing that the way the commission is doing things is not the right way and that there is in fact a better, fairer way for respondents' (Managing Regulatory Investigations 2009, emphasis added).

This search for a 'better way' has contributed to what many a respondent described as the increasingly formal and litigious character of the regulatory process. By nature, the administrative process is intended to be relatively informal and to proceed in as expeditious a manner as possible. This was indeed true of the commissions and SROs for much of their history. However, regulatory hearings have come to assume the trappings of full-blown trials with all of the procedural and evidentiary formalities contained therein, including the formal swearing of documents, a greater disclosure burden and extensive motions and adjournments:

> When I started with this stuff maybe twenty-five years ago it was on card tables in a rented room. It was very informal, but it got to the heart of the

> matter. Now there's the flag of Canada, there's a lot of judicial trappings to it, and I think it's maybe drifted somewhat from the inquiry nature of it.
>
> (BCSC #1: 13)

In the assessment of a senior regulator, this progressive juridification is a direct reflection of the greater stakes of the regulatory process and the involvement of high profile counsel seeking to obtain advantage for their clients on procedural rather than substantive grounds:

> A big challenge for all of us has been the criminalization of securities law. In the old days when there were administrative proceedings you didn't get people hiring [high profile lawyers] to represent them. You do today because there's a lot at stake . . . And that tends to bring in a complexity in the process because they of course want to introduce procedural practices that exist in criminal court but aren't really supposed to apply in an administrative context.
>
> (IDA #6: 3)

These developments, 'where no longer is the actual case being argued, but process' (IDA #5: 12), have come to represent a significant drag on regulatory proceedings:

> The type of cases we do are increasingly complex, the litigation takes longer. And that is in part because we are a body that is taken relatively seriously now by respondents and by defence counsel who will bring every motion imaginable to slow it down; who will challenge our jurisdiction because it's not clear; who will challenge our ability to get documents because it's not clear. So they're doing their job, but their job results in our cases, in particular cases with good regulatory messages, being slowed down and sometimes stopped.
>
> (IDA #4: 6)

While initiated by legal counsel, regulators are not entirely free from blame for this creeping formalism, as they have gone further than may be necessary in formalizing their policies and procedures. Again, this is likely a reflection of the backgrounds of those holding key positions with former police officers and Crown Attorneys more inclined to see the merits, necessity and even the moral force of these claims than those with a different occupational upbringing. As noted by the following respondent in connection with the IDA:

> [The IDA] has become a little more formal than I think they have to be. They've established more processes than they have to because a lot of the people running it come from a law enforcement background. So they've made it in some respects more criminal than it has to be. I've heard them talk about 'people's rights' or whatever. In self-regulating processes, people have no rights.
>
> (OSC #4: 24)

Regardless of their origins, these dynamics of juridification and formalization are in fact essential to lawyers' work. They create degrees of complexity and forms of density that call for specialized legal knowledge (see Bourdieu 1987). In addition to expanding the market for their services, the introduction of procedural formalities also eases the handling of cases, providing additional points of argumentation and forms of defensibility that help to shift the deliberative features of a case away from its substantive merits to questions of procedural fairness. There is no doubt that this has had an effect on the regulatory process, consuming the energies of enforcement staff, shifting the calculus of case viability and distracting agencies from their primary mission: 'Professional norms can deflect the agency from its ostensible concern with efficiency and serving the public interest. Lawyers, it is argued, may divert the agency from its primary objectives by giving undue emphasis to procedural values such as due process' (Hawkins and Thomas 1989: 20). The not-so-subtle irony is that while these strategic plays have increased the procedural formalities of proceedings, they have also resulted in a greater reliance on settlements and less formal avenues of recourse and restitution. Loath to endure the risks and pitfalls of a complicated and drawn out hearing, regulators appear much more motivated to resolve cases informally. As we will see, this more urgent pursuit of settlements has not necessarily turned out the way counsel may have hoped.

Firm conflicts and the division of legal labour

Operating alongside the changing mix of lawyers working in the enforcement field and the cross-pollination of standards and criteria across regulatory, criminal and civil realms, is another key influence on this professional market: formal and informal rules governing legal practices at the level of the firm. As noted by Shapiro (2001), among others, one of the defining features of the legal profession is the impact of conflict guidelines. These prohibit lawyers from taking on cases that would place them in a conflict with existing cases and clients. The clearest example of this would be the inability of a firm to represent both the plaintiffs and defendants in a proceeding, notwithstanding the fact that different lawyers would be engaged to represent these respective positions. Such conflict guidelines certainly make sense and help to maintain the integrity of the legal process. However, they have a very real and in many ways self-limiting effect on the kinds of cases that lawyers may take on, the positions they are able to represent and, ultimately, the supply and availability of legal labour to different constituencies.

In the realm of securities enforcement, one of the more notable of these effects stems from the fact that many of the top law firms maintain a stable of clients that includes the major banks, insurance companies and investment firms, clients that provide a large volume of both repeat and highly lucrative business. It is thus not surprising that '[these firms] see their natural target market to be the defence side representing brokerages and banks and also getting underwriting work for them'

(Lawyer #12: 1). The difficulty is that these relationships effectively bar counsel from taking on cases that would require them to act against these firms, hence the overriding and near exclusive focus on the representation of these same firms as defendants in regulatory and/or civil actions. As one respondent explained: 'The difficulty in large firms, the conflict stuff just becomes much more prominent because of the line between business and legal confidence so that you find it's very hard to take cases against some of the larger market participants' (Lawyer #3: 2). Under these circumstances, it is rare for these lawyers to act on behalf of individual investors: 'The practice at this point is primarily dealer oriented. We rarely act for individual investors primarily because of conflicts, actually totally because of conflicts' (Lawyer #28: 1). Even in the absence of a direct conflict, the desire of top firms to curry favour with their major clients, and to maintain their reputation of upscale advocacy work, breeds an aversion to taking on cases involving lower status, marginalized or simply maligned members of the industry. These constraints are driven by 'perceptions about how representing notorious characters might cause you to somehow have your reputation damaged in the eyes of the people who are then going to hire you next week' (Lawyer #12: 2).

The conditions governing the supply of legal labour have had a series of knock-on effects. Frustrated with the restrictions placed on their practices and the need to troll from a limited pool of clients and cases, some lawyers have opted to defect to the boutique sector. This consists of a number of smaller firms offering more specialized legal services to a broader range of clients, thus freeing them from many of the conflicts encumbering their larger brethren. While this migration has fuelled the growth of this sector, and contributed to the diversification of this professional market, many of the recognized practice leaders remain concentrated in the top tier firms, drawn to the superior compensation and the greater prestige associated with these positions. Another consequence of these conflict guidelines is an imbalance in the supply or availability of legal labour. The lawyers who are the most skilled and experienced, and the most well endowed with symbolic capital, are monopolized by the industry while investors, even if they could afford it, are effectively shut out of the market: 'Investors often find out that it is difficult to get professional help because most of the large firms are committed to helping the big companies' (SIPA 2004: 42). The problem is thus not only one of affordability but also accessibility. Finally, conflict guidelines and the measure of selectivity in the clients and cases taken on by the larger firms have contributed to a particular economy of legal problems. The issues that are most likely to be litigated are those that impact the industry, while those of concern to regulators and investors are bound to remain unaddressed and/or unresolved. This is significant, for example, in the context of fiduciary duty, where case law has tended to favour the more narrow interpretations of the industry, an advantage secured through the levers of money and time, as well as recourse to private settlements in cases that threaten more investor-friendly precedents. While this overview of 'securities and enforcement litigation' as a distinct professional market has helped to shed light on the conditions under which counsel engage with the enforcement field, it remains to be seen how these are translated into two specific forms of advocacy work: legal gamesmanship and legal entrepreneurialism.

Legal games and regulatory encounters

Positioned on the boundary between law and finance, and tasked with interpreting the often ambiguous relationships between regulatory frames and market activities, the involvement of lawyers in the field of securities enforcement tends to take one of two forms. The first is the most recognizable, and includes the representation of market players in regulatory inquiries and proceedings. Through this process, counsel strive to shape the regulator's view of 'the case' and to produce a definition of the alleged misconduct that is most favourable to the interests of their client. The second contribution is less direct, consisting of efforts to mould the larger legal and policy environment in which they work, through their participation in policy networks and agitation around key strategic issues. Each of these is discussed in turn.

Legal gamesmanship

In any regulatory encounter, the first objective of legal counsel is to engage with enforcement staff this with the intention of discovering and then actively shaping the regulator's understanding of the events in question. The goal is thus to 'gauge the attitude of the regulator towards the client', to understand 'how is the regulator looking at you' and to assess 'as early as possible exactly where the regulators are going and why' (Managing Regulatory Investigations 2007). One of the more pressing issues in these early conversations is determining not only the scope of the inquiry, but also whether the client is a direct target of the investigation or simply a witness, with case strategies adjusted accordingly:

> If you have a client who's close to the bull's eye but not quite there you're trying to get them into the witness category ... If you've got somebody who's in the bull's eye, then it's a totally different strategy in terms of developing a rapport with the regulator and trying to get a sense of where they're at in their investigation so you can have these kinds of conversations and work out some kind of resolution that reduces the publicity against your client.
>
> (Lawyer #3: 6)

In return, depending on the stage reached in any investigation, regulators may offer a quick glance at their cards while being careful not to give too much away. Thus begins a game in which counsel and enforcement staff engage in various forms of bargaining and bluffing, signalling and posturing, all the while anticipating the viewpoints and future moves of the other player (Hawkins 2002; McBarnet 2004; Schmidt 2005). One respondent likened this entire process to the Cuban Missile Crisis (Crime and the Corporation 2006), a testament to the signalling that goes on between staff and legal counsel and to enforcement's roots in 'systematic misrepresentation, not only of intentions but of proximal purposes and intended outcomes on both "sides" of the game' (Manning 1993: 235).

The course of these initial encounters, and the subsequent fate of investigations, are further shaped by the nature of interpersonal relationships, considerations of credibility and mutual trust, and related forms of 'soft knowledge': 'Because all parties enter enforcement actions with limited information, "soft" knowledge – instincts, impressions, and reputations – plays a vital role' (Schmidt 2005: 156). Legal counsel who are trusted and who have had good relationships with regulators in the past may receive more favourable treatment, particularly in these early encounters: 'In my experience, particularly where Staff has *experience with* and *confidence in* the caller, Staff may elaborate somewhat helpfully on what the investigation entails (subject matter and time frame) and, rarely, any preliminary conclusions and theories that Staff may have in mind' (Campbell 2005: 5, emphasis added). This is not to suggest that they will fully divulge the details of the case, but they may provide an indication of the range of activities that are of regulatory interest, thus allowing counsel to formulate case strategies at a much earlier juncture. Here forms of social and symbolic capital, including the contacts and connections forged through secondments and prior working relationships, have the potential to impact the enforcement process with the selection of counsel often driven by their status and reputation in both the legal and regulatory community. While possessing the initial upper hand, regulators are obliged to respond to these queries, given their dependence on counsel for the production of information (Reichman 1998) and the benefits yielded by more cooperative relationships. This would include speed, a valuable commodity given the tight timelines under which regulators are required to work. Rather than a straightforward confrontation, the relationships between counsel and regulators are thus defined by various forms of mutual dependency and reliance, a complementarity of needs and interests within which gaming occurs and battles are fought.

A further source of influence on regulatory encounters are the personalities of those involved: 'Personalities, like reputations, are mercurial but crucial forces in enforcement processes, shaping perceptions by all parties of what can be achieved, altering strategies, and changing roles' (Schmidt 2005: 179). A number of respondents from both legal and regulatory communities spoke to the significance of personality as exactly this kind of barometer, indicating how cases would probably be handled and the types of strategies bound to bear the most fruit:

> I tend to see things as completely personality driven. I see it as more a function of the people who are involved on the regulatory side having sufficient experience in the area, experience with dealers and with us, to be able to work together … My whole practice on the regulatory side is about that.
>
> (Lawyer #28: 4–5)

In the words of another respondent: 'It's often more strategies based on personality. So in some investigations I've been involved in, you can develop a good rapport with the investigator' (Lawyer #3: 6). This knowledge of the players involved 'informs the investigation to some extent. And so you get a sense of what that person is like and how high on their priority list this case is. And also their predisposition because two investigators can approach the same set of facts and come out with a different conclusion' (Lawyer #3: 7). Conversely, the absence of these 'personal relationships with the people on the other side' (Lawyer #24: 1) can frustrate these encounters: 'If you don't know how to deal with [personalities] it's like taking your head and knocking it against a cement wall. It really is. I take time to know some of the personal details ... I think what it does is it makes it easier to sell a position' (Lawyer #1: 5). Questions not only of credibility, but also likeability, respect and familiarity, thus impact the enforcement process: 'If I trust someone, I'm much more upfront with them ... the relationships you develop are very important' (OSC #10: 8). With these various forms of 'soft knowledge' shaping initial expectations and postures, the actual course of engagements hinges on a number of considerations and strategies used in various combinations, depending on the players involved.

Regulatory stakes and legal hazards: multiple jeopardy

The first of these is the need to determine at a very early juncture, and then subsequently to manage, the exposure of the client not only to the regulatory allegations at hand but also potential spin-off proceedings: 'An investigation at the regulatory level is not the end of your client's issue, it may be just the beginning. And that's something that you consider when you're advising a client on a regulatory investigation' (Lawyer #26: 13). Assessing these additional forms of jeopardy is especially critical, given the multiple legal avenues to which the regulated may be subject, including other regulatory investigations, criminal charges, civil suits, and the greatest fear of all for most respondents, the involvement of foreign, namely US, regulators:

> You can spend a lot of time dealing with the OSC trying to resolve an issue and you then still may have to go to the MFDA and they may take a different position, then you have to go to the IDA and they may take a different position and then you've got all the other securities regulators across Canada. The fact that you reach an agreement with the OSC doesn't necessarily mean that the IMET is going to think that that's sufficient. They have their own investigation. And then you have the SEC and the police forces in the US.
>
> (Lawyer #19: 4)

One respondent likened this need to deal with multiple regulators and police agencies, as well as potential civil plaintiffs, to 'dancing with four different partners, each of whom wants a different step' (Crime and the Corporation 2006), a sentiment echoed by a former regulator:

> Invariably in these types of investigations, the conduct that is under investigation is not merely of interest to the criminal regulators, but it's also of interest whether it be to the strike bar, class actions, civil litigators, I mean they're all over it. And then you will not only have the criminal interests, but you have the regulatory interests. So, you've got this guy and he's looking to the right and he sees the regulator. He's looking to the left and he sees criminal law enforcement. He's looking straight ahead and he sees civil litigators. And he's gotta figure out a way of protecting his interests in respect of all three of those arenas. Not an easy challenge.
>
> (Former OSC #2: 5–7)

And yet, while the 'piling on' of downstream regulatory and legal actions is certainly a theoretical possibility, the actual odds are much more remote and may themselves be part of counsel game play. Professed concerns with the exposure created by their dealings with regulators may be used to limit the amount or form of information that is turned over, or to ensure that additional protections are built into working arrangements and informal disclosures. Along these same lines, while the involvement of US regulators may be the most feared, in practice it is also the least likely. The same can be said of Canadian criminal authorities. While exposure to civil litigation remains a very real threat, the likelihood of this resulting purely from a regulatory investigation is also far more remote than is implied by legal counsel.[5] Regardless of whether they are perceived or real, these additional forms of legal jeopardy represent a key stake of regulatory encounters and inform strategies of disclosure, as well as degrees of cooperation.

Another form of exposure subject to strategic management is the media which, as noted in Chapter 2, counsel complain is increasingly used by regulators not only as a basis for case selection, but also a source of pressure and means of leveraging their investigations to produce desired outcomes: 'There are all these levers that can be used today and a big part of that leverage is the public theatre, the media, and people use that' (Journalist #1: 4).[6] The fact that playing to the media 'causes some people discomfort' (Lawyer #10: 4) is clearly evident in the sense of indignation expressed by a senior member of the defence bar: 'They have PR people at the OSC dumping news stories. It's a real Yankee world. I don't find it impressive at all . . . It turns it into a battlefield' (Lawyer #6: 4). Responding to these pressures, defence counsel have become increasingly aware of the need to manage potential publicity, developing media strategies at the very outset of cases. In addition to creating a degree of defensibility around the client, these strategies also include questioning the motives of regulators and dropping hints of regulatory over-zealousness. The media is, once again, very much part of the gamesmanship of regulatory encounters, with benefits potentially flowing in both directions.

Strategies of cooperation

Given these legal and reputational stakes, once legal counsel have an understanding of the basic contours of a case, one of the first sources of strategic play involves how to respond to regulatory requests for information and for access to clients, and thus the appropriate form and degree of cooperation with enforcement staff. On the one hand, there are tremendous pressures, both formal and informal, as well as incentives to cooperate. The perception that counsel and clients are being uncooperative may fuel regulatory suspicions and trigger a more aggressive approach: '[regulators] place importance on appearances and often take a greater "negative" interest in apparent confrontation' (Campbell 2005: 6). As noted in the previous chapter, cooperativeness and the degree of compliance with regulatory requests also factor into judgments of character, and may thus further mitigate or exacerbate the course and severity of regulatory actions. Conversely, the benefits of cooperation are extensive including, in a criminal context, the avoidance of charges, lesser charges and/or lower penalties and, in a regulatory context, the narrowing of allegations, a reduction in sanctions and the decision not to undertake formal proceedings. In weighing these pressures and incentives, cooperation may be the only option.

On the other hand, this degree of cooperation comes with significant risks and uncertainties. First, it is unclear exactly what qualifies as 'cooperation'. While agencies in both Canada[7] and the US[8] have taken to formalizing, if not the benefits, at least the obligations to cooperate with regulators in the form of 'credit-for-cooperation' policies, counsel complain that little real guidance is provided by such documents, with evaluations subject to the whims of enforcement staff in individual cases: 'It's a joke. It's absolutely meaningless in my experience ... If they asked me for my advice, I tell them that what they give up, which is a chance of non-detection combined with a chance of avoidance, is nowhere close to the benefit they get by going up voluntarily' (Lawyer #12: 15). Second, there are concerns that in order to receive this 'credit', respondents must waive privilege over key documents and other forms of evidence. This is viewed as a significant loss of strategic control, to say nothing of a valued bargaining chip, as well as a threat to the institution of privilege itself. Third, there is the concern that, in being overly responsive to regulatory requests for information and voluntary attendance at interviews, legal counsel will leave themselves exposed to the very legal hazards they seek to avoid. These fears of knock-on proceedings are especially acute in the criminal context, as the police cannot guarantee that information or statements, once disclosed, will remain confidential. Given the inability to compel witnesses or targets to cooperate with the police, the result is the freeze in information flow noted in Chapter 3:

> There's a lot of people who won't cooperate, particularly when you add in the added dimension that anything they say to the police not only could be used by the police but could end up haunting them again with the regulator or the civil litigator that's waiting at the door to come in with action. So I can tell you as a defence counsel my advice to the client is 'tell them on the advice of counsel you have nothing to say at this time'. And yeah, that puts law enforcement in a difficult position, but it is the correct advice.
>
> (Former OSC #2: 10)

From a policing perspective, this is an endless source of frustration:

> One of the biggest drawbacks to the IMET program is that they're more worried about civil litigation than they are the criminal investigation because the civil can cost them so much . . . if the criminal investigation comes forward and proves actual criminal intent that's gonna hurt them even more in the civil world because civil litigators can then jump all over that. And that happens with the witnesses also. They're more worried about being sued civilly than they are about a criminal investigation.
>
> (IMET #2: 7–8)

These multiple forms of legal jeopardy have also impacted relations with regulators, as the best protection for respondents is to force regulators to use their formal subpoena powers to interview key witnesses or targets, thus ensuring that any disclosed information is not passed on to the police or other interested parties, or at least is limited in its subsequent usage.[9] However, given that regulators prefer voluntary disclosures, as they require less work and afford maximum flexibility in deciding whether a case will be retained in-house or passed on to other authorities, such a stance may itself be interpreted as a sign of uncooperativeness.

A similar set of considerations comes into play with respect to decisions on whether or not to turn over the results of internal investigations and reports, and in what specific form these disclosures should be made (that is, the full report versus summaries or excerpts). Pursuant to credit-for-cooperation policies, there is an expectation that firms, when faced with evidence or allegations of wrongdoing, will first conduct their own internal investigation and then hand over the results to regulators. As one conference participant explained, 'regulators love internal investigations' (Crime and the Corporation 2006), as the reports provide both themselves and the police with a roadmap and 'a factual basis for claims against the wrongdoer' (IMET #7: 4) that is bound to reduce their own investigative load and increase the speed of the investigation.

Again, this creates a very real dilemma for defence counsel. On the one hand, an internal investigation and report bestow certain advantages. Besides signalling their willingness to cooperate with regulators, internal reports can also be used to shape the regulator's view of a case, highlighting some forms of conduct and lines of responsibility while downplaying others, thus narrowing investigations in terms of the number of issues and individuals in play (Managing Regulatory Investigations 2007). However, on the other hand, these reports may find their way into the hands of other agencies and interested parties, thus risking further regulatory and legal actions and exposing clients to added legal and reputational risks. A delicate touch is thus required, with counsel employing different strategies depending on the circumstances and communicative needs of the moment:

> For some of the assignments, counsel wanted a better relationship with the regulators and so we've actually briefed them on a periodic basis . . . And I've

> had other files where the only thing the regulator got at the end of the day was a final report and the offer to interview us if they wanted to.
>
> (Accountant #1: 10)

In working their way through these various considerations, one strategy used by legal counsel is to signal a willingness to cooperate while limiting, or at least clearly circumscribing, the forms of usable evidence passed on to authorities (Mann 1985; Shapiro 1987; McBarnet and Whelan 1999; McBarnet 2004, 2005). As noted by one respondent: 'Sometimes you've got to be careful about how you [cooperate]. You can appear to be quite cooperative without having to give somebody an audit trail to do their own enforcement proceeding' (Accountant #1: 10). For their part, regulators are clearly aware of this strategy:

> We have a lot of bereft cooperation, the appearance of cooperation. They'll give us all the documents we don't want, and all the documents we do want there are fights over. But we're cooperating. They come and they'll meet with us, they'll talk to us, they'll be nice to us. I'd much rather some of the lawyers on Bay Street would just tell us to f-off.
>
> (OSC #4: 21)

In addition to more overt forms of resistance, this strategy can also include such passive-aggressive moves as disclosing facts without their proper context, what McBarnet (2005) refers to as 'non-disclosing disclosure' (175). The objective here is to 'bluff and minimize disclosure before shifting position if necessary and laying one's cards on the table' (McBarnet 2005: 173) without necessarily appearing uncooperative. When all else fails and cooperation is unavoidable, counsel can then seek additional protections which, while far from iron-clad, can at least raise the stakes should they be violated and place added moral pressure on regulators to honour their agreements: 'Before I go into an interview now I put a statement on the record that goes on for about five minutes about what they cannot do with the evidence they're about to get from the client' (Lawyer #26: 3). They can also engage in such strategies as carefully patrolling interview transcripts and other evidentiary footprints to ensure that they reflect the 'whole story', rather than simply the regulator's view of events (Campbell 2005). Regardless, from the perspective of regulators, the incentives to cooperate have done little to alleviate the barriers to accessing information and obtaining timely disclosure with outright resistance and more subtle circumvention representing the strategies of the day and key stumbling blocks for investigators.

Strategies of delay

A somewhat different, although by no means mutually exclusive, tactical course involves the efforts of legal counsel to engage in strategic delay. The issue is thus not simply *whether* to engage with regulators and the police, but rather *how* to manipulate and extend the time frame in which this occurs, while exerting as much control over the flow of information as is possible under the circumstances. This is a battle waged on a number of fronts. One of the more common of these fights is over privilege, with counsel seeking to throw a blanket of privilege over as many documents and communications as possible, including reports and investigations,[10] and then demanding a lengthy process of review in order to access these materials. According to regulators, these confrontations are increasingly common, with legal counsel working to expand the 'net of privilege' and 'frighten off regulators' (Managing Regulatory Investigations 2007):

> One of the emerging things which is quite troublesome because to me it speaks to the integrity of counsel involved is that … a lot of counsel are starting to use bogus claims of privilege as an excuse for not turning over probably incriminating documents. We have one pile right now where we have a list of 100,000 documents that they are claiming privilege on, and a lot of it is internal communications within the issuer itself. Well, I don't know how internal communication within an issuer can be privileged. You're talking about the business, you're not talking about legal advice. I don't know what the resolution of that issue is going to be because it's a growing problem.
>
> (OSC #12: 5)

A senior police investigator put the problem in the following terms:

> Right now their opinion is that it's all privileged. There's certain things we've asked for that they've not given us because they're saying it's privileged. Privilege is legal advice so lawyers saying 'Don't talk to the police' or 'Don't do this'. But holding every document that that person held as privileged because that person's suing you? That's not right. That's not privilege.
>
> (IMET #2: 9)

While counsel must remain aware of the signals sent by asserting privilege (Crime and the Corporation 2006), this does provide the benefit of slowing investigations and controlling the scope of cases. The removal of key documents or pieces of data from the evidentiary record may be just enough to nudge the case in the desired direction yet another means of patrolling the record.

In moving to the criminal realm, opportunities for delay increase exponentially. The police lack many of the investigative powers enjoyed by regulators, are less able to demand information, and are forced to rely on various forms of cooperative disclosure obtained through the time-honoured practice of begging and borrowing. In addition to fights over privilege and the dragging of heels before turning over requested documents, counsel employ a number of additional tactics to delay investigations, including using busy court schedules and scheduling conflicts to put off interviews, in some cases indefinitely, invoking Charter challenges that greatly increase the duration and complexity of proceedings and, what is perhaps the greatest pet peeve of all for the police, battles over disclosure:

> If you're a defence counsel, the way that you win a case is by generating delay because delay always helps the defence ... the best way to do it is through the disclosure process, to ask for things that you didn't get, and then when you don't get it, make it look like it was an unprincipled refusal on the Crown, and that puts the Crown at fault. That's the way to win the case'.
>
> (IMET #6: 7)

According to one estimate, 30 per cent of the cost of IMET investigations involves cataloguing, tracking and duplicating information to make sure copies will be available for the defence, exacerbating the already burdensome documentary requirements and formatting demands of securities cases. This has resulted in a situation where disclosure considerations have begun to drive the evidence-gathering process, as investigators limit the number of documents that are seized so as to minimize their disclosure obligation: 'You have to be selective about the stuff you let through the door' (IMET #21: 1). What is interesting about this particular delaying tactic is that it rests on the success of counsel in expanding the ambit of decisions that were initially intended to be relatively narrow, or at least more tightly circumscribed. A perfect example of this is the fact that in the original decision which established disclosure as a precedent in Canada, *R v Stinchcombe*, the obligation was tied to a number of specific conditions which have since been expanded to include all manner of materials relating to a case, no matter how peripheral: 'People have forgotten that the courts laid four or five conditions of what you're expected to do but the practice has become "well, give them everything but the kitchen sink". And then if you don't give them the kitchen sink the case gets thrown out four years later' (Dialogue with the OSC 2006).

These kinds of procedural challenges help to explain the comment by a senior IMET investigator that much of what the police do in the course of their investigations 'has nothing to do with the case', but involves responding to attempts by counsel to 'run interference' (IMET #7: 2): 'It's not unusual to go into an interview with four to eight lawyers sitting there dissecting every question you ask and looking at every document before it's posed ... It's just a game. I mean it's just a shell game' (IMET #2: 2). While perhaps not as acute, a similar sense of frustration is no doubt shared by those on the regulatory side of the fence, where delay is seen as a key tactic in avoiding enforcement (Dialogue with the OSC 2006), one that has again become more and more common with the growing powers of enforcement agencies and stakes of regulatory proceedings: 'Because the fines are getting more stringent and more is at stake, the respondents in these cases will use a variety of legal tactics which they have a right to do which will tend to extend the delays' (Dialogue with the OSC 2004).

Strategies of resolution: settlements

A final set of tactical concerns involves the resolution of enforcement matters. There was universal agreement amongst respondents in both regulatory and legal circles that the vast majority of cases are resolved either through an informal warning and/or undertaking or a formal settlement, with very few cases making it to the hearing stage. The following respondent put an interesting spin on the normalcy of settlements:

> I think the last time I looked at the stats about 80 per cent of our matters settle and the ones that don't settle tend to be, for want of a better word, wacko. People on the fringe who don't understand the process and will just fight it because they can.
>
> (OSC #4: 10)

No doubt settlements are the preferred course as they afford a less expensive and more expeditious resolution to cases, while allowing for a greater degree of predictability and control:

> My experience has been that the regulators are most anxious to avoid, if at all possible, a contested hearing ... And that's because it makes sense from a regulator's point of view; they want certainty; they want to reduce the costs that are associated with a hearing, and the best way to do that is to reach a settlement agreement.
>
> (Former OSC #2: 2)

And yet, by the same token, legal counsel complain that the bargaining power of regulators is such that they are able to extract settlements from respondents in cases which may not be deserving of these concessions on their merits. Once again, this comes down to media exposure and the sense among respondents that they cannot afford the reputational damage associated with a formal hearing which 'may be difficult to repair' (Managing Regulatory Investigations 2007).

Even where a settlement is deemed appropriate, there are extensive negotiations over the content and language of the agreements themselves: 'You'd be surprised as to how much energy goes into the drafting of settlement agreements, what is included, what isn't included ... skilled counsel can really work their magic in minimizing either that which goes public or the nature of what is ultimately disclosed for the public' (Former OSC #2: 3). The timing of settlements is also a matter of negotiation. Legal counsel strive for settlement dates when coverage and readership are likely to be at their lowest, such as just before a long weekend, or insist that the settlement and statement of allegations be issued 'contemporaneously so it's one day's news not two day's news. It's not something that the [media] can generate into four or five stories' (Lawyer #3: 6). Given the downside risks combined with the clear strategic benefits, a number of counsel are recognized as having built their practices around a reputation for cooperation and quick settlements. In the words of one of the recognized pioneers of this strategy:

> I built my practice on a non-adversarial approach so that regulators came to expect when they see my name on a file, they will get somebody who will fully cooperate, not put up roadblocks into their obtaining documentation, dealing in a responsible way with the regulatory issues arising from an investigation and settle if at all possible. And it would only ever go to a hearing if it was an issue that was essentially on principle that for some reason the dealer or the sales rep wanted to have dealt with and not settle. So what that meant is I wasn't faced with regulators who were afraid to talk to me because it would show up in an affidavit ... And what I found is over time my approach came to be adopted by more of the other litigation lawyers that practice in the area.
> (Lawyer #28: 14)

The rationale for this strategy goes well beyond its expediency and the interests of counsel in building up a reserve of goodwill that might be tapped in future cases. There is also the matter of discouraging the regulator from taking a deeper look and potentially discovering additional forms of misconduct or lines of responsibility (Former OSC #2).[11] There is thus most certainly a method to their madness. Alternatively, despite these strategic advantages, this may be one of those points where client interests become secondary to the importance of maintaining good relations with regulators, thus mitigating against more aggressive legal maneuvers. There is also the worry that, in their efforts to cooperate and settle, firms may engage in actions, such as waiving privilege over counsel's work product, that are 'seriously prejudicial to the individual employees involved' (Campbell and O'Toole 2007: 3), thus triggering a form of organizational scapegoating that is part-and-parcel of the gamesmanship underlying the enforcement process.

Legal entrepreneurialism

While these struggles over the terms and outcomes of individual cases represent their primary point of engagement with the field of securities enforcement, legal counsel also maintain an active interest in the larger terrain on which these battles are fought, seeking to shape their legal habitat and the conditions under which they are required to work. Representing what can best be described as a form of legal entrepreneurialism, this involves creative efforts on the part of counsel to ask questions about key legal and policy issues, to challenge regulators on points of practice and procedure and to assert various claims about the need for reform. These efforts unfold through a number of different avenues of varying degrees of formality.

On the one end of this spectrum is the influence afforded to legal counsel by virtue of their positions on the advisory panels, executive boards and governance bodies of the major regulatory agencies, a kind of back-stage pass that allows them to provide input and shape the regulatory agenda from within without having to relinquish their positions in the private sector. Resembling a form of 'corporatism' (Johnson 1993; Andrews 2006), these appointments reflect the formal insertion of legal counsel into the regulatory process and thus their bequeathal of an institutionalized right of influence over regulatory policy and practice. While much less direct, an equally important source of advocacy work flows through the participation of counsel in the formal comment process, as well as the various reports and commissions on the regulatory system where, akin to the classic sketch comedy where a single actor plays multiple roles, they appear as sponsors, authors *and* respondents. The comment process, used by regulators to solicit feedback on policy issues or proposed regulatory changes from affected constituencies, consumes the most time and energy yet may be the less effective of the two, means of registering objections rather than significantly altering the proposed regulatory course. In contrast, the business of report writing, bolstered by periodic appearances before government committees, accords counsel a much more active role in shaping the agenda for inquiries and inserting their own voice into published findings.

A second form of legal entrepreneurialism is more ad hoc and targets a very different point in the enforcement process. This involves efforts on the part of legal counsel to shape the legal environment by means of their advocacy work in specific cases, that is, their decisions about which cases to take on and their pursuit of particular strategies, motions and lines of argumentation. Counsel are continually on the hunt for cases with fact patterns that would allow them to challenge the authority and jurisdiction of the regulators, to litigate around controversial issues and to establish favourable precedents for the future. If the objective of inserting themselves into the policy process is to engage with macro issues in the hopes that this will trickle down in the form of advantages in daily enforcement encounters, the interventions in specific cases and on particular points of law are designed to set precedents and policies that will be generalizable across enforcement contexts and will help to refashion regulatory policy from below. Their involvement in this form of juridification also affords counsel the opportunity to naturalize what are in essence rhetorical claims converting them into the technicalities of legal judgments, thus rendering them authoritative, universalized and removed from the field of contention (Bourdieu 1987; Riles 2005). Besides formal rulings, the benefits of litigating the 'right' cases also extend to the production of a form of symbolic messaging that may be useful in framing future battles, what Galanter (1981) refers to as:

> A whole set of messages that can be used as resources in making (or contesting) claims, bargaining (or refusing to bargain) and regulating (or resisting regulation). Through the wrong end of the telescope, the work of courts is seen not primarily as the resolution of disputes in official settings, but the projection of bargaining and regulatory endowments into a world unevenly occupied by indigenous regulation, a world in which the influences that emanate from courts mingle with those from other sources (31).

Often ambiguous and subject to interpretation, court decisions provide further fodder for bargaining in the shadow of the law and thus endowments, or bargaining chips, for those who are able to first interpret and then use these messages to their own advantage.

Moving to the more informal end of the spectrum, there are endless opportunities for interpersonal contacts and connections between counsel and regulators, a reflection of the intermingling of professional and regulatory networks and the close working relationships between these groups. One of the more intriguing of these forms of networking are the numerous conferences held each year and attended by legal counsel, members of the industry and representatives of the major regulatory agencies. While ostensibly for the purpose of educating market players on the regulatory issues of the day, in reality these conferences serve as occasions for counsel to press regulators on areas of concern and make them more aware of the stakes and interest positions associated with specific policies, practices and proposals. With the major law firms often footing the bill, these conferences resemble a combination of complaint department and suggestion box. If not directly altering maligned policy stances, they are at least useful in shaping the terms of reference through which relevant issues are defined and assessed, as well as creating an audience of the affected that regulators may be more likely to bear in mind when contemplating future moves.

Through these various avenues, the entrepreneurialism of legal counsel has drawn attention to a long list of grievances. These range from specific causes or pet peeves, such as the push for 'no contest' pleas allowing respondents to enter into settlement agreements without making potentially damaging admissions of guilt, the desire for a clearer definition of credit for cooperation and its implications for legal privilege as well as the clarification of privilege itself, and the unfairness of having to foot the bill for hearings, regardless of whether they win or lose, to more fundamental areas of contention that strike at the heart of the regulatory enterprise involving questions of authority, jurisdiction and fairness. Examples of the latter would include: (1) the push by counsel to make the regulatory process subject to Charter-based principles and constitutional protections; (2) skirmishes around the OSC's use of its public interest power; and (3) an extensive campaign to split the investigative and adjudicative functions of the OSC, based on allegations that commissioners are biased towards cases brought forward by enforcement staff who are said to enjoy a clear 'home-court advantage' (Lawyer #12: 8). The issue of bias is especially intriguing, as it represents one of the most high profile and enduring lines of advocacy work and dovetails with a number of other criticisms of the enforcement process, a clarion call for all that is wrong with the regulatory system (see Osborne et al. 2004). Equivalent to a call of foul play in a school-yard tussle, such complaints strike at the heart of the authority and fairness of the regulators, a position dripping with irony as the 'lengthy, criminal-law like trials' (Osborne et al. 2004: 32) that allegedly make life difficult for counsel and their clients reflect the interventions of lawyers themselves, the calcifications of previous advocacy efforts.

The bias issue is also revealing in the sense that it is based more on the posturings of legal counsel interested in pushing back on recent regulatory gains, and obtaining a leg up on their regulatory counterparts, than a well substantiated and truly genuine policy concern. In fact, many of these reports openly admit that they are responding only to the *perception* of bias, with few documented incidents and little in the way of concrete substantiation. As noted by a former regulator and present consultant, it is not even the specific issue of bias or the establishment of a separate adjudicative tribunal that is key, but the effort to reinsert some kind of balance to the regulatory process, a means of reintroducing arguments and positions that have either fallen on deaf ears or which may be deemed too risky in the current climate:

> They are looking at anything that will help to re-introduce natural checks and balances into the enforcement field. And if that means creating an adjudicative panel where they can make their criticisms of staff without fear of undermining their own position, I think that's it. My guess is that most of the securities specialists only care about structure because they think it might reintroduce the judgments they would otherwise not get.
>
> (Former BCSC #1: 10)

Of course, it is far from coincidental that these arguments have followed a more active posture on the part of the OSC and other regulators, as well as the entry of new players with slightly different case strategies: 'What happened when the enforcement increased is that litigators rather than traditional securities lawyers began to come before the commission. Litigators raised the issues you'd expect them to raise and that they should raise. One of them was bias. They came to believe it' (Twelve Minute Securities Lawyer 2005). All of this calls into question the sincerity of these critiques and again invokes the larger field of play:

> It does seem perverse ... that intense discussion of the need for a new tribunal arises when the OSC ... is taking its enforcement role more seriously than it may have in the past. This leads to speculation that complaints about bias are another weapon in the legal arsenal of respondents and their lawyers.
>
> (Condon 2006: 15)

Emerging from this advocacy work, it would appear that the forms of tactical advantage desired by legal counsel extend well beyond fights over specific laws and policies, instead encompassing a much larger set of pressure points, discursive frames and dramatic posturings designed to tilt the enforcement field back, or perhaps more, in their favour. Legal counsel are not so naïve as to think that these efforts will lead to actual changes in policy or the immediate implementation of their requests. In fact, there have been very few instances where regulators have responded to their wishes; to do so would constitute too clear a sign of outside influence. It is also the case that counsel have had greater success in altering the legal landscape through court-based interventions, as revealed by recent decisions around privilege and the applicability of the Charter to administrative tribunals,[12] rather than these more general regulatory exhortations. Instead, the purpose of registering their complaints and serving notice on particular issues is to make regulators think twice about how they deal with these questions in the future, to require more confidence and greater investments of symbolic capital in staking their positions, and to draw lines in the sand designating the reasonable boundaries of these practices, thus exercising a more subtle form of influence that has paid dividends in the past. For example, the protests that greeted the OSC's allegedly more aggressive media strategy were not followed by any formal reversal of course, but rather greater discretionary circumspection about when and how to publicize investigations. Legal entrepreneurialism is thus itself a form of posturing, a means of defining and redefining the stakes, parameters and rules of the enforcement game.

And yet, here again the realities of the professional market intrude to restrain these efforts as the preferred course for confronting regulators, through formal proceedings and court challenges, is also the most costly. Many clients are unwilling to shoulder the financial load and tolerate the reputational risks. Absent these more direct assaults, legal counsel are relegated to stamping their feet at conferences and relying on rhetorical volleys that may or may not hit their mark. Questions of affordability and client tolerance for risk thus join contradictory mandates, agency conflicts, the possession of symbolic capital and modes of detection and narrativity as one of the many contingencies of the enforcement enterprise.

Conclusion

Rather than being tightly coupled with law, this chapter has revealed securities enforcement to unfold through informal and often private contexts of interaction, posturing and bargaining in which 'the law', ambiguous as it is, represents both part of the field of struggle, and a strategic resource, bargaining chip and source of leverage waged in the pursuit of particular positions and endgames. These forms of gamesmanship, which include the strategic use of the jurisdictional challenges and enforcement gaps noted in Chapter 3, as well as attempts to minimize the vulnerabilities to detection and to challenge the narratives of client culpability noted in the previous chapter, exist alongside efforts to shape regulatory policies and working assumptions in the context of larger issue networks. In each of these respects, there is no doubt that lawyers play a critical role in the enforcement process, a role that is shaped through the distinct features of securities and enforcement litigation as a professional market governed by the production and supply of legal labour and the comingling of professional and client interests. It is here that expertise in the form of symbolic capital is critical, as lawyers are valued for, and influence the enforcement process through, the mobilization of degrees and credentials, interpersonal contacts and connections, and particular manners of speaking 'the law'. Likewise, the ability to engage in strategic bargaining and to seed and subsequently reap the benefits of issue networks hinges on the possession of forms of credibility that make their positions appear convincing and credible, that lend legal technicalities their air of permanence and incontrovertibility and which increase the stakes of taking on cases where credibility may be an, or is at, issue. Thus, the contributions of lawyers hinge both on their role as advocates and their position in a larger market in symbolic capital, connections and assurances.

Two additional insights emerge from this discussion that are germane to securities enforcement and which help to set the stage for the final chapter. First, while unfolding within the designated confines of individual agencies and assuming a distinctly organizational form, much of the substance of enforcement is actually rooted in loosely coupled professional or occupational networks that intersect with, but transcend, these institutional boundaries. These consist of forms of occupational knowledge grounded in law, finance and accounting, as well as interpersonal contacts and connections sustained by the movement across and between agencies and the private sector. While one may be tempted to see in these relationships further evidence of regulatory capture (Gunningham 1987; Shapiro 1987), to the extent that they exert a conservative influence over enforcement this is more likely the result of 'shared orientations and forms of knowledge' (Dorn 2010: 32). These define the basic parameters of what is sensible, reasonable or appropriate in the context of regulatory encounters, thus potentially foreclosing alternative approaches or courses of action. As 'epistemic' (Haas 1992; Scott 2001) or 'regulatory' (Meidinger 1987; Canan and Reichman 2002) communities, these professional networks also reveal a certain shared understanding of the nature, rules and objectives of enforcement, hence the agreed-upon countervailing effects of market efficiencies and regulatory activism. This suggests that, in order to understand enforcement, one must thus look beyond organizations to the workings of professional networks and to see within these networks forms of knowledge that help to define the terms and limits of the enforcement enterprise. More on this later.

Second, as a commodified form of labour delivered under the auspices of a particular professional market, the expertise and advocacy efforts of lawyers are neither equal, nor equally available. Those with the requisite financial resources will be granted access to the 'best' lawyers, that is, those possessing the greatest skills *and* the strongest reputations. Conversely, those who are less financially well endowed will be relegated to less well known and less credible representatives (Reichman 1992; McBarnet 2004). This speaks not only to the very real differences in the ability to mobilize law in the furtherance of one's interests, but also a convertibility of financial into symbolic capital that accords the greatest legal advantage to the largest players: 'Firms that can command high levels of regulatory authority are most likely to take control of the rules of the game in ways that authenticate their actions at the same time they marginalize, if not discredit, the actions of more subordinate members of their community' (Reichman 1992: 261). The product of this economy of expertise is the injection of a further degree of selectivity into the regulatory process as variations in symbolic capital, among other attributes, are translated into different likelihoods of detection, investigation and 'prosecution'. Returning full circle to the issue of regulatory outcomes, the question to be addressed in the final chapter is whether or how the influences on the enforcement enterprise examined in each of the previous chapters, legal advocacy and symbolic capital among them, contribute to the production of a distinct regulatory vision.

Notes

1 Here it is the police who face the greatest challenge this given that the '[The Criminal Code] is really designed for interpersonal relationships. Murder, rape, assault. The fraud provisions are really designed for interaction between people' (OSC #4: 12). Moreover, as noted by Sliter (1994): 'The problem lays with trying to incorporate some very conjectural economic principles and concepts into criminal law; definitions that were meant for use in economic models for academic discussion, not to be incorporated into the implicit definitions necessary for effective criminal legislation' (60).
2 Despite this growth, the majority of lawyers involved in enforcement work supplement this part of their practice with more stable and lucrative activities such as mergers and acquisitions, structured financings, public offerings, corporate finance and advisory work (eg assisting committees with their disclosure obligations), based on the reality that 'you can't run a full-time career just doing securities regulation and enforcement' (Lawyer #23: 1).
3 During the tenure of David Brown, the secondment program was suspended and has not been formally reinstated, with the OSC relying instead on the in-house development of legal talent.
4 This was justified by one respondent through a direct comparison with criminal procedures: 'Why don't we have access to that information because certainly in other contexts there is the ability of defence counsel to get that kind of information? For example, when police obtain a search warrant, the defence counsel can subsequently get the information provided in support of that search warrant' (Managing Regulatory Investigations 2009).
5 This is also true of class action lawsuits, which are much less common in Canada compared to the US given higher legal thresholds, less favourable class proceedings legislation, the limited availability of contingency fee arrangements and their foreignness to Canadian legal culture. While there were fears that the 2005 legislation in Ontario allowing for secondary market liability would trigger a wave of civil lawsuits, this has not come to pass for many of the reasons cited above.
6 One of the key points of tension between the OSC and legal counsel on this issue is whether, and at what point, investigations should be made public. While the stated policy of the agency is not to publicize investigations, there was a period under the chairmanship of David Brown that the OSC adopted a more aggressive media strategy, hiring a PR person or 'spin doctor' (MFDA #1) and publicizing a number of high profile investigations. Perhaps owing to the vocal feedback from the industry and legal counsel, the OSC's media presence has been much more muted of late.
7 For example, the OSC's credit-for-cooperation policy is outlined in OSC Staff Notice 15–702 (http://www.osc.gov.on.ca).
8 The US has perhaps the most infamous credit-for-cooperation policy outlined in what is known as the 'Thompson Memorandum'. This includes in the definition of cooperation the waiver of attorney-client privilege and the refusal to pay legal fees for employees, officers or directors under investigation, both of which have upset the legal establishment and triggered a vocal backlash (eg Committee on Capital Markets Regulation 2006).

9 While these protections are more or less iron-clad as they relate to the police, subject to the limits and ambiguities noted in Chapter 3, they are much weaker in the context of civil claims and downright dodgy with respect to foreign authorities such as the SEC and the Department of Justice, who appear more than willing to use testimony produced under these circumstances.

10 The ability to assert privilege over internal corporate investigations is limited to the report itself and does not extend to the facts uncovered during an investigation (Securities Superconference 2009). The difficulty, of course, is that without the surrounding narrative and interpretive context, it may be difficult to make sense of the facts; yet another example of non-disclosing disclosure (McBarnet 2005).

11 On the subject of speedy settlements, this same respondent noted that one of the factors driving this willingness on the part of regulators to engage in quick settlements was their need to meet tight deadlines for media releases (Former OSC #2).

12 Two recent cases are especially noteworthy here (see Rubin 2008). In one, the Supreme Court of Canada not only reinforced the sanctity of privilege but also framed it in terms of a quasi-constitutional right, thus invoking Charter-based protections. As a matter of practice, this means that regulators can no longer make requests for documents on the understanding that they will be reviewed to determine if privilege is warranted. Rather, these determinations must be made by counsel prior to the documents being handed over, a potentially fatal blow to the use of credit-for-cooperation policies to direct document production. A second landmark ruling by the Supreme Court of Canada holds that administrative tribunals have the right to find Charter violations and create legal remedies. While intended to give applicants the ability to seek administrative redress in cases where their rights have been violated, it is conceivable that this widening of the Charter ambit may be used as further leverage for the position that tribunals such as the OSC should themselves be subject to constitutional protections and guarantees.

Chapter 7

Regulatory vision and the politics of knowledgeability

Introduction

Daniel Drew, the renowned fraudster from the 1800s, once boasted: 'Law is like a cobweb: it's made for flies and the smaller kinds of insects, so to speak, but lets the big bumblebee break through. When technicalities of the law stood in my way, I have always been able to brush them aside easy as anything' (in Sutherland 1983: 57). This is indeed the prevailing image of financial regulation, one that continues to charge critics who assert that enforcement is geared to the pursuit of the smaller players while the larger ones are allowed to roam free. While this book has concerned itself with the practices underlying the enforcement enterprise, rather than its outcomes or products, the question inevitably arises as to the nature and composition of enforcement caseloads and the extent to which they are characterized by recognizable patterns and, conversely, gaps and omissions. This final chapter takes up this very question, tracing the forms of financial activity that are more rather than less likely to be picked up, problematized and taken on by the enforcement agencies conceived as a sliding scale of probability rather than a definitive basket of cases.

However, in proceeding down this path, the intention is not to relapse into old categories and familiar distinctions seeking in the composition of enforcement files actors of a particular size or influence. It may very well be the case that the larger players come out ahead (Galanter 1974). And yet, even if it were true, this is a statement in the absence of an explanation, one that overlooks the details of the regulatory craft. Informed by the more close-up view of enforcement developed over the course of this book, the objective instead is to examine the links between recurring patterns in case features and the influences, logics and contingencies highlighted in each of the previous chapters, understood as limits bearing on the knowledgeability of finance and contributing factors to a particular regulatory vision. Fleshed out through oceanographic and photographic metaphors, it is the distinct features and distinctly politicized nature of this regulatory vision that reveals enforcement's roots in a politics of knowledgeability that is vastly different from the forms of accommodation and capture so often imputed to the financial sphere. Building towards a different view of the possible futures in this and other realms of financial governance, this is an analysis that begins with a closer look at the visions of financial disorder.

Visions of financial disorder

In almost every study of regulation to date, the conclusion is invariably the same: the response of regulatory agencies to problems in the marketplace is highly selective, focusing on certain types of activities and players to the exclusion of others. On this count, the results of this study may be unremarkable. The selectivity of enforcement was a recurring theme of policy reports and public commentaries (eg Cory and Pilkington 2006; Jackson 2006). It also figured prominently in the comments of respondents themselves, who cited numerous examples of incidents that had either not been detected by regulators or which were passed on, in some cases through personal referrals, never to be heard of again. In response to a question about regulatory gaps one respondent replied: 'I would have to say yes. There's cases where clients consult me worried, and with just cause worried, and nothing happens' (Lawyer #3: 12). In the more critical assessment of another respondent: 'There's dozens and dozens of cases where there have been fairly clear cases of insider trading and there's been no action taken by the securities commissions ... there's a whole host of other cases where there's been misconduct where they just haven't done anything' (Lawyer #22: 2–3). Some attributed these lapses to an avoidance of the more 'serious' or 'sophisticated' cases; 'a lot of the serious stuff they don't know how to figure out' (Accountant #1: 3). Others invoked 'fruit-based' and 'iceberg' metaphors, the former likening case selection to a process of 'cherry picking', with regulators targeting the 'low hanging fruit' (Lawyer #21: 5), and the latter noting that the number of cases picked up by regulators is indeed quite small relative to the much larger mass of problems lurking beneath the surface and extending into the depths of the markets.

The notion that enforcement is not only selective but targets the most visible and readily accessible cases is reinforced by many of the dynamics examined in previous chapters, from which can be distilled a number of specific attributes of market activities bound to impact their susceptibility to detection and investigation. The first attribute is *magnitude*, with forms or patterns of activity that are subtle and distributed across a number of transactional sites less likely to attract the attention of enforcement staff. A second is *range* or *scope*, including not only activities that are dispersed in time and space, but also those that cross jurisdictional lines. A third attribute is *impact*, a form of magnitude that relates less to the nature of the activity itself and more to its effects on the markets and individual investors. Activities that cause a discernible loss to a clearly recognizable victim are more likely to result in official enforcement actions, while those whose harms are indirect and less subject to quantification, are less likely to appear in agency caseloads. The fourth is *blameworthiness*. As noted in Chapter 5, cases involving activities that are clearly intentional and perpetrated by players of questionable character are typically deemed more deserving of, and conducive to, enforcement actions. A fifth attribute is *clarity* or *perspicuity*, which encompasses both the ability to describe in the clearest evidentiary terms possible the details of an incident, and the absence of both legal ambiguity and reliance on subjective judgments. Activities involving less stable legal ground are not only more difficult from the technical standpoint of making one's case; they are also likely to invite run-ins with legal counsel, thus escalating the risks of a case and concomitant demands on symbolic capital. A sixth attribute is *embeddedness*. Forms of misconduct that are embedded in legal transactions and extend across different relationships and lines of activity stand a good chance of escaping regulatory scrutiny (Zey 1993). A seventh and final attribute is *stakes*. With agencies possessing a limited reserve of symbolic capital, whether incidents are pursued often hinges on the institutional risks and public exposures that they generate. Cases that are risky and would require an inordinate expenditure of symbolic capital are thus likely to be avoided.

Given these attributes, the incidents likely to 'make it' into the regulatory fold are defined by their distinctiveness and atypicality. These are the cases that are: (1) noticeable, standing out from the noise of the financial surround by virtue of their magnitude, impact, profile and blameworthiness; (2) limited in scope and visible from a single regulatory viewpoint; (3) readily reconcilable with available legal frames; and (4) conducive to the evidentiary and formatting demands that make for successful cases. They are also the cases that can be managed within the resourcing limits and time constraints of the enforcement process, with time emerging as an especially critical concern for agencies such as RS, which must tread through a morass of false positives and technical offsides in their pursuit of more serious problems in the marketplace:

> The majority of alerts relate to comparatively minor issues ... While we need to continue to be vigilant in these areas, the large volume of these alerts requires surveillance officers to spend the majority of their time on them. This leaves little time to analyze and detect more complex manipulations that pose a much more serious threat to investors and market integrity.
>
> (RS 2003: 17)

Time pressures also act as powerful constraints on assessments and investigations, as the fate of many cases hinges on both the possibility of a successful resolution and the speed with which this outcome can be effected and thus matters moved through the enforcement process.

Collectively, these case features result in what may be described as a tilting of enforcement caseloads towards files involving outsiders or players of marginal status and position. This is especially true given the normative undertones of the enforcement process and the moral calculus that invariably comes into play, as agencies direct the strongest regulatory response towards those viewed to be in violation of key normative frames involving the appropriateness and respectability of conduct. Many of the cases populating agency files thus involve boiler rooms and other forms of clearly manipulative activity, questionable practices associated with the 'Over-the-Counter Bulletin Board' and the 'Pink Sheets', and serious forms of registrant misconduct ranging from cases of misappropriation, to unauthorized trading, to the sale of unregistered or fictitious securities, to personal financial dealings with clients (Securities Litigation 2006). This is reflected in the comment from one respondent that the OSC's 'bread and butter' cases include the failure to register as a market player, the distribution of unregistered securities and out-and-out scams, including selling securities with no underlying value, with the focus in each of these instances being on 'untrustworthy people' (Securities Litigation 2006). Things are not much different for the IDA: 'Our most serious cases involve fraudulent activity on the market or in the marketplace, usually involving people that are not registered by us. So people that we do not have jurisdiction over. But these non-registered individuals are using our members, our firms, and our registrants to conduct their activity' (IDA #2: 5).[1] These are hardly the suitability cases or accounting manipulations of greatest concern to the investing public. The mere fact that the OSC was forced to consider whether a pigeon qualified as a security speaks to this work on the edges of the markets.[2]

Moreover, to the extent that more mainstream players and investment activities are targeted by regulators, the emphasis appears to be on rather narrow lines of responsibility. Alleged breaches are attributed to individual miscreants or 'rogues', while the larger contexts that inform even the most egregious of actions, including compensation systems, managerial pressures and standard practices and operating procedures, are overlooked: 'The big producer being unassailable until oops he's a rogue broker. I think there's way too much of that that's tolerated and countenanced' (Lawyer #8: 9). In fact, in many cases it is the firms themselves that inform regulators of the misconduct and build the case against their employees, an insider's perspective that regulators cherish but lack in most other instances. Thus, it is likely that regulators will not only target individuals rather than firms, but will also adopt a narrative and case logic that frames misconduct in highly individualistic terms (see also Hawkins 2002; Spalek 2001).[3] In the words of a former investment adviser: 'The vast majority of new issues go down. There's too much risk. And if they blow up or implode … the firm does not stand behind them. They say you are responsible' (Investor Advocate #2: 1). Engaging with this wider arc of responsibility is both inefficient from an enforcement perspective and inconsistent with the more expeditious approach to case management promoted by senior officials.

With this it would appear that we have travelled along a different track only to arrive at the same destination. All signs seemingly point to the fact that enforcement is not only selective, but that this selectivity is informed primarily by considerations of size and stature, with the bulk of enforcement activities reserved for the smaller, more marginal and inherently incorrigible players, the so-called 'miscreants' (Snider 2009: 187). The exception is a peppering of cases involving clearly egregious conduct on the part of high profile, mainstream players, which demand a strong regulatory response by virtue of their notoriety, regardless of whether or not they fit the typical case profile. And yet, here again, status is key as it is the background of the players involved that triggers the regulatory response. The underlying sentiment is that, save for those occasions where they overstep established boundaries and force the regulatory hand, size and status clearly matter. In the end, it is the larger players that receive the most forgiving treatment with their 'offences' either downplayed as technical violations meriting a warning or a slap on the wrist, or overlooked altogether. Sliding further down this slippery slope, the inevitable conclusion would appear to be that securities enforcement is, if not captured, at least predisposed to overlook the missteps on the part of the mainstream players, and is thus complicit in their wayward capitalism (Shapiro 1984).

The difficulty is that this emphasis on size as a window into the instrumentalities of the regulatory system continues to offer a limited and decidedly narrow view of the enforcement enterprise. First, despite the finding that the activities of smaller, more marginal players are over-represented in enforcement caseloads, a more careful and comprehensive review reveals a much more colourful picture, with agencies netting an assortment of players arising out of a variety of circumstances. Second, regardless of its veracity, the focus on size and stature has the effect of allowing a *description* of the regulatory caseload to stand as an *explanation* for the enforcement process, while overlooking the possibility that status is simply a crude proxy for the more subtle attributes noted above, and not an especially useful one at that. Size also leads right into the 'black box' trap, reducing enforcement to the drivers (resources) or levers (expertise) through which the larger players are able to game the regulatory system: size in, size out.

Instead of the more superficial features of reported cases, from which the determinative essence of enforcement can then be inferred or read back, the results of this study direct attention to the intervening and intersecting logics, technologies and politics that enliven this regulatory project as an historically constituted social field. It is the nuances, details and little struggles that matter most. These influences contribute to what can best be described as a distinct regulatory vision, a perspective or viewpoint on the social world of the markets that is constituted and mediated by contradictory mandates, inter-agency struggles, differences in symbolic capital, detection technologies and formatting demands, and legal couplings. These are significant not as drivers or interests, there are no levers to be pulled nor ghosts in the machine animating regulatory pursuits, but rather constraints that shape the knowledge work performed by regulators. Reflecting this emphasis on questions of knowledge and knowledgeability, it is the forms (the structures, limits and boundaries) rather than necessarily the contents (points of inclusion and exclusion) of this regulatory vision that are most critical, and which implicate the enforcement enterprise in the 'construction of a broader field of financial visibility' (Thrift 2002: 203). Having shifted the terms of reference, it remains to be seen what this regulatory vision looks like, and how it emerges from the influences examined over the course of this book.

Regulatory vision: inside the 'camera obscura'

The notion that securities enforcement is organized in terms of a particular kind of vision finds its inspiration in what can loosely be described as the anthropology of knowledge, a perspective more than a tradition, which examines how knowledge is produced and the social as well as material, technical and discursive conditions of its production. While this is an outlook that boasts a number of different theoretical moorings, many of which have been examined in previous chapters, one contribution that is especially useful in working through the question of regulatory knowledge is the work of Charles Goodwin. An anthropologist by training, Goodwin (1994, 1995) explores the socio-cognitive devices and structures of intelligibility associated with professional or expert knowledge. This informs his understanding of 'professional vision' as a 'socially organized way of seeing and understanding events' (Goodwin 1994: 606) that is distinct to areas of professional practice such as archaeology and law and which is informed by particular logics, discursive practices and measurement devices. These allow for dynamics such as 'coding', 'highlighting' and 'representing', which format the material world in a way that is professionally relevant and allows for the production of 'professional knowledge' (Goodwin 1994). The result is a viewpoint *on* the world that contributes to a particular view *of* the world.

Goodwin (1995) further builds on this approach in an engaging study of an oceanographic research vessel. While oriented to a seemingly common object of study, the ocean and its depths, he examines how each group of scientists on board, through their various positions, tools and representational devices (eg sampling grids and depth recorders), produce distinct representations of the ocean and its scientifically relevant features: 'though all of these groups are in precisely the same place and probing exactly the same patch of sea, each will in fact see something quite different there' (Goodwin 1995: 246). It is these mediated forms of knowledgeability that define the relationships between scientists and the spaces of the ocean: 'Human beings perceive space from within socially-organized settings and conceptualize, articulate and traverse space through a rich collection of tools that have been appropriated from the cognitive activities of our predecessors (maps, graphs, ships and so on)' (268).

There are clear parallels here with the science and technology studies tradition,[4] as well as the work of Riles (2005) and Valverde (2009). Goodwin devotes considerable attention to the materialities of knowledge production, including the effects of measurement devices, diagrams and other representational technologies. He also emphasizes the mediated or mediatory nature of this knowledge work, noting the role of these very same devices in producing a particular image or rendition of objects which then becomes the subject of analysis: 'A clear demonstration of the situated nature of the perceptual processes examined here is found in the way in which they require for their accomplishment the tools that build the setting that makes the activity possible in the first place' (Goodwin 1995: 256). In the language of STS and the social studies of finance, these devices, technologies and discursive frames are performative in nature, rather than simply mirroring the social or financial world (see Pryke 2010). Interestingly, Goodwin's work and the concept of professional vision also resonates with the emphasis placed by Bourdieu on questions of social space and associated notions of positioning, relationalism and referentiality. For Goodwin, as for Bourdieu, knowledge is not only 'instantiated in situated social practices' (Goodwin 1995: 257), the product of a distinct place in the social or natural world, but also unfolds through the *relative* distances between players, positions and objects. Critical linkages thus emerge for both of these authors between space, distance and forms of knowledgeability.

Applying these insights to the analyses of securities enforcement undertaken in this book, it would appear that the enforcement enterprise may itself be conceived in terms of a distinct professional, or more appropriately, regulatory vision. While caution must be exercised in pushing the analogy too far, or taking it too literally, enforcement staff are not unlike the scientists onboard Goodwin's research vessel. They are similarly positioned on the surface of the market and are far removed from its depths with which they have limited engagement and which they can only approximate using the tools, channels and strategies available to them. This includes a reliance on the proclivities of investors, informants or firms to voluntarily report suspected cases of troublesome activity, as well as on their own detection technologies, themselves bound to a narrow range of market indicators, information sources and attributions of 'normality'. Moreover, as with oceanographic research, there is a very real physical dimension to the forms of space and distance underlying the regulatory enterprise, as reflected in the organization of urban financial centres and the geographical separation of regulators from the markets. Commensurate with these physical and geographical emplacements, the field of enforcement may be viewed as a kind of manufactured or built space, a regulatory architecture that is defined by particular dimensions, scales and relationships between form and function that are constitutive of its perspective on the markets. This is not to suggest that enforcement is somehow set in stone (or marble), but rather to convey the fact that it is invariably defined by a certain physical dimensionality.[5] There is also a sense in which both ocean exploration and market regulation, partly as a function of these forms of physical distance and spatial separation, rely on artificial, often computer generated, approximations of their object of study, which then become the primary reference point and datum to be explained and accounted for. Representations of the ocean and the markets thus possess a distinctly derivative quality.

And yet, in the case of enforcement, these physical dimensions of space and distance also assume a uniquely social form. Regulators are equally far removed from the social world of finance, and have limited access to the forms of sociality and intelligibility that are so critical to understanding the markets and their movements. With different social backgrounds and operating in distinct social networks, regulators are likewise distanced from the forms of symbolic authority, credibility and sophistication that inform claims of expertise and which are so central to the regulatory project, tethered as it is not only to various kinds of strategic encounters but also, and more importantly, to the ability to appear credible and to advance one's position with a degree of interactional confidence. When combined with organizations that are themselves risk averse, these forms of social distance and deficits in symbolic capital contribute to the pursuit of safe cases, thus binding enforcement staff to more conventional narratives and invocations of intentionality, responsibility and blameworthiness, as well as forms and patterns of offending that offer readily assessable and easily sustainable evidentiary pathways and whose illegalities are conductive to the formatting demands of the legal process. This includes an individual and organizational aversion to cases rooted in ambiguous areas of law, as well as forms of legal and professional judgment that demand greater investments of symbolic capital, raising the stakes of enforcement actions and generating pause amongst the risk averse.

Another unique feature of the enforcement field is that it is subject not only to specific legal obligations and formatting demands, but is itself legally encoded. The distances between regulators and the markets are further deepened by their confinement to, and operation within, distinct regulatory territories and jurisdictional spaces. By virtue of the technicalities of jurisdiction, the organic movements of the markets are artificially divided into discrete spheres of authority, which limit the ability to take action against detected misconduct, as well as to discover wrongdoing in the first instance. Restricted in their ambit, authority and perspective, regulatory agencies are bound to a narrow view of the markets and are thus susceptible to various forms of oversight and inattention. This jurisdictional casting also sets the stage for inter-agency conflict and politicking, as it engenders forms of dependency and mutual reliance which, given different objectives, interests and perspectives, translate into competing approaches to cases, thus widening enforcement gaps and exacerbating the disconnect between regulatory territories and the markets. These extend from the more formally designated jurisdictional divides to operational distinctions, such as those between regulators and the police, carved not so much in law as in the ways in which these legal conventions have been interpreted and institutionalized over time. It is on this subject of inter-agency conflict that the work of Bourdieu allows us to push beyond Goodwin and the STS tradition, neither of which are sufficiently attuned to the politics underlying knowledge practices. These politics go beyond mere forms of inclusion and exclusion, or salience versus silence (Goodwin 1994: 628), to include localized forms of struggle, jealousy and turf protection, themselves part of the materialities of enforcement.

Politics, and political optics, also inform the activities of enforcement agencies from a more organizational or managerial perspective, as one of their primary concerns *as* organizations is with maintaining a strong public image. This is essential in this regulatory context, given that public confidence in the markets is so closely tied to confidence in the agencies themselves, a matter of perception which in the absence of clear benchmarks spurs a tireless effort to manage their public face and associated reputational risks. These concerns percolate throughout the entire enforcement enterprise, influencing what counts as a strong case, creating an aversion to risk that limits creativity and aggressiveness and contributing to the development of new ways to signal agency competencies. Strategic engagements on the ground, including decisions around case processing, interactions with legal counsel and the avoidance of legal risks and landmines, are all informed by this larger symbolic register. The difficulties associated with these efforts are exacerbated by the contradictions at the heart of the regulatory mandate. Agencies must consider the effects of their activities on the markets at the same time as they face various forms of resistance by stakeholders who, in referencing the dual mandate, allege that regulators are intruding unnecessarily on the autonomy of the markets and stifling creative energies, a sounding board enlivened by various forms of legal entrepreneurialism and mediated by the financial press. Should enforcement agents be seen to be overstepping their bounds, they are deemed overly aggressive and unreasonable, thus further jeopardizing their public image and undermining their regulatory capital. It is these various double binds that create not only managerial dilemmas, but also a degree of slippage between the front-line activities of enforcement staff and the kinds of discursive and symbolic displays produced by agency management and disseminated for stakeholder consumption. Unlike the professional domains examined by Goodwin, the field of securities enforcement is thus highly politicized, an arena where perceptions truly matter, and in which fundamental contradictions create hazards that further shape the vision of the various agencies and their perspectives on the financial world.

Following from these various aspects of, and influences on, the regulatory vision of enforcement agencies, some of which mesh nicely with Goodwin's approach, others less so, is a second organizing metaphor: that of the 'camera obscura'.[6] Invoked by a number of social theorists and philosophers,[7] as a metaphor for ways of seeing the social world, the camera obscura helps to capture the uniquely contextualized and distinctly mediated nature of enforcement's regulatory vision. As with the oceanographic metaphor, it is attuned to the realities of space, distance and perspective, yet offers a somewhat better appreciation of the ambiguity, incompleteness and unique sense of separation with which regulators must contend, a reflection of their position more as detectives than scientists. Removed from the actual flow of market activities, regulators must view the markets not only from a distance, to be overcome via technological approximations and best guesses, but also through the confines of a distinctly limited and partial perspective. This is reflected in the fact that the image that is produced is dependent, first, on where the camera is trained, a reflection of a particular physical and geographical emplacement or positioning and, second, on the architectural features, design elements and technologies (eg the size of the aperture, the use of various mirrors and lenses) built into the camera itself. The image is thus technologically enhanced and mediated, as is the perspective of enforcement agencies themselves. There is also the question of lighting and the interplay of light and darkness, with areas of shadow potentially limiting the sharpness and clarity of the image, a kind of chiaroscuro effect that follows less from the natural scene and more from the success with which the regulated are able to embed their activities in various forms of shadow.[8] The result is a 'built perspective' that not only restricts the regulatory vision but also creates distinct challenges in terms of intelligibility. There is always the issue of what lies outside the frame and how the established viewpoint impacts or limits one's appreciation of the larger picture, a question of contextuality that is critical to understanding the markets. Thus, the vision of the markets is not necessarily incorrect or false, but somewhat partial and incomplete, with many of the aforementioned enforcement gaps reflecting neither an absolute contrast between light and shadow nor an intentional glance in another direction, but rather the kinds of shadings, frames, limited perspectives and forms of obscurity that are embedded within, and which are constitutive of, the regulatory vision itself and which make some forms of financial activity more difficult to make out than others. Enforcement, as with the camera obscura itself, is thus much more than simply a black box.

Like the oceanographic metaphor, the camera obscura is certainly not without its limitations, chief among which is the fact that the enforcement process is not simply a camera passively recording the movements of the markets and producing a poor copy or replica of financial disorder. Securities enforcers are actively engaged in the very constitution of those markets and are thus themselves key market players. As with other calculative devices and representational technologies, the regulatory vision underlying the enforcement enterprise possesses a constitutive or performative character (Callon 1998; Callon and Muniesa 2005; Muniesa et al. 2007; Preda 2006, 2009a; Pryke 2010; Miller 2008). Enforcement is 'an active force transforming its environment, not a camera passively recording it' (MacKenzie 2006: 12), and is one of the 'material and discursive assemblages that intervene in the construction of markets' (Muniesa 2007: 2). This element of performativity is evident in the fact that, by taking action against particular forms of misconduct, enforcement agencies define the nature and parameters of acceptable market behaviour. Market actors are no doubt aware of, and are responsive to, these signals and in turn strive to modify the shape and detectability, if not the substance, of their activities so as to avoid these regulatory 'hot zones'. Conversely, some forms of questionable and potentially harmful activity are likely to be perpetuated by virtue of their exclusion from these regulatory frames and thus their status as 'safe bets'. These dynamics help to account for the thunderous protests whenever regulators invoke their public interest powers. The playing of this 'wild card' disrupts established notions of acceptability and normalcy, breeding uncertainty and drawing into question the accepted rules of the enforcement game. As noted by McBarnet (1992): 'In defining what is a violation, law also defines what is not … In defining what is to be controlled, law also defines the limits of legal control. Boundaries mark the point for keeping out as well as keeping in' (70). By acting against misconduct, as per their regulatory vision, enforcement agencies enact regions of acceptability and deviation, thus influencing the very nature of market activities in the process.

This notion of boundaries or borders points to a second form of performativity. The work of defining financial disorder not only contributes to the production and reproduction of the substantive distinctions between acceptable and unacceptable, legitimate and illegitimate, players, activities and transactions. It also lends credence to the very notion that a line *can be drawn* between these entities, while contributing to its very naturalization and depoliticization (Preda 2009a).[9] This informs the endless references by respondents to the metaphors of 'lines', 'fences' and 'perimeters' as a means of distinguishing between what they see as the 'two ends of the market' (Dialogue with the OSC 2006): the 'top end legitimate market and the bottom end scam market' (Dialogue with the OSC 2007):

> You have people inside the fence and outside the fence. People inside the fence want to settle and be good citizens because they want to continue to play in the sandbox. They may fight a bit but they will eventually settle the matter. The people that are doing stuff outside the fence, which is often fraudulent activity, will not settle.
>
> (OSC #4: 10)

By equating misconduct with egregious activities and morally questionable actors, thereby distinguishing the inadvertent indiscretions of the well intentioned regulators from the self-evident knavery of the interloping ne'er-do-wells, these accounts reproduce the imagined line between legitimate and illegitimate offences at the same time as they normalize and decriminalize the activities of those on the other side (de Goede 2005; Aitken 2006, 2007; Langley 2008a, 2008b; Preda 2009a).[10] This kind of messaging is not simply an exercise in symbolic management. It is embedded in the very materialities of enforcement, in the assessment tools, risk metrics, worksheets and other knowledge formats (Ericson and Haggerty 1997) that serve to settle the seeming chaos of market activities into workable frames, according to which transactions can be designated as 'normal' or 'deviant'. It is through these various dynamics of juxtaposition, framing and normalization that the practice of securities enforcement brings into existence a particular view of both the markets and financial disorder, thereby performing the distinction that separates different classes of players and activities and constituting the markets as both regulated and distinctly *regulatable* social spaces (Miller 2001; see also Williams 2008a). Securities enforcement is thus part of the framing of finance (Preda 2009a), the designation of a 'constitutive outside' (Mitchell 2002: 291) through which boundaries are drawn 'between legitimate groups, together with the institution they support, on the one hand, and a tolerated "rest", on the other' (Preda 2009a: 67).

Despite these limits, the metaphor of the camera obscura goes furthest in capturing the unique features of enforcement as a way of envisioning the markets, a perceptual architecture constituted through the materialities of space, distance, dimension and perspective. It is also helpful in accounting for the limitations of the regulatory enterprise in a way that does not reduce them to the bald politics of capture or accommodation. Without question, securities enforcement is responsive to, and is informed by, the interests of financial capital. Likewise, there is little doubt that the blind spots and regulatory lacunae that follow from the emphasis on readily detectable and easily substantiated breaches are not randomly distributed, tending to shadow the activities of the more sophisticated and better-positioned players. These are the very players most able to draw from their intimate knowledge of and closeness to the markets, to access transactional tools and disguises and to mobilize their sizeable financial and reputational capital in order to shield themselves from the regulatory gaze and ensure that even if detected their activities will be dismissed or at least downplayed as going regulatory concerns.

The essential point is that while these aspects of the enforcement field may be used to the advantage of the more sophisticated players, they are not necessarily of their own making. They are the product neither of rational design nor instrumentalized machinations, but rather the situated contingencies and contextualities of enforcement, of the forms of technological, calculative and documentary mediation necessitated by the distances between regulators and the markets, of the legal technicalities, formatting demands and types of expertise needed to convert these visions of misconduct into viable cases, and of a disjointed regulatory architecture formed through historical accretion, the soldering of competing organizational mandates and forms of political conflict and compromise. Thus, while it may be true that 'financial capital' is able to influence the rules of the game and the range of regulatory motion, it is by no means determinative of the field of play. Conversely, it is unfair to allege that enforcement agencies have blinders on, although it is true that their perspective is limited both by their instruments of perception and by their place within, and terms of engagement with, the financial world. Far from sitting in the dark, they are nevertheless bound to a particular field of vision.

Out of sight, out of mind: regulatory gaps and omissions

Having outlined the basic parameters of enforcement caseloads and their roots in a distinct view of the markets, the one question that remains concerns the activities and forms of financial disorder that are able or are allowed to exist beyond the regulatory gaze. This is a matter of the constitutive outside recast to reflect an interest not in the forms of borderline or marginal activities that help to legitimate the actions of those at the centre but, rather, practices and actors which by the very fact and conspicuousness of their absence from the enforcement fold are accorded a degree of legitimacy, thus reinforcing the parameters of what is deemed acceptable versus unacceptable, or at least revealing the thresholds of regulatory tolerance.

There are a number of qualifications to this trek into the unknown. First, in linking these lacunae to specific offence categories, such as insider trading, the implication is not that these are areas of absolute neglect. Rather, within each of these categories there are particular forms or variants of the activity in question that face a comparatively smaller likelihood of discovery and investigation. The omission is relative rather than absolute. Second, the object of exploring these gaps is not to put forth an ontology of 'real' harm in which the actual cases pursued by the enforcement agencies are juxtaposed with the 'true' or 'real' harms allowed to persist beyond their regulatory borders. The focus is on the discovery of general blind spots and areas of inattention, not the disclosure of undiscovered and unsubstantiated harms. Finally, many of these gaps include activities that sit somewhat awkwardly on the boundaries of legality and illegality, often bearing a 'semblance of legality' (Twelve Minute Securities Lawyer 2005) that may necessitate their exclusion from enforcement caseloads. Other activities exist near or even beyond the pale of regulatory jurisdiction, thus barring agencies from taking action, were they so inclined, absent the strengthening or even redrawing of jurisdictional lines. With agencies confined to the public markets, this would include: (1) the pools of 'dark capital' circulating in the form of non-public offerings or private placements; (2) trading between private parties in the over-the-counter market; and (3) many of the activities of hedge funds and other institutional investors. The point in all of this is that from the perspective of regulators and regulated alike, many of these gaps may be deemed unfair or misguided, an unjustified casting of aspersions onto entirely legitimate activities. This is fair enough, but the intention is not to produce a menu of grievances that can and must be pursued in the next enforcement cycle, but rather to sketch the general contours of activities that tend to remain in the shadows whether due to their invisibility or their resistance to control. These can be linked to three core areas of market activity: (1) trading; (2) products and sales practices; and (3) disclosure and transparency.

Trading

Despite their prominent place in the stated priorities of enforcement agencies and the massive stores of regulatory energy devoted to their detection and investigation, the first notable gap in enforcement caseloads involves forms of insider and manipulative trading.[11] As has been noted at various points in this book, even in its more conventional form where information is relayed by corporate insiders and then knowingly used as the basis for a trade, insider trading stands a good chance of escaping the attention of enforcement agencies. However, these lapses become even more pronounced when it comes to more subtle and sophisticated forms of trading, where the odds of detection are indeed exceedingly remote. Here the size-based fluctuations that inform surveillance technologies make it difficult to pick up small or non-dramatic movements in volume and price executed over longer time frames, through multiple exchanges and transaction points and across jurisdictional divides. As noted by one respondent: 'The problem with established patterns is that you're not going to find them because they are set up so well ... If they do it right they can hide it for a long time' (Former RS #1: 11). Even if traces of illegal activity are detected, the fact that they have been routed through multiple exchanges using transactional disguises such as offshore and nominee accounts makes it difficult to trace the trades and establish the identities of those behind them. There are also opportunities for insiders to use non-public information in more creative and less direct ways, further concealing their activities while building in added layers of deniability and defensibility. For example, insiders may feed information to independent traders, benefiting indirectly from subsequent movements in the stock price (eg more valuable stock options), or purchase derivatives tied to their stock:

> Often when we look at insider trading, it's kind of the tip of another iceberg. It could show principals of a company who are not treating their information carefully. It could show that principals are feeding information to players in the market to run a box around their stock. So they leak inside information to do other things, not just make the money but manipulate the stock.
>
> (RS #3: 4)

This is to say nothing of the far more pernicious and intractable problem of ambiguity and slippage in exactly what qualifies as 'inside' information, and thus the issue of information leakage noted in the previous chapter. The reality is that the markets are awash in information of different types as well as degrees of confidentiality. The difficulty from a regulatory standpoint is that much of this information is likely either to be of a non-specific nature, involving rumours, leaks or 'less obvious bits of non-public information' (Masters 2007: 1) falling well below materiality thresholds or only indirectly affecting the price of a security, or to be obtained by virtue of a relationship other than a true 'insider' position (see Dorn 2011):

> One of the realities of the insider trading work we do is that people who are taking advantage of information are virtually never the true insiders of a corporation. They are people who seem to have found other ways of getting access to this information. And finding out that there has been a connection and where they received this information is a lot trickier than simply finding the CFO traded right before the release of financial statements.
>
> (Dialogue with the OSC 2007)

These forms of information leakage are widely cited as the basis for the well documented and eminently suspicious surges in stock price that often precede major public announcements, as word of possible or impending deals spreads through the conversational fibres of the industry:[12]

> In a small marketplace there's a lot of conversation. Deals don't happen. Deals are massaged and worked on. And in offices where there aren't 300 traders, there might be only 20, you're going to know if somebody is working on a deal at the other end of the table. So it leaks.
>
> (RS #3: 8)

One form of this leakage that has proven especially resistant to detection involves employees of investment banks, brokerage firms or other professional advisory firms with knowledge of impending transactions (eg a merger or acquisition) leaking this information to institutional investors, particularly hedge funds, in exchange for lucrative trading commissions.[13] Thanks to the Galleon case in the US and its various spinoff investigations (see Rusli 2011), there is now well-documented evidence for what many have long suspected: that insider trading is a major issue in the hedge fund sector, with the spotlight firmly trained on so-called 'expert network' firms that put hedge funds in contact with experts in various industries, sectors and even companies, many of whom are former or current employees and some of whom are alleged to have passed on 'inside' information. This fits nicely with the observation by Reichman (1993) that: 'The growth of these institutional players has enhanced the field of play for information brokers of all kinds. The institutionalization of the market means that there are now more concentrated, powerful outlets for manipulating and exploiting the market' (73). There have also been instances where hedge funds have been accused of intentionally spreading false rumours about companies in which they hold short positions, a form of market manipulation:[14]

> We're looking into whether hedge fund or money manager types who spread rumours and then trade on the basis of that. If somebody phones [a reporter] and says 'I think you should write about company x', knowing that that article will influence the price but they are not insiders of the reporting issuer, whether or not that sort of manipulation is going on and is illegal is an issue. (OSC #6: 4)

Here the intent-based nature of manipulative trading provisions frustrate regulatory efforts, as the circulation of rumours is unlikely to fit the legal definition of making a misrepresentation 'with the intent of effecting a trade': 'There is also the problem of intent: did a trader know certain rumours were false when he or she fed them to someone else? Or was this merely the decades-old tradition of trading information, and then sifting through the noise in search of some added advantage' (Stewart 2008: B9). Coupled with a narrowly drawn and notably ambiguous legal framing that excludes much of what would rationally pass as 'inside' information or 'manipulative' activity, this shifting morphology of the markets has created new opportunities for questionable trading practices, while impeding regulatory efforts. The fact that the major financial players are 'all part of a network; everybody knows everybody in the little world' (Lawyer #8: 11) thus both facilitates questionable trading and confounds its regulation.

Products and sales practices

Another area of market activity where gaps are bound to emerge is sales practices at the client-broker interface, and the types of products that are developed and sold to investors. The most visible and widely publicized form of product-related abuse, beyond more blatant cases of misappropriation or unauthorized trading, involves suitability, where brokers are alleged to have recommended transactions that are unsuitable given the investment objectives and stated risk tolerance of their clients. The classic example is recommending a tech stock to a client with a risk profile better suited to government bonds or guaranteed investment certificates (GICs). However, as with insider and manipulative trading, there is a less visible yet potentially far more damaging band of activity that infrequently attracts sustained regulatory attention. This involves not the suitability of investments per se, but rather the very quality of the products sold by the industry. There are numerous instances where products of questionable soundness have been peddled to investors, often under false pretences and absent full disclosure. Examples include initial public offerings (IPOs) that are aggressively marketed as a means of clearing firm inventory or boosting the value of the firm's own holdings, a reflection of the strange yet institutionalized conflict of interest whereby firms are able to own the very shares they are promoting as underwriters:[15]

> If you have an account with a major securities dealer, if you're not a savvy individual you won't realize when they call you up and say 'I think you should buy whatever' that they've got that leftover in inventory from an underwriting they did a couple of months ago and it's a dog. They can't flog it to the institutions because they're sophisticated and they know they shouldn't buy it, but you don't know that. And you'll buy because you've built a personal relationship and you like the person and think they are looking out for you. But they aren't. They're getting paid themselves for doing it, the firm's pushing them to do it, the firm is going to get the benefit, conflict is written all over it, and you're getting screwed. And that happens every day across the country.
>
> (Accountant #1: 15)

As noted by another respondent, this is one of those areas where questions of product quality dovetail with manipulative trading and promotional practices:

> There are a lot of companies that are engaging in huge promotions of companies that aren't worth very much and they're well known and we're just waiting for them to blow up, but no one seems to be paying too much attention to them. [The regulators] just doesn't seem to have the will to dig into these complex cases.
>
> (Journalist #1: 8–9)

Another concern is that the majority of new issues, up to 80 per cent according to the estimate of one former broker, regardless of their quality decrease in value with asymmetries in information driving investor exit options and thus the ability to secure profits or mitigate losses. According to one respondent this very scenario, in which institutional investors were able to exit the market prior to retail investors, played out in an IPO involving a now defunct Canadian company:

> [Company X] was royalty. So it gets sold out. The stock starts sliding back down and at the [point where it had lost half its value], a research analyst working for one of the major banks was told by senior management that the company is going bankrupt, 'We've got institutional clients who still have positions, we've got to get them out of it. Phone the institutional client and tell them to blow it out. At the same time I want you on the morning calls talking about how good it is. And put out buys on it so the retail market will create additional demand to absorb the institutional supply'. [They] refused. And so they packaged [them] off and [they] got a $1 million severance. And then they found somebody else who was more ethically challenged or had two kids and a mortgage and that's what was done. And that happens.
>
> (Investor Advocate #2: 5)

The IPO market is far from the only source of dubious investments, as firms are always on the prowl for new investment products offering higher than normal returns and comparatively low risk. One such example is the income trust[16] market, which became very popular in Canada in the early 2000s for exactly the reasons noted above. The problem was that many of these trusts were weak in their fundamentals, paying out more than they were earning and inflating distributions to attract new investors, often through bank loans and lines of credit. There were also cases where accounting manipulations were used 'to tart the thing up' (Investor Advocate #2: 8) prior to sale. Unable to sustain the promised payouts, a number of the trusts subsequently collapsed, with investors suffering extensive losses.[17] And yet, despite evidence of weak, bordering on fraudulent issues, enforcement was sparse, with many of the underwriters responsible for promoting and distributing these products protected by 'regulatory outs', such as limited liability provisions: 'The securities commissions have just sat on the sidelines and haven't seriously done anything' (Accountant #2: 1). Another notable example is Asset Backed Commercial Paper (ABCP),[18] a product sold to investors as a low-risk alternative to the GIC that proved much more volatile than expected, given exposure to the sub-prime market in the US.[19] Quality-related issues also plague more mainstream products, such as principal protected notes[20] and mutual funds that are marketed to investors without clear disclosure of the commissions and fees which eat away at long-term returns. In responding to these and other products, regulators face many of the same hurdles as in suitability cases, including high powered legal counsel, extensive reputational risks and the challenge of discerning regulatory breaches from products of poor quality or distinguishing between the meaningful disclosure of product costs and fees and the mere technical compliance with regulatory rules. As always, the vigour of regulatory efforts are further sapped by the availability of other avenues of recourse and recovery.

Disclosure and transparency

While the first two bands of activity involve interactions between traders, investors, issuers and a number of other market participants, the third is primarily issuer-centred and involves a failure on the part of companies to provide clear, timely and meaningful disclosure regarding their financial status and operations. This takes two different forms and concerns two different sets of regulatory provisions. The first is the obligation, as per to continuous disclosure policies, for public companies to disclose 'material' changes bound to affect the value of their stock. This could include a merger or acquisition, the landing of a major new client or the securing of regulatory approval for a new product. The failure of public companies to provide adequate disclosure is a perennial problem for regulators, given both ambiguities in the interpretation of key concepts, such as 'materiality' and 'timeliness', and competing interests not necessarily around whether but when to disclose. Disclosing a deal prematurely, prior to its formal consummation, could be misleading while potentially undermining the transaction by, for example, driving up the cost of acquisition:

> If you disclose then you may drive the stock price up and the deal won't close. So that's an issue. Also if you disclose before you've got the full commitment of your partner or the acquirer, then you might scare off the acquirer. So there are real issues about when you disclose because the world is leaky and so there's the issue of selective disclosure in the marketplace.
>
> (Lawyer #3: 12)

Conversely, tardy disclosures create opportunities for informational asymmetries and the very forms of informational leakage discussed earlier. Difficulties also arise where disclosures are overly detailed, with critical bits of information secreted away in footnotes[21] or other remote regions of disclosure documents without the necessary interpretive context:

> The issues [with disclosure] relate to not just whether you disclose something, but the manner in which it is disclosed. If you look at enough public disclosure on enough types of things you'll see that there's either disclosure that's badly drafted or it's intended to bury people in so much detail without any analysis, without any structure, without any real framework that unless you're in the transaction itself you'll never understand it. So the quality of disclosure goes not just to what you disclose and how timely it is and how often you disclose, it goes to the manner in which it is presented and are you actually trying to help people understand what the issues are.
>
> (Lawyer #14: 2–3)

Given this ambiguity in the very nature of what constitutes adequate disclosure, more often a matter of subjective judgment than law,[22] it is not surprising that disclosure cases infrequently appear in the caseloads of enforcement agencies:

> There are certain types of offences they try to stay the heck away from because they just plain don't understand them. Any disclosure types of things, Bre-X before it became a total fraud, YBM until it blew up, a whole range of disclosure issues across the range of Canadian public issuers that they just won't touch because they don't understand and don't think they can win.
>
> (Lawyer #21: 2)

Another respondent alleged that this reticence applies to even the most winnable of cases:

> Enforcement doesn't seem to go there. Some of the stuff where companies come out with a statement, if they wanted to they could go in and look at who was on the management committee meetings two months before and what were the discussions. I was involved with a high profile case and it was such an easy case for them to make and they didn't make it. It was very, very sad to see that. It was a good one involving information that should have been made public a lot sooner. And they could easily have done it.
>
> (Accountant #1: 8)

Making matters worse is the problem of institutional compartmentalization and the turf battles within agencies themselves. Front-line responsibilities for monitoring continuous disclosure fall to compliance departments, which are inclined to keep these cases in-house, treating them as compliance matters best resolved through negotiation and compromise. If what respondents suggest is true, perhaps this is a wise decision; however, it does little to boost the enforcement cause, with incomplete or misleading disclosure rarely the subject of sustained interest or activity.

A second issuer-centred enforcement gap involves misrepresentations as to the financial health of companies. This was the very issue in the cases of Enron and WorldCom in the US and Nortel in Canada, where company officials used various accounting tricks to produce misleading accounts of their company's financial health.[23] The stakes underlying these forms of 'financial conjuring' (Tsing 2000: 121) have increased dramatically in recent years, a product of the obsession with shareholder value (Lazonick and O'Sullivan 2000; Williams 2000; Froud et al. 2006) and pressures to meet aggressive earnings and profit targets, that is to 'generate the numbers that corroborate the story' (Froud et al. 2006: 9), lest companies incur the wrath of unhappy shareholders, analysts and fund managers (Zorn et al. 2005). Perhaps more so than any other form of conduct, regulators have been faulted for their failure to detect and subsequently respond to cases of questionable accounting: 'Any of those financial statement ones seem to be quite problematic' (Accountant #1: 3), a tepid response that follows from a number of factors.

First, these cases are notoriously difficult to detect, as the very fact that financial manipulation is involved, often of a rather subtle nature, precludes discovery through the usual channels. Instead, these cases typically come to light through legal actions, the allegations of whistleblowers or media reports, if at all. Accounting irregularities are thus firmly embedded in the private contexts of organizational activities, with few discernible ripples.

Second, as any enforcement agent will tell you, these are among the most complex cases to investigate and prosecute, owing to their foundation in accounting rules and regulations, namely US and Canadian GAAP,[24] which are themselves ambiguous, subject to interpretation and tolerant of and conducive to forms of creative accounting that are technically legal yet in practice misleading (McBarnet and Whelan 1999; McBarnet 2005, 2006): 'The important point is this: even where accounting is technically proper and can claim to be "perfectly legal", where it creatively exploits rules and regulatory gaps rather than engages in outright fraud, it can still be highly misleading' (McBarnet 2005: 209). One respondent spoke very candidly to this ambiguity and the associated difficulties from a regulatory perspective:

> GAAP is inherently a problem to us. Once you have auditors involved, like, what does it mean? What about if the auditors knew and said it was okay? And is it fraudulent or not? . . . I don't think we've done a GAAP case. Certainly not since I've been here. Because what do you do? I mean I don't know what a lot of those things mean.
>
> (OSC #10: 14–15)

In the words of another respondent: 'If you say you've got a cure for breast cancer, buy my company, it's easier to prove that that's known to be false than which side of a journal entry you decide to go with on a GAAP case' (OSC #6: 2). Canadian GAAP is thus a 'pretty flexible tool' (OSC #6: 4). These areas or zones of ambiguity have only expanded in recent years, as production has shifted from material goods and services to various forms of intellectual property which sit very awkwardly with traditional accounting rules and treatments (Rosen and Rosen 2010).

Regulatory actions in accounting cases are also impeded by unfavourable case law. Perhaps the best example of this is the 1997 Supreme Court of Canada decision in *Hercules Management v Ernst and Young*, which held that auditors cannot be held liable for allegedly deceptive or incomplete audits given that the purpose of the audit is to oversee corporate management and not to assist individual shareholders in the assessment of a firm and its financial health: '[The CAs] argued successfully that they have no obligations to individual investors for annual audited financial statements. So what is the purpose of the audited financial statements which then the investors are supposedly using as their main input? And the answer is well they're useless' (Accountant #2: 1). A seasoned defence attorney echoed this sentiment: 'I think *Hercules* was wrongly decided . . . if somebody elected me king for a day, I'd overturn *Hercules* and make auditors liable to shareholders . . . *Hercules* is a joke' (Lawyer #12: 11). Regardless of its merits, this ruling paved the way for a more limited liability regime, with notable regulatory repercussions, one that continues to be propped up by accounting firms through their suppression of legal claims or the settlement of cases that hold the promise of less favourable precedents.[25]

Finally, accounting cases are unattractive from a regulatory point of view, given that they involve professional judgments and thus require that regulators not only understand the complexities of accounting rules, but also that they are willing to question the integrity of professional accountants. While the former creates a significant burden in terms of access, knowledge and understanding, the latter demands a sizeable investment of regulatory capital, especially given the vigour with which accounting firms defend themselves from these kinds of accusations. By virtue of these stakes, these cases tend to be very resource intensive: 'Easily they could scoop up all the resources that you have and you still wouldn't have enough … you're dealing with major organizations that have the financial wherewithal to put up a stellar defence' (OSC #4: 21). There is also the issue of locating credible expert witnesses willing to testify against their colleagues. With few exceptions, the professional esprit de corps surrounding accountants and lawyers mitigates against this kind of participation, thus further jeopardizing cases and depriving regulators of much needed regulatory capital:

> The GAAP issue is an interesting one because it sort of raises a side issue. The fewer the number of big firms, the harder it is to find people who will say that's not GAAP, and we've had a number of cases where we thought the accounting was very bad, and in the view of the accountants here was not GAAP. Often you find that the most an accountant will tell, at the prospect of being a witness, is 'Well, I can't say it's not GAAP. I wouldn't have done it that way. It's not good GAAP, but it might be GAAP'. So we've had a number of those cases where we just haven't been able to do anything at all.
>
> (OSC #12: 5)

In the context of these encounters, professionals have further access to a number of due diligence defences which can, and have been, effectively used as a kind of regulatory shield in instances where their conduct has been called into question, 'a form of auditing that cloaks itself in due process and offers anodyne and carefully constructed and constrained opinions' (Power 2003: 195). Being naturally risk averse and lacking in symbolic capital and authority, these various difficulties result in a natural disinclination on the part of enforcers to proceed against anything but the most bold and blatant of misrepresentations, or where their hand has been forced by disclosure through other means, most often civil lawsuits and the media: 'We need a certain type of case' (OSC #7: 5). In the assessment of a former member of the OSC:

> We had a lot of difficulty when I was at the commission in trying to convince the senior staff members to do accounting cases because it's unclear in most people's heads unless you're an accountant. Then they were afraid to take on

> the big four firms. So they're not that easy to do. You've got to go for the obvious ones.
>
> (Accountant #1: 5)

This is to say nothing of the fact that, as with disclosure cases, the first responder to these incidents is likely to be corporate finance, with few cases making it over to enforcement, yet another sign of the fissures that exist not only between but also within regulatory agencies:

> Probably we would not get [GAAP cases] even referred to us. Because if we get a complaint coming in that someone's financial statements are askew, it would immediately go to our corporate finance people and they have the in-house GAAP experts. So they would look at that and they would make a determination as to whether they felt that the statements were prepared in accordance with GAAP or not.
>
> (OSC #5: 9)

That accounting irregularities represent a major blind spot in the regulatory vision of enforcement agencies highlights the limits of their capabilities, at the same time as it reveals the range of conditions and contingencies brought to bear on their work. Deeply embedded in the fabric of corporate operations and buried in a mass of documents, signs of abuse are often not visible even to the trained eye, with potential glimpses tied to periodic and highly formulaic disclosures that are themselves difficult to piece together. Much of what is required to distill tangible illegalities from the flow of transactions thus remains out-of-frame. Should more concrete and readily digestible indications of misconduct emerge, there is the added difficulty that accounting rules are ambiguous and difficult to reconcile with available legal frames, and are clothed in forms of professional judgment that crisscross the epistemic communities of accounting, law and finance, each of which mobilize different interpretive visions, forms of deniability and zones of discretion. These professional insertions quickly ramp up the stakes of these cases, demanding a significant outlay of symbolic and financial capital while exposing agencies to substantial jeopardy should things not go their way, dangers that are especially acute in instances where they may be perceived to be over-stepping their rightful mandate or jeopardizing the interests of shareholders who may themselves be invested in keeping up appearances for the sake of their investments. Regardless of the merits of the claim or the strength of their conviction, regulators may not be able to call the corporate bluff, abandoning their hand in the process. In view of these various obligations and lingering traps, accounting cases reveal that what is most critical in evaluating the work product of regulators is not necessarily, or exclusively, the *limits* of their perspective, defined in terms of gaps, misses or blind spots, but rather the specific *conditions* governing the production of regulatory knowledge of, and about, the markets. This is a subtle yet significant distinction that further directs attention away from the brute force of the regulated and towards the knowledgeability of finance, thus couching the policing of the markets in the epistemic politics of the enforcement field.

Conclusion: the politics of knowlegeability

At the heart of the social science enterprise is an attempt to engage with the problem of knowledge. That is, to examine the conditions under which knowledge is framed and formatted, rendered intelligible and authoritative, and performed as a matter of practice, thus reflecting and constituting the social world of which it is a part. The issue here is not simply how knowledge is produced but the practices, logics and interests governing its production, conditionalities that invariably shape and mediate its insertions into contemporary social relations. This notion of the conditionality of knowledge and knowledge effects is perhaps best expressed in the work of Foucault and, in particular, his concept of 'discursive formation'. This refers to a loosely structured field of intelligibility rooted in a common discursive object, such as medicine, and governed by specific rules of formation, 'the general enunciative system that governs a group of verbal performances' (Foucault 1989: 130). These rules, part of the order of discourse, determine the possibilities and limits within which the objects of discourse are shaped and imagined, thus pre-figuring not only that which can reasonably be stated in a given discursive terrain, but also that which is held to be 'true'. Discourses are thus governed by the:

> Limits and forms of the sayable. Not everyone has the ability to speak the truth and to have one's utterances recognized as being in the true. Rather, the right of speech is heavily circumscribed. It is bound to the possession of qualifications, the occupation of designated institutional sites, and by conformity to accepted modes of enunciation. The question is thus, 'Who, among the totality of speaking individuals, is accorded the right to use this sort of language (langage)? Who is qualified to do so?'
>
> (Foucault 1989: 55)

While grounded in a very different intellectual tradition, this is not unlike Bourdieu's own interest in the 'performative efficacy of discourse' (Bourdieu 1991: 106), and the conditions governing the production of effective performances. As he notes in the context of medicine, in a vein eerily similar to that of Foucault: 'Medical statements cannot come from anybody; their value, efficacy, even their therapeutic powers and, generally speaking, their existence as medical statements cannot be dissociated from the statutorily defined person who has the right to make them, and to claim for them the power to overcome suffering and death' (Bourdieu 1991: 56).[26] Interestingly, de Goede (2005) sees this very same principle at work in the financial realm:

> Finance is defined through general regulative practices that determine what can and cannot be legitimately said within its domain. These regulative

> practices determine what it is possible to speak of within the historically constituted financial sphere; which events are recorded as evidence and which utterances are recognized as valid. These same limits govern which statements are considered futile and irrelevant to the financial domain; which evidence is inadmissible, which utterances are invalid (95).

Despite their differences, what ultimately underlies these accounts is not only a problem of knowledge but, more specifically, a particular politics of knowledgeability. What counts as legitimate knowledge, and the conditions under which this knowledge can be produced and by whom, are informed by the political dynamics of access and exclusion, authority and silence, and performative and discursive rules and limits. These politics need not be attached to a specific class or group but circulate within discourse determining the limits of the 'sayable'.

This book has concerned itself with these very dynamics and has sought to examine the extent to which the practices and limits of securities enforcement are shaped through, and are contingent upon, the production of regulatory knowledge or, more accurately, a politics of regulatory knowledgeability unique to this domain. It is in this respect that the constraints and influences that shape securities enforcement, themselves expressions of the social and physical distances, differences and positions that define the enforcement field relative to the markets, reflect the conditionalities of regulatory knowledge and thus the conditions under which knowledge of the markets is not only produced, but also recognized as authorized and legitimate.

Following from this, there are four specific forms of politicized conditionality that underlie the enforcement project and circumscribe both the viewpoints and powers of speech accorded to members of the regulatory establishment. The first is *accessibility*. Removed in time, space and affinity from the ongoing flow of transactions and the private spaces and relationships in and through which they are consummated, enforcement agencies are relegated to the digital and documentary footprints left behind by this activity and/or the willingness of parties to these transactions to come forward, both of which have their own complications. The second dilemma is one of *intelligibility*, as enforcement staff are faced with the challenge of not only accessing information of and about the markets, but also deciphering and interpreting the accumulated data, documents and testimony. This includes rendering these pieces of evidence in the form of coherent storylines that satisfy the managerial, documentary and formatting demands of the enforcement process and which will be deemed sensible and intelligible by other players. A third dilemma involves the matter of *reconcilability*, that is, the ability to produce a formatted version of events that can be reconciled with existing legal codes, a dynamic that turns less on the application of 'the law' and more on the ability to mobilize particular framings of the illegalities in question. After all, it is not the mere production of *knowledge* of the markets that is at stake in enforcement, but the production of *legal knowledge*. Finally, as distinctly social performances, the success of enforcement actions depends on attributions of *credibility* that provide the social authority needed, first, to produce convincing accounts of market misconduct and, second, to have these accepted as legitimate by other players in the regulatory game.

Taken together, it is these points of knowledgeability that inform the politics at play in the field of securities enforcement and which shape the possibilities and limits of successful regulatory performances. They represent, if not the rules, at least the conditions governing the production of legitimate regulatory knowledge and they are the grounds for the skirmishes between regulators, regulated and various stakeholder groups as they struggle over the collection, interpretation and legal rendering of the various signs of market trouble. While regulators possess a formally institutionalized authority and right to speak the truth of the markets, their ability to do so is in practice constrained, some would say undermined, first, by a limited viewpoint yielding snapshots of marginal sharpness and clarity and, second, by a strict set of regulative practices (de Goede 2003) that govern how these visions of the markets are to be converted into positive assertions of financial offence, while at the same time allowing for their validity and legitimacy to be challenged at every turn.

And yet, the fact that these limits and points of struggle may be understood in epistemic, rather than instrumental or structural terms, points to possibilities for change grounded not in a radical rupture or collective protest, but rather more subtle points of disruption. This is one of the benefits of thinking, along with the STS tradition, about the enforcement process in terms of its materialities, contingencies and vulnerabilities, its intersections with devices, formats and legal technicalities that are irreducible to larger political and economic forces yet which nevertheless exert power or truth effects (Foucault 2000). As noted by Law (2008), rather than being awed by 'large systems', what is needed is an effort to 'make the problem smaller, or better, to make it more specific. To deal with the materialities of specific practices. To discover difference. And then to intervene in ways that might make a difference to those differences' (637; see also Latour 2005: 250; Langley 2008a, 2008b). As will be revealed in the conclusion to follow, it is these very points of fragility, rupture and vulnerability that present opportunities for intervening in the mediations and conditionalities governing the production of regulatory knowledge, and thus re-evaluating the scope and scale of the enforcement effort.

Notes

1 According to the 2010 Enforcement Report produced by the Canadian Securities Administrators, the umbrella group that compiles data and coordinates policy across the various securities commissions, 66 per cent of cases concluded by the commissions in 2010 involved illegal distributions. This is consistent with the previous two reports. The next highest category, at 12 per cent, is registrant misconduct (CSA 2011).

2 This refers to a case from rural Ontario involving individuals who had invested in a pigeon farm with the status of the investment, which turned out to be a classic Ponzi scheme, and the OSC's ability to assume jurisdiction and seek penalties hinging on whether pigeons could be defined as securities (OSC #7: 4–5).

3 A telling example of this kind of attributional bias and its pervasiveness in the industry is a case involving fraudulent trading in the accounts of two Quebec retirees. In his decision at the conclusion of the civil trial, the judge lambasted CIBC for what he viewed as their complicity in the matter, including their failure to properly supervise the broker in question (*Markarian v CIBC World Markets*). And yet, during a regulatory conference shortly thereafter, a prominent member of the defence bar referred to the very same case as the straightforward matter of a 'rogue broker' (Securities Litigation 2006).

4 In fact, Goodwin draws directly from the work of Latour (eg Latour and Woolgar 1979; Latour 1987).

5 Questions of space as well as architecture figure prominently in the work of Foucault. This is perhaps best embodied in his use of the panopticon as a metaphor for the architectural and spatial configurations underlying contemporary systems of disciplinary governance (Foucault 2000). The difference, of course, is that in the context of securities enforcement, as with most forms of financial governance (Williams 2009), these architectural features contribute to partial or obscured views which actually impedes efforts at control.

6 One of the first forms of modern photography, this is a device consisting of a covered box or darkened room with small hole on one side. This hole, or aperture, allows light from an outside scene to enter the box where it is then reproduced on the opposite wall in the form of a moving image. While free of obvious distortion, and with colour and perspective preserved, the image is projected in inverted form with a sharpness that varies according to the size of the aperture. In its more advanced versions, such as those appearing in fairs and exhibitions in the 1800s, lenses were used to cast larger and sharper images, which were then righted through a series of mirrors and projected onto a central screen to be viewed by assembled onlookers (Terpak 2001).

7 Appearing in works by Freud and Nietzsche, the camera obscura is perhaps most famously invoked by Marx as a metaphor for the distorted nature of capitalist ideology (see Paolucci 2001: 78). Wickham and Freemantle (2008) also identify the camera obscura as one of a handful of technologies that allowed for a new way of seeing socially, providing the grounds for a distinctly sociological form of thought.

8 Chiaroscuro is a technique used in painting, and subsequently in cinematography, to provide realistic perspective, depth and dimension to rendered images through the use of contrasting areas of light and shadow. While this is undertaken in an effort to produce more realistic portrayals of the 'natural world', this same metaphor is invoked by Jackson and Carter (1995), through their term 'organizational chiaroscuro', to capture the strategic efforts on the part of organizations to limit their visibility through the purposeful 'management of what is lit and what remains in the shadow' (879). Applied to the context of securities enforcement, the notion is that regulators are confronted by a scene engineered, intentionally and unintentionally, to create areas of shadow that invariably obstruct and obfuscate their views of the markets.

9 This is similar to de Goede's argument that the juxtaposition of financial speculation with gambling was essential to the legitimation of speculative activity in the early 1900s. In this respect, the problematization of gambling established a 'pattern of normalization' ... 'which made possible ... the emergence of speculation as a legitimate practice' (de Goede 2005: 54).

10 As noted by a number of commentators, one of the common elements underlying responses first to the dot com bust and then to the sub-prime crisis were accounts which highlighted the role of greedy individuals and cited prosecution and the strengthening of criminal enforcement as the necessary response (Spalek 2001; Fooks 2002; McBarnet 2006; Langley 2008b). The result was both the individualization of the crises and the normalization of more systemic industry practices and players: 'Pointing the finger at

predatory lenders, and their cozy relationships with the credit-rating agencies ... rather conveniently secures the identity of responsible "prime" lenders and borrowers' (Langley 2008b: 490).

11 While insider trading involves trading based on non-public information obtained by virtue of an insider position or relationship, manipulative trading is the attempt to artificially influence the price of a security through strategies such as 'wash sales' or high volume trading that stimulate market activity allowing traders to benefit from subsequent price swings. In practice, these forms of trading are less clearly distinguished, as most insider trading involves a degree of manipulation and vice versa.

12 This effect has been documented in both the US and Canada. One study revealed that 41 per cent of US companies receiving buyout bids exhibited abnormal or suspicious trading in the days and weeks before the deals became public (Morgenson 2006), while another study using Canadian data detected unusual trading patterns prior to the announcement of 33 of 52 mergers (Critchley 2008).

13 This includes an SEC inquiry into whether major Wall Street firms are warning favoured customers about pending large trades, a form of front-running. The close ties between hedge funds and investment banks were also the subject of the SEC's investigation of Goldman Sachs. In this case, the investment bank was alleged to have developed an investment fund composed of toxic sub-prime mortgages based on the urgings of a hedge fund (Paulson & Co), which then bet against the fund through the purchase of credit default swaps, profiting to the tune of $1 billion.

14 Legal actions have been initiated by a number of companies, namely Biovail, Overstock.com and Fairfax, alleging that hedge funds have conspired with independent research firms (eg Gradient Analytics) to produce falsely negative reports on their companies and have then shorted their stock, profiting from the ensuing slide in stock price once the reports were made public. There have also been allegations that false rumours and collusion among short-sellers triggered the collapse of a number of firms with exposures to the sub-prime market, with the SEC promising to crack down on this practice, to which the industry response has been disdain and laughter in equal measure. Beyond the absence of clear prohibitions against these activities, the elements of collusion and conspiracy make them especially difficult for regulators to tackle.

15 Under the newly enacted Volcker Rule, one of the most controversial features of the Dodd-Frank Act, this kind of proprietary trading is now prohibited in the US, although investment banks continue to lobby regulators on the specific interpretations of the provision and the rules governing its implementation. There are no comparable rules in Canada or the UK.

16 These are essentially asset packages that have been taken public in the form of an IPO. They are yield-oriented, paying out their pre-tax cash flow in the form of distributions rather than reinvesting in the company.

17 These problems, among others, spurred the Canadian Government to take action on 31 October 2006, introducing a series of measures to curtail the income trust market, a move that cooled the market as intended yet triggered significant losses amongst trust holders.

18 Asset-backed commercial paper consists of 30-day and 60-day notes designed to pay investors interest generated by bundles of mortgages, car loans, derivatives and other assets.

19 In light of widespread industry resistance to the regulators' use of their public interest powers, it is noteworthy that a recent legislative report faulted the OSC for the 'narrow interpretation of its public interest jurisdiction in responding to the ABCP crisis' (Standing Committee on Government Agencies 2010: 10).

20 These products are based on the guarantee that the invested principal will be returned upon maturity along with any gains, a no-risk option that provides investors with the

opportunity to engage in riskier investments. However, their fee structure makes PPNs expensive to hold, while their returns are on average no higher than a diversified fixed income portfolio. They also tend to have longer maturity periods allowing inflation to erode the principal-back guarantee, and include prohibitive penalties for early redemption.

21 The creative use of footnoting is perhaps best illustrated in the case of Enron, where the company's reliance on special purpose vehicles to 'manage' its debt was disclosed, albeit through overly detailed and convoluted footnotes, a form of concealment by a thousand details.

22 On the subject of judgment, while regulators often encounter difficulties in having their determinations of violation stand in disclosure cases, the discretion of issuers is legally codified in the form of the 'business judgment rule'. This holds that a degree of deference must be paid to the good judgment of executives regarding the timing and appropriateness of disclosures, thus creating a discretionary bubble around these transactions that regulators may be unable to pierce.

23 It has also emerged as an issue in the recent sub-prime crisis, with allegations that firms such as Lehman Brothers misled investors as to the degree of their exposure to the sub-prime market.

24 As part of an international movement towards the harmonization of accounting rules, Canada has recently transitioned from GAAP to International Financial Reporting Standards (IFRS). Designed to eliminate discrepancies and allow for more seamless and consistent comparisons of corporate performance across jurisdictions, it remains to be seen whether or how this will impact the quality of financial reporting and the ability of regulators to pursue questionable accounting practices. Some commentators have already identified problems with IFRS, which they believe will only make matters worse (Rosen and Rosen 2010).

25 For example, Deloitte and Touche was the target of a major class action lawsuit for its role in the collapse of Philip Services. The firm settled the suit for $50.5 million, the largest amount ever paid by a Canadian accounting firm in a securities class-action case. This private settlement allowed the firm to avoid the courts and thus a potentially unfavourable precedent around auditor liability. Another notable case is Castor Holdings, in which a group of investors filed suit against the company's auditor Coopers and Lybrand for $1 billion, alleging that it was negligent in failing to properly audit Castor and misrepresented the health of the company. A potential test case for about two dozen related lawsuits, the proceedings have been subject to numerous delays and procedural wrangling, leaving the suit, launched as long ago as 1997, unresolved at the time of writing.

26 The difference of course, among others, is that Bourdieu is more concerned with the legitimacy of these statements and their roots in larger structural configurations, whereas for Foucault knowledge and knowledge effects operate solely through the orders of discourse in the absence of forms of subjective recognition or intervention.

Conclusion

Moving forward?

This book originally set out to move beyond the narrow confines of contemporary debates on the 'effectiveness' of securities enforcement and to explore the practices, contours and parameters of enforcement as a particular kind of knowledge work. This included, among other things, bracketing the question of effectiveness and eschewing the mere tendering of proposals as to how the enforcement enterprise might be improved in the future. Having shed some light on the black box of enforcement and revealed a different side of the regulatory enterprise, the question arises as to whether it is now appropriate or even necessary to remove these brackets and to delve more earnestly into the policy terrain, mining the analysis for potential reforms to securities enforcement.

While not wishing to offer anything that would come close to a fully formed suite of recommendations, the insights gleaned from the preceding chapters do provide the grounds for a few tentative steps in this direction. This begins with the need to steer clear of the existing menu of policy options, including structural change at the commission and SRO level and the establishment of a national securities commission, the latter championed by many as a cure-all for the Canadian regulatory system, despite decades of wrangling over its constitutional and political implications, to say nothing of the failure of such nationalized structures to prevent major scandals elsewhere.[1] Despite being advanced under the banner of investor protection, many of these 'reforms' are rooted more in the alleged disadvantages encumbering legal counsel and their clients, mere variations on the theme that securities regulation must become more efficient and responsive to the interests of its stakeholder-clients.

And yet, there is a lesson to be learned here, as the success with which securities professionals have advanced their own view of the 'enforcement problem', a function of their professional capital and the strength and sophistication of their well institutionalized stakeholder voice, suggests that in order to challenge these views what is needed are different sites and forms of discursive authority, and thus a recasting of the politics of knowledgeability in the field of securities enforcement. This concluding section begins by examining whether there are voices currently outside of the regulatory and legal establishment that may fill such a role. Bearing in mind the potential as well as limitations of these competing voices, a number of opportunities are then invoked for moving beyond the prevailing policy agenda. Informed by the limits, challenges and politics examined over the course of the book, these are presented as nascent points of intervention, a kind of staging area for future work in this field.

'Competing' voices

While the industry and its legal representatives possess the strongest and most authoritative voice on matters of regulatory and enforcement policy, there are a number of stakeholder groups that have sought to challenge this dominant position, some through soft lobs from the centre and others through more sustained attacks from the margins. Included in the former group would be shareholder advocacy associations, led by the Canadian Coalition for Good Governance, which have lent their voice to criticisms of the regulatory system in general and the ineffectiveness of enforcement in particular. As noted in Chapter 3, the problem is that these groups are tied to the interests of a fairly narrow, albeit very influential, constituency, namely large institutional shareholders including the major Canadian pension and mutual funds. As such, their advocacy efforts are geared towards a correspondingly narrow set of policy concerns, corporate governance and executive compensation among them. On issues of relevance to the average investor, they have much less to say, a stance informed by the fact that they are 'less [reliant] on the regulators to solve their problems for them' (RS #2: 18) and are sensitive to the competitive disadvantages associated with a more active enforcement regime, including the possible netting of their own members. Thus, beyond demands for a more heavy handed response to the truly egregious offences, these kinds of advocacy groups are hardly a source for meaningful change.

Investor advocacy groups: Small Investor Protection Association (SIPA)

Outside of the formal shareholder advocacy movement, one of the only remaining agitators for change are coalitions of retail investors. These are the individuals with the largest stakes in the enforcement process, having lost significant amounts of money on their investments, allegedly as a result of industry malfeasance, and possessing few other alternatives for recourse or restitution. And yet, retail investors lack a strong voice on enforcement matters. In contrast with legal counsel and industry representatives, snugly ensconced in advisory committees and executive positions, representation from retail investors has been and continues to be negligible in the Canadian context,[2] the exceptions being periodic town halls and other public gripe sessions and the odd appearance before government investigative or oversight committees.

Recognizing both the problems with enforcement and the absence of formal investor participation in the regulatory process, a number of individuals have stepped forward to challenge the regulators on a host of issues. While much of this advocacy work is loosely coordinated, with contributions from a small handful of the most vocal advocates, many of whom have been victimized by the industry either as investors or as employees, these efforts have been coordinated to a degree under the auspices of a national investor protection group, the Small Investor Protection Association (SIPA). Founded by a retired engineer, himself a victim of broker misconduct, this is a voluntary organization of roughly 600 members which runs on a shoe-string budget and offers advice on how to deal with questionable practices and products, as well as participates in various forms of advocacy work including the publication of reports, working papers, op-ed pieces, testimony at government proceedings and appearances at regulatory conferences. This advocacy effort has focused on a number of issues, including: (1) greater representation of small investors on the governing bodies of the enforcement agencies; (2) demands that the regulators provide restitution as a part of their mandate; (3) advocacy around specific cases in which regulators have been accused of dropping the ball; and (4) the need for better arbitration programs and opportunities for civil recourse.

Despite achieving a degree of notoriety on both the regulatory and political stage, as well as a handful of small gains for retail investors, the impact of SIPA and its most vocal members has been rather modest. This stems from a number of factors, most of which revolve around questions of symbolic capital and credibility, and the politics of knowledgeability examined in the previous chapter. The first of these limits stems from the fact that the investor advocacy movement is so closely tied to these core personalities, thus lacking a more institutionalized investor voice: 'Whilst there are many committed and active individuals, there is no real, coherent, national, well-resourced consumer voice representing the interests of all Canadian retail investors in securities regulation' (Black 2006: 555). This contrasts with the UK and Australia, both of which possess independent consumer panels that are consulted on a range of issues relating to regulation and the financial services industry. One latecomer to the advocacy landscape that may help to bridge this gap is the Canadian Foundation for the Advancement of Investor Rights (FAIR), an agency founded by a prominent securities lawyer with a mandate to advance the interests of investors and the integrity and fairness of the Canadian capital market. However, some investor advocates have expressed concern about the representativeness and authenticity of this effort, spearheaded as it is by a legal insider with funding provided by the SROs and the board of directors consisting of the usual suspects recruited from the legal and financial communities. One advocate has gone so far as to call this a 'front' for the industry, designed to fill the advocacy gap and thus delegitimate the calls on the part of organizations such as SIPA for an independent, national consumer protection agency (Investor Advocate #2).

Second, with the advocacy movement driven by individual personalities, it has proven extremely vulnerable to accusations of bias and non-representativeness. The perception that these investor advocates are motivated by self-interest, even self-aggrandizement, and have their own axes to grind has been seized on by critics who question not just their motives but their credibility: 'There is a strong perception among regulators that many consumer advocates' concerns relate too much to their own personal experiences and grievances ... The lack of credibility of some consumer advocates in the eyes of the regulators leads to a high degree of mistrust and hostility' (Black 2006: 634). A number of respondents offered similar, although in many cases less diplomatic, assessments of the personalities involved:

> I would characterize the investor advocates who I know as people who have a very limited understanding of the industry, who see things in black and white, and who, when they weren't investor advocates, were engaging in some other form of misconceived advocacy or activism. I see them as providing very little to the process, almost nothing.
>
> (Lawyer #28: 6–7)

The account of another respondent is equally disparaging: 'The problem that the small investor has is that the people who set themselves up as advocates for them have lost all touch with reality. And so their champions have zero credibility' (Former OSC #1: 7). This notion that investor advocates are motivated by their own self-interest and 'have their own little axes to sharpen' (IDA #5: 16), was even acknowledged by a fellow investor advocate: 'We've tried to bring people in and integrate them and we failed miserably because people have their own issues. They have to get beyond their own issues' (Investor Advocate #1: 9).

Besides their position on the margins of the enforcement field and their ascribed status as unreasonable and self-interested outsiders, the success of investor advocates in drawing attention to their cause and gaining traction on key policy issues has also been hampered by their approach, which is seen to be lacking tact, decorum and sophistication.[3] For example, during Q and A sessions at public conferences, advocates are known to take over the floor and, rather than ask questions, hurl what are viewed as unsubstantiated allegations of regulatory incompetence, confrontations that come across as awkward, somewhat unfair and certainly out-of-sync with the more courteous tone of the event as a whole. This general lack of sophistication and credibility is made worse by a tendency to adopt quite conspiratorial views of enforcement's failures. As part of a written submission to a Senate committee, one of the more high profile advocates argued that: 'The system is not set up for the investor. It is set up for the industry. In my view, every aspect of it is co-opted by the industry. It is full circle. They have captured it' (Kyle 2005). Whether or not this is true is to an extent beside the point, as the extremity of these views provide the grounds for their immediate dismissal, even by sympathetic ears. Thus, lacking both firm institutional connections and symbolic capital, these kinds of allegations are limited in terms of their impact, easily reduced, at least in the eyes of industry and regulatory audiences, to a form of carnivalesque effrontery, with little of the credibility or traction needed to advance the investor cause. This is indicative of a form of censorship that 'condemns the occupants of dominated positions either to silence or to shocking outspokenness' (Bourdieu 1991: 138).

Beyond the loosely institutionalized and highly personalized nature of the advocacy movement, a third limitation involves its discursive frames of reference and, in particular, what may be construed as an extremely limited and somewhat narrow view of both 'victims' and 'offenders'. In this respect, it is interesting that many of the investor advocates, and SIPA itself, are invested in the very same narratives of victimization and offending circulated by regulators and the industry. Thus, emphasis is placed on older, naïve, innocent and entirely vulnerable investors who have been cheated out of their retirement savings through the schemings of unethical investment advisers. Consistent with this frame, images and stories of senior citizens are featured prominently in the publications and other materials produced by SIPA and are front-and-centre in its efforts to dramatize the harms associated with financial misconduct. In addition to the age of the victims, the accounts of investor advocates also emphasize the physicality of investment harms, cast in terms of rather simplistic comparisons with conventional street crime. One SIPA report compared a major financial loss to the experience of incest (SIPA 2004: 51), while a prominent investor advocate likened these offences to 'financial assaults':

> We view white-collar crimes as financial assaults. We don't see why some disadvantaged poor kid stealing some bread ends up with two years in jail and someone who's gone through financial assault, and I think you're aware sometimes this involves premature death, diseases, heart attacks, or even suicide ... [receives a minimal penalty].
>
> (Dialogue with the OSC 2007)

Investor advocacy discourses are also highly moralistic and framed in decidedly pejorative terms, as is evident in a SIPA (2004) report, which asserts that:

> Some leaders of the investment industry have displayed a widespread practice of greed and dishonesty. Corporate fraud and breaches of securities laws appear rampant. There are fears that moral and ethical codes are breaking down in our society. It is time for Canada's leaders who have a sense of right and truth to take affirmative action to prevent further degeneration of Canadian society (33).

Weakened by the charges of inaccuracy and imprecision that invariably accompany this kind of hyperbole, these discursive framings are associated with two unintended consequences. First, they dramatically narrow both the appeal of their cause and the size of the investor pool from which to recruit future members and expand their ranks. By limiting the face of the aggrieved investor to senior citizens, the impression given by SIPA is that this is a problem faced by people in their retirement thus excluding a much larger, and potentially more vocal and engaged, group of investors.[4] Second, scenarios where clearly unscrupulous investment advisers take advantage of innocent and vulnerable victims merely reinforce dominant narratives of blameworthiness, while making it more difficult to assert grievances in cases where the involvement of the investor may be more questionable or where the harm may be less clear.

This somewhat ironic, and no doubt unintended, complementarity with the industry also extends to positions on policy issues. For example, spurred by the general disdain with which they hold the SROs, a number of investor advocates have appeared before legislative hearings, openly opposing proposals that the SROs be granted statutory powers, despite the fact that these would only enhance their investigative capabilities and jurisdictional reach, potentially to the benefit of retail investors. Moreover, the grounds on which these critiques are advanced, such as unfairness and a lack of stakeholder accountability, are eerily similar to those employed by the industry in its protests against these very same proposals. Other examples include: (1) advocate support for the proposed separation of the investigative and adjudicative functions of the OSC, the favourite pet issue of the industry that, if anything, would result in more litigious proceedings and lower penalties for those accused of breaching securities laws; and (2) resistance to the RCMP's pursuit of subpoena powers in securities cases. In the opinion of one advocacy group,[5] the latter 'would violate the Charter of Rights and Freedoms and therefore would not serve either the securities crime victims or the accused perpetrators very well. We need to adopt reforms in a balanced justice system that has appropriate checks and balances and public accountability mechanisms' (NPSCF 2008: 7). Were there members of the industry in the audience, they would have nodded their heads in silent agreement.

Together these limits have seriously undermined the success of the investor advocacy movement and its ability to shift the terms of policy debates to better reflect the interests of the larger community of investors, the prototypical financial outsiders. Despite their passion and vitriol, advocacy efforts have been hampered by a lack of formal access to, and representation within, the regulatory process, a reflection of the notoriously 'closed' and 'self-contained' character of financial policy communities (Underhill 1997: 38), and the efforts of legal counsel and other industry advocates to monopolize available outlets for the expression of grievances.[6] The advocacy movement has also been hurt by a relative absence of social and symbolic capital, a by-product of its reliance on a handful of dominant personalities valued for their 'insider' knowledge, yet easily marginalized by their casting as self-interested outsiders and discourteous trouble-makers. As a consequence, investor advocates have been largely marginalized and silenced (Black 2006: 561), relegated to hurling insults from the sidelines. The advocacy movement has also been hamstrung by its own, decidedly narrow, discursive framing of 'victims' and 'offenders', as well as the population of affected investors, one of the unintended consequences of the effort to bolster the compellability of their cause. Within these connections between access, expertise and symbolic capital, we can once again see the workings of a distinct politics of knowledgeability.

Investor advocates are marginalized by virtue of the conditionalities underlying the production of legitimate knowledge in the financial and regulatory sphere, and the contrast drawn between the confident voices of securities professionals and the vague discontent of the amorphous pool of small investors. As noted by Langton (2008):

> [Retail investors] are at a great disadvantage in terms of both expertise and market power relative to the financial services industry firms with which they do business. The same circumstances that make small investors vulnerable – an imbalance in market knowledge and resources – also leaves them at a disadvantage in terms of crafting rules. They don't have lobbyists to promote their interests to policy-makers. Nor do they have teams of lawyers to pick apart regulatory proposals and craft arguments that can swing the details in their favour (xx).

In light of this imbalance, and lacking other sources of discursive authority on which more aggressive moves might be staked, regulators are bound to remain on the current path.

Materialities, vulnerabilities and interventions

While this recognition of the politics and forms of knowledgeability at work in the enforcement field has proven useful in accounting for the shape of securities enforcement as a matter of practice, as well as the limitations of advocacy efforts, it also offers a unique window into various points of vulnerability and thus opportunities for intervention. However, before moving down this path, a number of qualifications are in order. First, these are presented not as formal policy recommendations, but rather as possible lines of future inquiry, debate and discussion. Moreover, they are not attached to any definitive normative project or commitment to make enforcement 'better' per se, as this would leave the discussion vulnerable to the same old normative trap. Rather, the intention is to identify ways in which the positions of regulators and advocates might be strengthened, through various forms of legal, interactional and symbolic advantage, while leaving aside the question of whether or how this would actually translate into a more 'effective' enforcement system. Finally, following from the notion that the foundations for these kinds of changes lie not in larger structural transformations but rather interventions in the materialities and technicalities of enforcement practice, emphasis is placed on specific points of engagement, while recognizing that these materialities, perhaps somewhat ironically, assume not only a material but also a symbolic and discursive form. Thus, appropriate points of intervention would include the recognized deficits in symbolic capital on the part of regulators and advocates alike, as well as limits to the discursive framing of financial problems and regulatory solutions. With these provisos in hand, the opportunities for intervention can be divided into two distinct, yet interrelated, clusters. The first includes those directed to enforcement agencies themselves while the second, building on the notion that a shift in the political and discursive landscape is needed in order to press the regulatory cause and generate new sources of symbolic authority, focuses on investors and investor advocacy.

Enforcement politics, practices and conventions

Given that one of the key impediments affecting regulators and the police is not only their social, physical and experiential distance from the markets but also their relative deficit in social and symbolic capital, from and into which a number of other limits flow, it is natural that efforts to bolster the regulatory cause would first seek to enhance the credibility and authority of those working on the regulatory side of the fence. This is, of course, an extremely difficult task, given the intangible nature of symbolic capital as well as the reality that lawyers, as one of the primary groups whose respect regulators seek, may only ever value their own capital, credentials and connections. Shifting the metrics of credibility and authority is thus certainly an uphill battle. And yet, there may be positive moves in this direction. For example, following the credo to first do no harm, it would be sensible for regulatory agencies to resist allowing outside counsel to be parachuted into key managerial positions, the recommendation of a number of commissions and reports. Following from this, efforts should be made to foster internal forms of experience, expertise and confidence, potentially through better training and retention programs, as well as new recruitment strategies.[7] In the case of the police, this could also include an effort to relocate at least part of their IMET operations to the downtown core, thus providing them with a presence in the financial district and the ability to access the social and informational networks at the heart of the markets. Collectively, these changes would need to be accompanied by the recalibration of internal systems of reward and punishment, as well as the modification of the larger organizational culture to allow for a greater emphasis on risk taking, creativity and the ability to take chances, rather than the current posture of narrow perfectionism and strategic defensiveness.

A second point of intervention involves the adoption of a more open, creative and aggressive stance on seemingly settled legal conventions, including interpretations of privilege, disclosure, privacy and the relationship between regulators and the police. As noted at various points in the book, these conventions have become depoliticized and ossified over time, an encasement that belies their contingency and contextuality, as well as vulnerability to different interpretations and legal imaginings. A number of respondents spoke to this very possibility, particularly around the question of information sharing between regulatory and criminal realms, where opportunities exist for a more aggressive interpretation of the restrictions on information flow. The continued pursuit of subpoena powers for the police in securities cases would also represent a positive move, although one that would require a delicate treatment of Charter-based concerns. These efforts to unsettle established legal practices would no doubt hinge on, and would have to be accompanied by, the aforementioned realignments of internal reward structures, a more aggressive approach to institutional risk, and not only a substantial narrowing of the capital deficit between regulators and private litigators but also the cultivation of other sympathetic audiences, particularly the courts. Despite their renowned organizational inertia, the fact that the criminal courts, among others, have grown increasingly intolerant of the procedural delays initiated by defence counsel (Makin 2008), may offer a degree of traction for a more aggressive approach on these questions of legal precedent and procedure.

Finally, there may be opportunities for reducing some of the jurisdictional gaps that currently divide the field of securities enforcement and contribute to the awkward disconnect with the markets themselves. This could include arrangements for better information sharing between agencies, as well as more clearly defined protocols for joint and parallel investigations, particularly in cases where an SRO and a commission may each wish to stake a jurisdictional claim. Efforts might also be undertaken to provide for the greater integration of data streams, for example, allowing RS (now IIROC) to access trading data from other exchanges and jurisdictions. This would certainly require a deft handling of turf issues, although the greater challenge might be developing the technological capacity needed to store, process and mine these massive volumes of data. This is one of those barriers that is distinctly technical in nature. Opportunities also exist for revisiting the protocols for transferring cases of insider and manipulative trading from the SROs to the commissions, including the standardization of these arrangements across jurisdictions and the possibility of joint investigative teams for cases of common interest, a working relationship that would be facilitated were the SROs to be granted statutory powers, thereby levelling the legal playing field. Regardless of the chosen course, it is unlikely that mere institutional realignments, such as further consolidation at the SRO level or the merging of provincial commissions into a fully nationalized regulator, will have an appreciable effect on these coordination difficulties, grounded as they are less in the institutional structure of enforcement and more in its working practices. While limiting the number of partners, these moves would also do little to address the SRO/commission divide, which is where many of these tensions flourish and cases are allowed to founder.

Investor activism and financial citizenship

To the extent that the aforementioned moves at the enforcement level require a more aggressive and confident posture on the part of the enforcement agencies and a critical sense of institutional legitimacy, their success is bound to depend on the larger court of political and public opinion. In contrast with the current situation where regulators face, on the one side, a strong, well organized and entrenched industry and legal lobby, and on the other a disorganized and in many respects ill-informed and indifferent community of investors, what is needed is a much stronger investor presence. This would help to generate political momentum for the kinds of changes discussed above, providing both a source of pressure on regulators and a well of legitimate authority from which they might draw in pressing forward with these interventions and rebuffing the inevitable objections from legal counsel and other affected parties.

One of the first steps here would be the establishment of a more institutionalized as well as representative investor voice, a site through which advocacy efforts could be coordinated and efforts made to reach a much larger population of investors.[8] Most critically, this would include a dedicated research function and a full-time professional staff, with personnel in key management and administrative positions recruited not only from the ranks of those victimized by the industry, but also senior representatives of the financial and legal community with an interest in advocacy issues at the retail level. A number of respondents mentioned that there are individuals with this type of background who would be interested in this work, but who have been put off by the lack of organization and the dubious credibility of existing advocacy efforts. The formation of such an agency would no doubt face a number of significant hurdles, including the need to secure an independent, stable and long-term source of funding for its recruitment, research and advocacy work. There is also the danger that this would be framed as yet another consumer agency, thus artificially narrowing, or conversely dramatically expanding, its mandate and leaving it susceptible to colonization by other consumer groups or agencies.[9] And yet, despite these hurdles, it is exactly this kind of more credible and well structured investor representation that is sorely lacking in the current environment, particularly in the Canadian context.

In addition to its public face, this makeover of investor stakeholdership also requires capacity building of a slightly different sort. This certainly includes addressing the very low levels of investment knowledge and financial literacy (Government of Canada 2005). However, the form of investor education that is most needed is very different from that typically proposed, which more often than not consists of information about financial products and investment opportunities, salted with warnings about shady investments that are too good to be true, and framed in terms of a neo-liberal discourse of responsibilization and personal empowerment (Aitken 2006, 2007; Froud et al. 2006; Erturk et al. 2007; Williams 2007; Langley 2008a). The problem with these accounts, beyond their limited value and failure to provide truly educative experiences and opportunities for investors, is that they perpetuate and in fact reinforce discourses of investor complicity and victim blaming (Spalek 2001). Armed with the requisite information and warnings, it is the alleged responsibility of the individual investors to protect themselves from misconduct and to take immediate action should problems arise with their investments. The result is the privileging of an increasingly narrow discourse of 'true' victimization, thus further limiting the need for, and legitimacy of, regulatory protections. Here knowledge is strangely equated not with power but with culpability, as these kinds of investor education initiatives have the 'useful effect of allowing [the retail financial industry] to depict consumers as more knowledgeable and therefore more able to be subject to the principle of caveat emptor, buyer beware' (Leyshon et al. 1998: 51).

In contrast with these prevailing trends in investor education,[10] what is needed are programs which enhance the capabilities of investors through the delivery of knowledge rather than simply information, as well as skills and competencies that improve the confidence, comfort level and, ultimately, the credibility of investors: '*Education* involves building people's capacities: their skills, competence, knowledge and understanding' (Black 2006: 566, emphasis added). This echoes the assessment of a former regulator and respected member of the advocacy community:

> A lot of people think you can fill [the knowledge] gap by simply giving facts. But if you don't have the ability to understand why these facts are relevant or what to do with them, you haven't accomplished anything. You have not levelled the playing field. And so the real problem is at a more fundamental level and that is we've got to work to produce people, *citizens*, who have the ability to apply knowledge'.
>
> (Consultant #2: 4, emphasis added)

Such capacity building would include changes to the educational strategies of advocacy groups themselves (eg SIPA). For example, many such groups provide lists of questions that investors are encouraged to ask when meeting with their advisers and deciding on potential investments. While potentially useful in smoking out shady advice, this approach overlooks the inequalities in symbolic capital and interactional competencies between investors and advisers, differences that are likely to undermine the usefulness of these kinds of 'ask your adviser' checklists. Investors may lack the confidence and credibility needed to ask these questions in such a way as to yield the most meaningful answers, pressing advisers when they appear evasive and probing for additional information. In this respect, education-oriented interventions must address the power imbalances at play in these advisory relationships, which cannot be resolved simply through an awareness of the questions to ask, but rather require a degree of confidence in the asking.

While investor education is certainly a necessary and worthwhile point of intervention, a means of narrowing gaps in capital, credibility and confidence, this must be accompanied by discursive shifts in the way that investing itself is framed. This starts with efforts to challenge the narrow discourses of responsibility so pervasive in both industry and regulatory parlance, and which serve to deflect questionable dealings onto negligent or insufficiently responsible investor-subjects. One positive step here would be to further clarify and encode the investor-adviser relationship as one of mutual obligation and reliance, rather than the current options of either capable autonomy, or outright dependence and vulnerability. In order to be viable, this notion of mutual or shared responsibility also requires a larger discursive shift in the very nature of investing itself, and its reframing as a social rather than simply individual practice and responsibility. Along these lines, instead of viewing investing as a form of consumption like any other (Harmes 2001: 210) and investors as consumers requiring assistance and protection commensurate with their purchasing decisions,[11] it may be necessary to conceive of investors as *financial citizens* and investing as a form of *financial security* and a fundamentally *social right*. To be clear, this requires a move beyond current musings on financial or economic citizenship which, given their neo-liberal trappings, conceive of investing as a contractual obligation of the responsible citizen (Aitken 2006, 2007; Langley 2008a) and 'financial competence as a marker of citizenship' (Leyshon et al. 1998: 50). In contrast, what is needed is a rights-based discourse that links investing not only to questions of collective financial security, but also to the invocation of a distinctly political right.[12] In the Canadian context, this recasting of investing could lay the foundation for the use of broader constitutional protections (for example, the Charter of Rights and Freedoms) to push for the recognition of investor rights and the ability to challenge existing regulatory and legal regimes on the grounds that they violate or fail to uphold these rights.[13] Similar benefits could also accrue from the fashioning of an Investor Bill of Rights or other such document which, even if articulated outside of a explicitly juridical or rights-based framework, could nonetheless provide a discursive point of reference or 'deliberative space' (Braithwaite 2005: 34) through which the very notion of 'investor rights' could be more seriously considered.

To be sure, these kinds of discursive moves will be difficult to bring about and will likely encounter significant challenges along the way, including: (1) opposition from the industry and other stakeholders as well as the regulators themselves; (2) difficulties in attracting the attention and interest of politicians and the investing public; and (3) challenges in transcending the differences in scale (see Valverde 2009) that currently mark off and separate the private sphere of investing and finance from the national political domain where citizenship-based rights apply and may be more actively invoked. In countering these barriers, the broadening of the appeal and the membership base of the advocacy movement and the move away from educational initiatives rooted in simplistic discourses of investor responsibility will help, as will the establishment of a more institutionalized and refined investor voice, a critical source of symbolic authority and a key base from which to engage in these various skirmishes and discursive moves. Regardless of the specifics of the approach, the importance of these kinds of shifts is only likely to increase in the near future, given the continued erosion of public and employer-funded pension and social security programs, and thus ever greater pressures on individuals to become active managers of their own financial fate. These stakes are further magnified by the fact that many of the aforementioned interventions in the enforcement arena are themselves dependent on this more authoritative and institutionalized investor voice, an alternative source of discursive authority that may help to shift the political optics and scales of institutional risk and thus provide regulators with the necessary momentum, legitimacy and authority should they opt to pursue a more vigorous regulatory course. It is within these efforts to reframe and depoliticize both investment and enforcement that we can see not only the constraints, but also the possibilities underlying the politics of knowledgeability.

Implications and suggestions for future research

To the extent that this book has lived up to its promise to provide a very different perspective on questions of enforcement and regulation in the financial sphere, it is hoped that it may serve as a foundation of sorts for future work in this area. Certainly, there is a desperate need for additional research on all aspects of financial governance from a distinctly social science perspective. Extending well beyond the formal confines of securities enforcement as a distinct disciplinary function, this includes: (1) more detailed and focused analyses of emerging regulatory technologies, including new surveillance, pattern recognition and artificial intelligence programs and their possibilities as well as limits; (2) the examination of other units within the major regulatory agencies, namely corporate finance and even public relations, and their connections to enforcement; (3) the existence of legal mechanisms, such as exemptions and exemption orders *as legal technicalities* and their role in restricting the scope and impact of regulatory efforts; and (4) a more in-depth account of investor advocacy as a particular type of social movement. Opportunities also exist for the analysis of governance arrangements in other types of markets, including commodities markets, which have yet to appear on the social science radar but carry critical *social* implications, both for our understanding of financial regulation and larger policy questions involving access to food and other essential commodities.

As with the analysis of securities enforcement undertaken in this book, these future inquiries should avoid the temptation to invoke grand narratives of financial or political power, or to focus on the products of regulation and their etiological drivers to the neglect of the details, practices and politics of the regulatory enterprise itself. A continued engagement with questions of knowledge and knowledgeability is essential to teasing out the more subtle workings of these financial and regulatory practices, as is a spirit of interdisciplinary cross-fertilization. As noted by Tinker and Carter (2003) in connection with the 'Enron' scandals: '[The cases] do not appear in neatly labeled packages addressed to "sociology", "finance" or "economics". Rather, they are phenomenological misfits, requiring a radical conceptual reconfiguration in order to be adequately appropriated' (577). Future research on the markets and their regulation would thus benefit from further dialogues between economic sociology, the sociology of professions and organizations, socio-legal and criminological studies, as well as the more theoretical contributions of Foucault, Bourdieu and others interested in problems of knowledge and their implications for contemporary forms of governance. However, rather than simply a joining of hands, it is critical that this cross-disciplinary exercise remain cognizant of the points of tension and discontinuity between these various literatures and thus make explicit the compromises invariably required as part of such an effort.

While the foundations of this project, and the most anticipated of the future lines of inquiry, are grounded in questions of ordering as they relate to the world of finance, the analytical approach developed in this book may also prove useful to studies of governance beyond the economic realm. As noted previously, the connection between knowledge and governance has long been a concern of the social sciences. However, the main thrust of this scholarship has centred on how power is exercised over individuals and populations by virtue of the *visibilities* afforded by knowledge-based practices, tactics and discourses (eg Rose 1999; Miller and Rose 2008). This book has the potential to broaden the scope of these inquiries by introducing the possibility that, in domains such as finance, power is associated less with a drive to visibility and more with *invisibility*, *incompleteness* and *obfuscation* (Williams 2005, 2009). It might also provide an opportunity to address some of the weaknesses within these perspectives themselves which have at times been accused of being overly formulaic or at least less than sensitive to the uncertainties, contingencies and unanticipated complications of governance projects (eg Williams and Lippert 2006). Here inspiration may be drawn from the book's emphasis not simply on the 'production of knowledge' but on the 'politics of knowledgeability', an expression of the *conditionalities* and *contextualities* imposed by space, distance, geography and architecture, as well as the forms of *mediation* associated with inter-agency struggles, organizational imperatives and the work of professionals as both bearers of symbolic capital and participants in various markets in expertise. Having examined securities enforcement as a fundamentally knowledge-based enterprise shaped by exactly these dynamics, it will be left to future research to mine the possibilities contained within this notion of the politics of knowledgeability, and to engage with the knowledge games and space(s) of play at the heart of contemporary forms of governance unfolding both within and beyond the borders of finance.

Notes

1 The success of any future Canadian securities commission is also likely to be undermined by the need for political compromise, as was evident in proposals that the agency's head offices be located in Alberta or BC, thousands of kilometers from the financial district of downtown Toronto and thus far removed from the social world of the markets.

2 One exception to this was the OSC's Investor Advisory Committee (IAC), which was established in 2005. Populated by individuals with strong credentials and an appreciation for key issues in the industry, the mandate of the committee was to provide input into the regulatory process from the perspective of the small investor. However, deprived of its own research budget and office space, granted limited autonomy and isolated from other consultative committees, the IAC was viewed by many of its members as being largely ineffective. Before these complaints could be aired or addressed, the committee was disbanded after just two years in existence. Two years later, in February of 2010, a new committee was struck: the Investor Advisory Panel. While still in its infancy, at least one former IAC member has alleged that the panel suffers from many of the same flaws as its predecessor, including a lack of independence and ability to determine its own agenda, inadequate resources and the inability to serve as anything other than a sounding board for commission initiatives (Reeve in Rosen and Rosen 2010).

3 The question of tact and sophistication was highlighted by one of the more 'controversial' consciousness-raising initiatives in which a SIPA member recruited a female acquaintance to kiss her girlfriend for 30 seconds in the middle of the downtown financial district with

the words 'TSX no win' and 'OSC not fair' emblazoned on their tank tops (Dobrota 2006: B7). While this certainly made headlines, it did little to boost the credibility of their cause. As noted by an otherwise sympathetic observer: 'I think he was wrong about it and I sent him a note saying that. Obviously he didn't care, his point is to keep raising the profile. Well, alright but I think some of this is self-defeating' (Journalist #2: 18).

4 One SIPA member commented during an interview that this strategy was deliberate, as younger investors are better able to recover from questionable financial dealings while senior investors, many of them retired, are not. This may be true, but it neglects the larger strategic considerations at play in this kind of enterprise.

5 This is one of a number of groups that advocates on issues of interest to senior citizens with investment-related matters a common area of concern.

6 Perhaps the best example of this kind of dynamic is a report produced as part of the IDA Task Force to modernize security legislation in Canada dealing specifically with securities enforcement (Cory and Pilkington 2006), which was well received and widely cited as a template of sorts for righting the enforcement ship. While the report was written by Justice Peter Cory and Marilyn Pilkington, a former Supreme Court Justice and a respected law professor, the authors admit in the text of the report to a limited knowledge of 'the highly specialized and complex field of securities law and the operation of capital markets' and thus their reliance on consultations with 'specialists in the field to identify the challenges to be addressed' (183). With these specialists selected primarily from the available pool of legal counsel and industry insiders, the report not surprisingly reflects dominant industry concerns with issues such as poor judgment and bias on the part of regulators.

7 This could also include the recruitment of senior people from the industry who have a genuine interest in regulation and for whom a move to the regulatory sector would be the final stage in their career, rather than a jumping off point to future opportunities.

8 At present there are no agencies in Canada dedicated to securities-based advocacy, with the Financial Consumer Agency of Canada limited to the retail banking and insurance sectors.

9 An example of this type of expansion is the Consumer Financial Protection Agency established by President Obama following the sub-prime crisis. With a jurisdiction that covers not only securities and investments but also credit cards, debit cards, consumer loans, credit reporting agencies and debt collection, there will always be a danger that securities-related advocacy efforts will be drowned out by other voices.

10 The most recent example of this trend is the Task Force on Financial Literacy, which issued its final report and recommendations in December 2010. Based on the core theme of 'shared responsibility', these recommendations covered everything from education on the 'role and benefits of professional financial advice' (44), to employer-operated automatic saving programs, to financial literacy programs for high school students.

11 This is reflected in what Stromberg (1998) refers to as a 'consumer' versus a 'securities' model, with the former clearly the more dominant: 'As consumers, they are not "investing". They are simply buying a recognized brand name ... While I have concerns about simply viewing investment funds as products or services that are sold like laundry soap, blue jeans or sports shoes, the reality is that this is how they are being positioned in the public eye and how they are being viewed by many of the key participants in the investment fund industry' (29).

12 According to Preda (2005), it was just such a view of investing as a natural right and grounds for the equalization of economic opportunity that, in the late 1800s and early 1900s, helped to transform it from a purely speculative endeavour to an economically rational and socially beneficial practice.

13 In the past, the Charter has been used with considerable success to encode the 'rights' of private industry (see Mandel 1994), as well as to challenge the jurisdiction, authority and working practices of both regulators and the police. And yet, very few if any efforts have been advanced on the investor front, where the notion of financial or economic rights remains very much under-developed.

References

Books and journals

Abel, R. (2003) *English Lawyers between Market and State: The Politics of Professionalism*. Oxford: Oxford University Press.

Abolafia, M. Y. (1996) *Making Markets: Opportunism and Restraint on Wall Street*. Cambridge, MA: Harvard University Press.

— (1998) 'Markets as Cultures: An Ethnographic Approach' in M. Callon ed., *The Laws of the Markets*, 69–85. Oxford: Blackwell.

Adler, P. and P. Adler eds. (1984) *The Social Dynamics of Financial Markets*. Greenwich, CT: JAI Press.

Aitken, R. (2006) 'Performativity, Popular Finance, and Security in the Global Political Economy' in M. de Goede ed., *International Political Economy and Poststructural Politics*, 77–98. Basingstoke: Palgrave.

— (2007) *Performing Capital: Toward a Cultural Economy of Popular and Global Finance*. New York: Palgrave.

Anand, A. (2010) 'Is Systemic Risk Relevant to Securities Regulation?', *University of Toronto Law Journal*, 60(4): 941–81.

Andrews, N. (2006) 'Corporatism and the Toronto Stock Exchange: A New Ontario Egg Board?', *Australian Journal of Corporate Law*, 19: 65–113.

Armstrong, C. (1997) *Blue Skies and Boiler Rooms: Buying and Selling Securities in Canada, 1870–1940*. Toronto: University of Toronto Press.

— (2001) *Moose Pastures and Mergers: The Ontario Securities Commission and the Regulation of Share Markets in Canada, 1940–1980*. Toronto: University of Toronto Press.

Atkinson, T. (2004) Presentation to the Canadian Security Traders Association Conference. 8 July 2004. Toronto, Ontario.

Baker, W. E. (1984) 'The Social Structure of a National Securities Market', *American Journal of Sociology*, 89: 775–811.

— (1990) 'Market Networks and Corporate Behaviour', *American Journal of Sociology*, 96: 589–625.

Baldwin, R. (1997) 'Regulation: After "Command and Control"' in K. Hawkins ed., *The Human Face of Law: Essays in Honour of Donald Harris*, 65–84. Oxford: Clarendon Press.

Baldwin, R. and J. Black (2008) 'Really Responsive Regulation', *The Modern Law Review*, 71(1): 59–94.

Bennett, W. L. and M. S. Feldman (1981) *Reconstructing Reality in the Courtroom*. New Brunswick, NJ: Rutgers University Press.

Benson, M. L. and F. T. Cullen (1998) *Combating Corporate Crime: Local Prosecutors At Work*. Boston: Northeastern University Press.

Beunza, D. and F. Muniesa (2005) 'Listening to the Spread Plot' in B. Latour and P. Wiebel eds., *Making Things Public: Atmospheres of Democracy*, 628–33. Cambridge, MA: MIT Press.

Beunza, D. and D. Stark (2003) 'The Organization of Responsiveness: Innovation and Recovery in Trading Rooms of Wall Street', *Socio-Economic Review*, 1: 135–64.

— (2005) 'How to Recognize Opportunities: Heterarchical Search in a Trading Room' in K. Knorr Cetina and A. Preda eds., *The Sociology of Financial Markets*, 84–101. Oxford: Oxford University Press.

Beunza, D., I. Hardie and D. MacKenzie (2006) 'A Price is a Social Thing: Towards a Material Sociology of Arbitrage', *Organization Studies*, 27(5): 721–45.

Bhattacharya, U. (2006) 'Enforcement and Its Impact on Cost of Equity and Liquidity of the Market', *Canada Steps Up: Report of the Task Force to Modernize Securities Legislation in Canada*, Vol. 6. Toronto: Task Force to Modernize Securities Legislation in Canada.

Black, J. (2001) 'Decentring Regulation: Understanding the Role of Regulation and Self-Regulation in a "Post-Regulatory" World', *Current Legal Problems*, 54: 103–46.

— (2002) 'Mapping Contemporary Financial Services Regulation', *Journal of Corporate Law Studies*, 2(2): 253–88.

— (2004) 'Law and Regulation: The Case of Finance' in C. Parker, C. Scott, N. Lacey and J. Braithwaite eds., *Regulating Law*, 33–59. Oxford University Press.

— (2005) 'The Development of Risk-Based Regulation in Financial Services: Just "Modeling Through"?' in J. Black, M. Lodge and M. Thatcher eds., *Regulatory Innovation: A Comparative Perspective*, 156–80. Northampton, MA: Edward Elgar.

— (2006) 'Managing Regulatory Risks and Defining the Parameters of Blame: A Focus on the Australian Prudential Regulation Authority', *Law and Policy*, 28(1): 1–30.

Blomley, N. (1994) *Law, Space, and the Geographies of Power*. New York: Guilford Press.

Blomley, N. and J. Bakan (1992) 'Spacing Out: Towards a Critical Geography of Law', *Osgoode Hall Law Journal*, 30(3): 661–90.

Blyth, M. (2003) 'The Political Power of Financial Ideas: Transparency, Risk, and Distribution in Global Finance' in J. Kirshner ed., *Monetary Orders, Ambiguous Economics, Ubiquitous Politics*, 239–59. Ithaca: Cornell University Press.

Board, J., C. Sutcliffe and S. Wells (2002) *Transparency and Fragmentation: Financial Market Regulation in a Dynamic Environment*. New York: Palgrave Macmillan.

Bourdieu, P. (1984) *Distinction: A Social Critique of the Judgment of Taste*. London: Routledge.

— (1986) 'The Forms of Capital' in J. Richardson ed., *Handbook of Theory and Research for the Sociology of Education*, 241–58. New York: Greenwood.

— (1987) 'The Force of Law: Toward a Sociology of the Juridical Field', *The Hastings Law Journal*, 38: 805–53.

— (1989) 'Social Space and Symbolic Power', *Sociological Theory*, 7(1): 14–25.

— (1991) *Language and Symbolic Power*. Cambridge, MA: Harvard University Press.

— (1993) *Sociology in Question*. London: Sage Publications.

— (2005) *The Social Structures of the Economy*. Malden, MA: Polity.

Bourdieu, P. and L. Wacquant (1992) *An Invitation to Reflexive Sociology*. Chicago: University of Chicago Press.

Braithwaite, J. (2005) *Markets in Vice, Markets in Virtue*. Annandale, Australia: Federation Press.

— (2008) *Regulatory Capitalism: How It Works, Ideas for Making it Work Better*. Northampton, MA: Edward Elgar.

Brown, D. (2004) Testimony Before the Ontario Standing Committee on Finance and Economic Affairs. 18 August 2004. Toronto: Legislative Assembly of Ontario.

Bruner, J. (1991) 'The Narrative Construction of Reality', *Critical Inquiry*, 18(1): 1–21.

Burk, J. (1988) *Values in the Marketplace: The American Stock Market Under Federal Securities Laws*. New York: de Gruyter.

Callon, M. (1998) 'The Embeddedness of Economic Markets in Economics' in M. Callon ed., *The Laws of the Markets*, 1–57. Oxford: Blackwell.

Callon, M. and F. Muniesa (2005) 'Economic Markets as Calculative Collective Devices', *Organization Studies*, 26(8): 1229–50.

Campbell, N. (2005) 'Regulatory Investigations: Dealing with the Regulator', Paper Presented at Regulatory Investigations: Effectively Managing Your Client's Exposure. Osgoode Professional Development Program. 13 June 2005. Toronto, Ontario.

Campbell, N. and B. O'Toole (2007) 'Regulatory Investigations: Conflicts of Interest and Privilege Issues', Paper Presented at Understanding and Managing Regulatory Investigations. Osgoode Professional Development Program. 23 April 2007. Toronto, Ontario.

Canadian Bankers' Association (2008) *Enhancing Canadian Competitiveness by Reforming the Way Securities are Regulated in Canada*. Submission to the Expert Panel on Securities Regulation. 15 July 2008.

Canadian Securities Administrators (2011) *2010 Enforcement Report*. Montreal: CSA.

Canan, P. and N. Reichman (2002) *Ozone Connections: Expert Networks in Global Environmental Governance*. Sheffield: Greenleaf Publishing.

Carruthers, B. (1996) *City of Capital: Politics and Markets in the English Financial Revolution*. Princeton, NJ: Princeton University Press.

Carruthers, B. and T. Halliday (1998) *Rescuing Business: The Making of Corporate Bankruptcy Law in England and the United States*. Oxford: Clarendon.

Carscallen, M., W. K. Gray and J. G. Pink (2003) *Regulatory Burden Taskforce: Report to the Ontario Securities Commission*. December 2003. Toronto, Ontario.

Clark, G. (2000) *Pension Fund Capitalism*. Oxford: Oxford University Press.

— (2003) 'Twenty-First Century Pension (In)Security' in G. Clark, and N. Whiteside eds., *Pension Security in the 21st Century*, pp. 225–51. Oxford: Oxford University Press.

Clark, G., N. Thrift and A. Tickell (2004) 'Performing Finance: The Industry, the Media, and its Image', *Review of International Political Economy*, 11(2): 289–310.

Clarke, L. (1999) *Mission Improbable: Using Fantasy Documents to Tame Disaster*. Chicago: University of Chicago Press.

Coffee, J. (1981) 'No Soul to Damn, No Body to Kick', *Michigan Law Review*, 79: 386–459.

Coleman, W. D. (1989) 'Self-Regulation in the Canadian Securities Industry: A Study of the Investment Dealers Association of Canada', *Canadian Public Administration*, 32(4): 503–23.

Committee on Capital Markets Regulation (2006) *Interim Report*. 30 November 2006.

Condon, M. (1998) *Making Disclosure: Ideas and Interests in Ontario Securities Regulation*. Toronto: University of Toronto Press.

— (2004) 'Technologies of Risk? Regulating Online Investing in Canada', *Law and Policy*, 26(3–4): 411–37.

— (2006) 'Rethinking Enforcement and Litigation in Ontario Securities Regulation', *Queen's Law Journal*, 32(1): 1–44.

Condon, M. and P. Puri (2006) 'The Role of Compliance in Security Regulatory Enforcement', *Canada Steps Up: Report of the Task Force to Modernize Securities Legislation in Canada*. Vol. 6. Toronto: Task Force to Modernize Securities Legislation in Canada.

Condon, M., A. Anand and J. Sarra (2005) *Securities Law in Canada: Cases and Commentary*. Toronto: Edmond Montgomery.

Cory, P. and M. Pilkington (2006) 'Critical Issues in Enforcement', *Canada Steps Up: Report of the Task Force to Modernize Securities Legislation in Canada*. Vol. 6. Toronto: Task Force to Modernize Securities Legislation in Canada.

Crawford, P. (2003) *Five Year Review Committee Final Report: Reviewing the Securities Act (Ontario)*. 21 March 2003. Toronto: Ontario Ministry of Finance.

Critchley, B. (2008) 'The Cost of Leaked M&As', *Financial Post*, 11 June 2008: FP2.

de Goede, M. (2003) 'Beyond Economism in International Political Economy', *Review of International Studies*, 29(1): 79–97.

— (2005) *Virtue, Fortune, and Faith: A Genealogy of Finance*. Minneapolis: University of Minnesota Press.

Dean, M. (2011) *Governmentality: Power and Rule in Modern Society*. 2nd ed. London: Sage.

Dezalay, Y. (1995) 'Introduction' in Y. Dezalay and D. Sugarman eds., *Professional Competition and Professional Power. Lawyers, Accountants and the Social Construction of Markets*, 1–15. New York: Routledge.

Dezalay, Y. and B. Garth (1996) *Dealing in Virtue*. Chicago: University of Chicago Press.

— (1997) 'Law, Lawyers, and Social Capital: "Rule of Law" versus Relational Capitalism', *Social and Legal Studies*, 6(1): 109–41.

DiMaggio, P. and W. Powell (1983) 'The Iron Cage Revisited: Institutional Isomorphism and Collective Rationality in Organizational Fields', *American Sociological Review*, 48(2): 147–60.

Dobrota, A. (2006) 'Shareholder Protest Has Bay Street's Undivided Attention', *Globe and Mail*, 18 July 2006: B7.

Dorn, N. (2010) 'The Governance of Securities: Ponzi Finance, Regulatory Convergence, Credit Crunch', *British Journal of Criminology*, 50: 23–45.

— (2011) 'The Metamorphosis of Insider Trading in the Face of Regulatory Enforcement', *Journal of Financial Regulation and Compliance*, 19(1): 75–84.

Edelman, L. (2002) 'Legality and the Endogeneity of Law' in R. A. Kagan, M. Krygier, and K. Winston eds., *Legality and Community: On the Intellectual Legacy of Philip Selznick*, 187–202. New York: Rowman and Littlefield.

Edelman, L. and M. Suchman (1997) 'The Legal Environments of Organizations', *Annual Review of Sociology*, 23: 479–515.

Emerson, R. M. (1991) 'Case Processing and Interorganizational Knowledge: Detecting the "Real Reasons" for Referrals', *Social Problems*, 38(2): 198–212.

— (1992) 'Disputes in Public Bureaucracies', *Studies in Law, Politics, and Society*, 12: 3–29.

Emerson, R. M. and B. Paley (1992) 'Organizational Horizons in Complaint Filing' in K. Hawkins ed., *The Uses of Discretion*, 231–47. Oxford: Clarendon Press.

Engel, K. and P. McCoy (2011) *The Subprime Virus: Reckless Credit, Regulatory Failure, and Next Steps*. Oxford: Oxford University Press.

Enrich, D. (2011) 'FSA Gives Peek Into Crime-Fighting Methods', *Wall Street Journal*, 2 February 2011.

Ericson, R. V. and K. Haggerty (1997) *Policing the Risk Society*. Toronto: University of Toronto Press.

Erturk, I., J. Froud, J. Sukhdev, A. Leaver and K. Williams (2007) 'The Democratization of Finance? Promise, Outcomes, and Conditions', *Review of International Political Economy*, 14(4): 553–76.

Ewick, P. (1985) 'Redundant Regulation: Sanctioning Broker-Dealers', *Law and Policy*, 7: 421–45.

Ewick, P. and S. Silbey (1995) 'Subversive Stories and Hegemonic Tales: Towards a Sociology of Narrative', *Law and Society Review*, 29(2): 197–226.

Expert Panel on Securities Regulation (2009) *Creating an Advantage in Global Capital Markets: Final Report and Recommendations*. Ottawa: Department of Finance.

Fligstein, N. (1996) 'Markets as Politics: A Political Cultural Approach to Market Institutions', *American Sociological Review*, 61(4): 656–73.

Fooks, G. (2002) 'Contrasts in Tolerance: The Curious Politics of Financial Regulation', *Journal of Contemporary Politics*, 9(2): 127–42.

Ford, R. (1999) 'Law's Territory (A History of Jurisdiction)', *Michigan Law Review*, 97: 843–930.

Foucault, M. (1989) *The Archaeology of Knowledge*. London: Routledge.

— (1991) 'Governmentality' in G. Burchell, C. Gordon and P. Miller eds., *The Foucault Effect: Studies in Governmentality*, 87–104. Chicago: University of Chicago Press.

— (2000) 'Truth and Power' in J. D. Faubion ed., *Power: The Essential Works of Foucault 1954–1984*, 111–33. New York: The New Press.

Frank, T. (2000) *One Market Under God: Extreme Capitalism, Market Populism, and the End of Economic Democracy*. New York: Anchor Books.

Froud, J., A. Leaver, K. Williams and W. Zhang (2006) 'The Quiet Panic About Financial Literacy' in L. Assassi, D. Wigan and A. Nesvetailova eds., *Global Finance in the New Century: Beyond Deregulation*, 74–88. Basingstoke: Palgrave Macmillan.

Galanter, M. (1974) 'Why the "Haves" Come Out Ahead: Speculations on the Limits of Legal Change', *Law and Society Review*, 9(1974–5): 95.

— (1981) 'Justice in Many Rooms: Courts, Private Ordering, and Indigenous Law', *Journal of Legal Pluralism*, 19: 1–47.

Geisst, C. R. (2004) *Wall Street: A History*. Oxford: Oxford University Press.

Globe and Mail (2006) 'The RCMP's IMET Has Little to Show for Itself', *Globe and Mail*, 22 May 2006: A12.

— (2010) 'The Waning of the RRSP', *Globe and Mail*, 12 January 2010: A16.

Goldwasser, V. R. (1999) 'The Enforcement Dilemma in Australian Securities Regulation', *Australian Business Law Review*, 27 (December): 482–513.

Goodwin, C. (1994) 'Professional Vision', *American Anthropologist*, 96(3): 606–33.

— (1995) 'Seeing in Depth', *Social Studies of Science*, 25: 237–74.

Government of Canada (2005) *Why Financial Capability Matters*. Synthesis Report on Canadians and Their Money: A National Symposium on Financial Capability. 9–10 June. Ottawa, Ontario.

Grafstein, J. (2006) *Consumer Protection in the Financial Services Sector: The Unfinished Agenda*. Report of the Standing Senate Committee on Banking, Trade, and Commerce. Ottawa: Government of Canada.

Granovetter, M. (1985) 'Economic Action and Social Structure: The Problem of Embeddedness', *American Journal of Sociology*, 91: 481–510.

Gray, J. (2007) 'A Good Country for Crooks: Canada's Losing War Against White-Collar Crime', *Canadian Business Magazine*, 24 September 2007.

Gunningham, N. (1987) 'Negotiated Non-Compliance: A Case Study of Regulatory Failure', *Law and Policy*, 9(1): 69–95.

— (1991) 'Private Ordering, Self-Regulation and Futures Markets: A Comparative Study of Informal Social Control', *Law and Policy*, 13: 297–326.

Haas, P. M. (1992) 'Introduction: Epistemic Communities and International Policy Coordination', *International Organization*, 46(1): 1–35.

Hancher, L. and M. Moran (1989) 'Organizing Regulatory Space' in L. Hancher and M. Moran eds., *Capitalism, Culture, and Economic Regulation*, 271–99. Oxford: Clarendon Press.

Harman, M. (2009) 'Court Rules SROs Can Pursue Former Members', *Investment Executive*, 28 September 2009.

Harmes, A. (2001) *Unseen Power: How Mutual Funds Threaten the Political and Economic Wealth of Nations*. Toronto: Stoddart.

Hawkins, K. (2002) *Law as a Last Resort: Prosecution Decision-Making in a Regulatory Agency*. Oxford: Oxford University Press.

Hawkins, K. and J. Thomas (1984) 'The Enforcement Process in Regulatory Bureaucracies' in K. Hawkins and J. Thomas eds., *Enforcing Regulation*, 3–22. Boston: Kluwer-Nijhoff Publishing.

— (1989) 'Making Policy in Regulatory Bureaucracies' in K. Hawkins and J. Thomas eds., *Making Regulatory Policy*, 3–26. Pittsburgh: University of Pittsburgh Press.

Hertz, E., and V. Lepinay (2003) 'The Markets of the Laws: From Relationships to Mechanisms in Securities Fraud Cases', Presented at the Constance International Conference on Social Studies of Finance. 16–18 May 2003. Konstanz, Germany.

Hutter, B. (1997) *Compliance: Regulation and Environment*. Oxford: Clarendon Press.

— (2005) *The Attractions of Risk-Based Regulation: Accounting for the Emergence of Risk Ideas in Regulation*. ESRC Centre for Analysis of Risk and Regulation. Discussion Paper No. 33. March 2005.

Insider Trading Task Force (2003) *Illegal Insider Trading in Canada: Recommendations on Prevention, Detection, and Deterrence*. November 2003.

Jackson, H. E. (2006) 'Regulatory Intensity in the Regulation of Capital Markets: A Preliminary Comparison of Canadian and U.S. Approaches', *Canada Steps Up: Final Report of the Taskforce to Modernize Securities Legislation in Canada*. Vol. 6. Toronto: Task Force to Modernize Securities Legislation in Canada.

Jackson, N. and P. Carter (1995) 'Organizational Chiaroscuro: Throwing Light on the Concept of Corporate Governance', *Human Relations*, 48(8): 875–89.

Johnson, D. (1993) 'The Canadian Regulatory System and Corporatism: Empirical Findings and Analytical Implications', *Canadian Journal of Law and Society*, 8(95): 95–120.

Katz, J. (1979) 'Legality and Equality: Plea Bargaining in the Prosecution of White-Collar Crimes', *Law and Society Review*, 13: 431–60.

Knorr Cetina, K. (2007) 'Economic Sociology and the Sociology of Finance: Four Distinctions, Two Developments, One Field?', *Economic Sociology: The European Electronic Newsletter*, 8(3): 4–10.

Knorr Cetina, K. and U. Bruegger (2000) 'The Market as an Object of Attachment: Exploring Postsocial Relations in Financial Markets', *Canadian Journal of Sociology*, 25: 141–68.

— (2002) 'Traders' Engagement with Markets: A Post-Social Relationship', *Theory, Culture, and Society*, 19(5/6): 161–85.

Knorr Cetina, K. and A. Preda (2005) 'Introduction' in K. Knorr Cetina and A. Preda eds., *The Sociology of Financial Markets*, 1–16. Oxford: Oxford University Press.

Kyle, R. (2005) Testimony Before the Standing Senate Committee on Banking, Trade, and Commerce. 4 May 2005. Ottawa: Government of Canada.

Lange, B. (1999) 'Compliance Construction in the Context of Environmental Regulation', *Social and Legal Studies*, 8(4): 549–67.

— (2002) 'What Does Law Know? Prescribing and Describing the Social World in the Enforcement of Legal Rules', *International Journal of the Sociology of Law*, 30: 131–50.

— (2003) 'Regulatory Spaces and Interactions: An Introduction', *Social and Legal Studies*, 12(4): 411–23.

Langevoort, D. (1996) 'Selling Hope, Selling Risk: Some Lessons for Law Behavioural Economics About Stockbrokers and Sophisticated Customers', *California Law Review*, 84(3): 627–701.

— (2002) 'Taming the Animal Spirits of the Stock Markets: A Behavioral Approach to Securities Regulation', *Northwestern University Law Review*, 97(1): 135–88.

Langley, P. (2008a) *The Everyday Life of Global Finance: Saving and Borrowing in Anglo-America*. New York: Oxford University Press.

— (2008b) 'Sub-Prime Mortgage Lending: A Cultural Economy', *Economy and Society*, 37(4): 469–94.

Langton, J. (2008) 'Listening to Retail Investors: New Committee Will Seek Input on Issues of Importance to Clients', *Investment Executive*, 28 April 2008.

Latour, B. (1987) *Science in Action*. Cambridge, MA: Harvard University Press.

— (1999) 'On Recalling ANT' in J. Law and J. Hassard eds., *Actor Network Theory and After*, 15–25. Oxford: Blackwell.

— (2005) *Reassembling the Social: An Introduction to Actor-Network Theory*. Oxford: Oxford University Press.

— (2010) *The Making of Law: An Ethnography of the Conseil d'Etat*. Cambridge: Polity Press.

Latour, B. and S. Woolgar (1979) *Laboratory Life: The Construction of Scientific Facts*. Princeton, NJ: Princeton University Press.

Law, J. (2002) 'Economics as Interference' in P. du Gay and M. Pryke eds., *Cultural Economy: Cultural Analysis and Commercial Life*, 21–38. London: Sage.

— (2008) 'On Sociology and STS', *The Sociological Review*, 56(4): 623–49.

Lazonick, W. and M. O'Sullivan (2000) 'Maximizing Shareholder Value: A New Ideology for Corporate Governance', *Economy and Society*, 29(1): 13–35.

Le Pan, N. (2007) *Enhancing Integrated Market Enforcement Teams, Achieving Results in Fighting Capital Markets Crime*. Ottawa: RCMP.

Levi, M. (1993) 'White-Collar Crime: The British Scene', *Annals of the American Academy of Political and Social Science*, 525: 71–82.

— (1995) 'Serious Fraud in Britain: Criminal Justice vs. Regulation' in F. Pearce and L. Snider eds., *Corporate Crime: Contemporary Debates*, 181–98. Toronto: University of Toronto Press.

— (2009) 'Suite Revenge?: The Shaping of Folk Devils and Moral Panics about White-Collar Crimes', *British Journal of Criminology*, 49: 48–67.

Levi, R. and M. Valverde (2008) 'Studying Law by Association: Bruno Latour Goes to the Conseil d'Etat', *Law and Social Inquiry*, 33(3): 805–25.

Levi-Faur, D. (2005) 'The Global Diffusion of Regulatory Capitalism', *The Annals of the American Academy of Political and Social Science*, 598(1): 12–32.

Lewis, B. (2003) 'Jail Time for Stock Crime: Corporate Fraud Law an Attempt to Restore Investor Confidence', *The Province*, 13 June: A45.

Leyshon, A. (2000) 'Money and Finance' in E. Sheppard and T.S. Barnes eds., *A Companion to Economic Geography*, 432–49. Oxford: Blackwell.

Leyshon, A. and N. Thrift (1997) *Money/Space: Geographies of Monetary Transformation*. New York: Routledge.

Leyshon, A., N. Thrift and J. Pratt (1998) 'Reading Financial Services: Consumers, Texts, and Financial Literacy', *Environment and Planning D: Society and Space*, 16: 29–55.

Lie, J. (1997) 'Sociology of Markets', *Annual Review of Sociology*, 23: 341–60.

Livesey, B. (2008) 'The Buck Stops Where?', *Canadian Lawyer*, 32(1), January 2008: 42–7.

Macaulay, S. (1993) 'Business Adaptation to Regulation: What Do We Know and What Do We Need to Know?', *Law and Policy*, 15(3): 259–70.

MacKenzie, D. (2004) 'Social Connectivities in Global Financial Markets', *Environment and Planning D: Society and Space*, 22(1): 83–101.

— (2005) 'Opening the Black Boxes of Global Finance', *Review of International Political Economy*, 12(4): 555–76.

— (2006) *An Engine, Not a Camera: How Financial Models Shape Markets*. Cambridge, MA: MIT Press.

— (2007) 'The Material Production of Virtuality: Innovation, Cultural Geography and Facticity in Derivatives Markets', *Economy and Society*, 36(3): 355–76.

— (2009) *Material Markets: How Economic Agents are Constructed*. Oxford University Press.

MacKenzie, D., F. Muniesa and L. Siu eds. (2007) *Do Economists Make Markets? On the Performativity of Economics*. Princeton, NJ: Princeton University Press.

Makin, K. (2008) 'Ontario Sets Targets to Reduce Court Delays', *Globe and Mail*, 4 June 2008: A9.

Mandel, M. (1994) *The Charter of Rights and the Legalization of Politics in Canada*. Toronto: Thompson Educational Publishers.

Mann, K. (1985) *Defending White-Collar Crime: A Portrait of Attorneys at Work*. New Haven, CT: Yale University Press.

Manning, P. K. (1993) 'Comment: Regulation as a Game?', *Law and Policy*, 15(3): 235–38.

— (1997) *Police Work* 2nd ed. Cambridge, MA: MIT Press.

Market Regulation Services (2003) *Submission to the Wise Person's Committee to Review the Structure of Securities Regulation in Canada*. Toronto: Market Regulation Services.

— (2006) *General Principles for Sanction Guidelines for RS Disciplinary Hearings*. Toronto: Market Regulation Services.

Markopolos, H. (2009a) Testimony Before the U.S. House of Representatives Committee on Financial Services. 4 February 2009.

— (2009b) Testimony Before the US Senate Banking, Housing, and Urban Affairs Committee. 10 September 2009.

— (2010) *No One Would Listen: A True Financial Thriller*. Hoboken, NJ: John Wiley & Sons.

Masters, B. (2007) 'Watchdogs Step Up Global Tracking of Insider Trading', *Financial Times*, 15 February 2007: 1.

McBarnet, D. (1992) 'Legitimate Rackets: Tax Evasion, Tax Avoidance, and the Boundaries of Legality', *Journal of Human Justice*, 3(2): 56–74.

— (2004) *Crime, Compliance, and Control*. Burlington, VT: Ashgate.

— (2005) 'After Enron: Corporate Governance, Creative Compliance, and the Uses of Corporate Social Responsibility' in J. O'Brien ed., *Governing the Corporation: Regulation and Corporate Governance in an Age of Scandal and Global Markets*, 205–22. Hoboken, NJ: John Wiley.

— (2006) 'After Enron Will "Whiter than White-Collar Crime" Still Wash?', *British Journal of Criminology*, 46: 1091–109.

McBarnet, D. and C. Whelan (1992) 'Regulating Accounting: Limits in the Law' in M. Bromwich and A. Hopwood eds., *Accounting and Law*, 99–111. Hertfordshire: Prentice Hall.

— (1999) *Creative Accounting and the Cross-Eyed Javelin Thrower*. Chichester: John Wiley.

McCahery, J. and S. Picciotto (1995) 'Creative Lawyering and the Dynamics of Business

Regulation' in Y. Dezalay and D. Sugarman eds., *Professional Competition and Professional Power. Lawyers, Accountants and the Social Construction of Markets*, 238–74. New York: Routledge.

McDowell, L. (1994) 'Social Justice, Organizational Culture, and Workplace Democracy: Cultural Imperialism in the City of London', *Urban Geography*, 15: 661–80

— (1997) *Capital Culture: Gender at Work in the City*. Oxford: Blackwell.

Meidinger, E. (1987) 'Regulatory Culture: A Theoretical Outline', *Law and Policy*, 9: 355–86.

Merry, S. E. (1990) *Getting Justice and Getting Even: Legal Consciousness Among Working-Class Americans*. Chicago: University of Chicago Press.

Meyer, J. W. and B. Rowan (1977) 'Institutionalized Organizations: Formal Structure as Myth and Ceremony', *American Journal of Sociology*, 83(2): 340–63.

Miller, P. (2001) 'Governing By Numbers: Why Calculative Practices Matter', *Social Research*, 68(2): 379–96.

— (2008) 'Calculating Economic Life', *Journal of Cultural Economy*, 1(1): 51–64.

Miller, P. and N. Rose (2008) *Governing the Present: Administering Economic, Social and Personal Life*. Malden, MA: Polity.

Minns, R. (2001) *The Cold War in Welfare: Stock Markets versus Pensions*. London: Verso.

Mitchell, T. (2002) *Rule of Experts: Egypt, Techno-Politics, Modernity*. Berkeley: University of California Press.

Mnookin, R. H. and L. Kornhauser (1978) 'Bargaining in the Shadow of the Law: The Case of Divorce', *Yale Law Journal*, 88: 950–97.

Moran, M. (1991) *The Politics of the Financial Services Revolution: The USA, UK, and Japan*. New York: St. Martins Press.

Morgenson, G. (2006) 'Whispers of Mergers Set Off Suspicious Trading', *New York Times*, 27 August 2006.

Muniesa, F. (2007) 'Market Technologies and the Pragmatics of Prices', *Economy and Society*, 36(3): 377–95.

Muniesa, F., Y. Millo and M. Callon (2007) 'An Introduction to Market Devices' in M. Callon, Y. Millo and F. Muniesa eds., *Market Devices*, 1–12. Oxford: Blackwell.

Nader, L. and C. Nader (1985) 'A Wide Angle on Regulation: An Anthropological Perspective' in R. Noll ed., *Regulatory Policy and the Social Sciences*, 141–60. Berkeley: University of California Press.

National Pensioners and Senior Citizens Federation (2008) *Submission to the Expert Panel on Securities Regulation*. 10 July 2008.

Neufeld, E. (1972) *The Financial System of Canada: Its Growth and Development*. Toronto: Macmillan.

O'Brien, J. (2005) 'Redesigning Financial Regulation: Elliott Spitzer, State-Federal Relations and the Battle for Corporate Control' in J. O'Brien ed., *Governing the Corporation: Regulation and Corporate Governance in an Age of Scandal and Global Markets*, 295–316. Hoboken, NJ: John Wiley.

Oliver, J. (2006) 'A Capital Journey', Speech to the Canadian Club of Toronto. 15 May 2006. Toronto, Ontario.

Osborne, C., D. Mullan and B. Finlay (2004) *Report of the Fairness Committee to David Brown, Q.C. Chair of the Ontario Securities Commission*. 5 March 2004. Toronto, Ontario.

Palango, P. (1998) *The Last Guardians: The Crisis in the RCMP and in Canada*. Toronto: McClelland & Stewart.

Paolucci, P. (2001) 'Classical Sociological Theory and Modern Social Problems: Marx's Concept of the Camera Obscura and the Fallacy of Individualistic Reductionism', *Critical Sociology*, 27(1): 77–120.

Parker, C. and J. Braithwaite (2003) 'Regulation' in P. Cane and M. Tushnet eds., *Oxford Handbook of Legal Studies*, 119–45. Oxford: Oxford University Press.

Parker, C. and V. Nielsen (2009) 'The Challenge of Empirical Research on Business Compliance in Regulatory Capitalism', *Annual Review of Law and Social Science*, 5: 45–70.

Pearce, F. and S. Tombs (1999) *Toxic Capitalism: Corporate Crime and the Chemical Industry*. Toronto: Canadian Scholars' Press.

Picciotto, S. (2002) 'Introduction: Reconceptualizing Regulation in the Era of Globalization', *Journal of Law and Society*, 29(1): 1–11.

— (2007) 'Constructing Compliance: Game Playing, Tax Law, and the Regulatory State', *Law and Policy*, 29(1): 11–30.

Picciotto, S. and J. Haines (1999) 'Regulating Global Financial Markets', *Journal of Law and Society*, 26: 351–68.

Poveda, T. (1994) *Rethinking White-Collar Crime*. London: Praeger.

Power, M. (1995) 'Auditing, Expertise, and the Sociology of Technique', *Critical Perspectives on Accounting*, 6(4): 317–39.

— (1997) *The Audit Society: Rituals of Verification*. Oxford: Oxford University Press.

— (2003) 'Evaluating the Audit Explosion', *Law and Policy*, 25(3): 115–202.

— (2004) *The Risk Management of Everything: Rethinking the Politics of Uncertainty*. London, Demos.

— (2007) *Organized Uncertainty: Designing a World of Risk Management*. Oxford: Clarendon Press.

— (2009) 'The Risk Management of Nothing', *Accounting, Organizations, and Society*, 34(6–7): 849–55.

Preda, A. (2001) 'The Enchanted Grove: Financial Conversations and the Marketplace in England and France in the 18th Century', *Journal of Historical Sociology*, 14(3): 276–307.

— (2002) 'Financial Knowledge, Documents, and the Structure of Financial Activities', *Journal of Contemporary Ethnography*, 31(2): 207–39.

— (2005) 'The Investor as a Cultural Figure of Global Capitalism' in K. Knorr Cetina and A. Preda eds., *The Sociology of Financial Markets*, 141–62. Oxford: Oxford University Press.

— (2006) 'Socio-Technical Agency in Financial Markets', *Social Studies of Science*, 36(5): 753–82.

— (2007) 'The Sociological Approach to Financial Markets', *Journal of Economic Surveys*, 21(3): 506–33.

— (2009a) *Framing Finance: The Boundaries of Markets and Modern Capitalism*. Chicago: University of Chicago Press.

— (2009b) 'Brief Encounters: Calculation and the Interaction Order of Anonymous Electronic Markets', *Accounting, Organizations, and Society*, 34: 675–93.

Pryke, M. (2010) 'Money's Eyes: The Visual Preparation of Financial Markets', *Economy and Society*, 39(4): 427–59.

Pryke, M. and P. du Gay (2007) 'Take An Issue: Cultural Economy and Finance', *Economy and Society*, 36(3): 339–54.

Public Works (2006) *Formative Evaluation of the 'Strategy For Enhanced Protection of Canadian Capital Markets' (Integrated Market Enforcement Teams Component) (Up to October 2005)*. Ottawa: Public Works and Government Services Canada.

Puri, P. (2005) *Enforcement Effectiveness in the Canadian Capital Markets*. Toronto: Capital Markets Institute.

Reichman, N. (1991) 'Regulating Risky Business: Dilemmas in Security Regulation', *Law and Policy*, 13(4): 263–95.

— (1992) 'Moving Backstage: Uncovering the Role of Compliance Practices in Shaping Regulatory Policy' in K. Schlegel and D. Weisburd eds., *White-Collar Crime Reconsidered*, 244–68. Boston, MA: Northeastern University Press.

— (1993) 'Insider Trading' in M. Tonry and A. Reiss eds., *Beyond the Law: Crime in Complex Organizations*, 55–96. Chicago: University of Chicago Press.

— (1998) 'Power and Justice in Sociolegal Studies of Regulation' in B. Garth and A. Sarat eds., *Justice and Power in Sociolegal Studies*, 233–71. Evanston, IL: Northwestern University Press.

Reynolds, G. (2006) 'Remedies in Criminal Regulatory Processes: Is the Charter Less Robust?' The Constitution in Regulatory Investigations and Proceedings. Ontario Bar Association Continuing Legal Education. 5 May 2006.

Reynolds, J. L. (2005) *The Naked Investor*. Toronto: Penguin.

Riles, A. (2000) *The Network Inside Out*. Ann Arbor, MI: University of Michigan Press.

— (2005) 'A New Agenda for the Cultural Study of Law: Taking on the Technicalities', *Buffalo Law Review*, 53: 973–1025.

— (2011) *Collateral Knowledge: Legal Reasoning in the Global Financial Markets*. Chicago: University of Chicago Press.

Rose, N. (1999) *Powers of Freedom: Reframing Political Thought*. New York: Cambridge University Press.

Rose, N. and M. Valverde (1998) 'Governed by Law?', *Social and Legal Studies*, 7(4): 541–51.

Rosen, A. and M. Rosen (2010) *Swindlers: Cons and Cheats and How to Protect Your Investments From Them*. Toronto: Madison Press Books.

Rothstein, H., M. Huber and G. Gaskell (2006) 'A Theory of Risk Colonization: The Spiraling Regulatory Logics of Societal and Institutional Risk', *Economy and Society*, 35(1): 91–112.

Rubin, S. (2008) 'The Armour Strengthens Around Privilege', *Globe and Mail*, 27 August 2008: B5.

Rusli, E. (2011) 'Hardball Tactics Against Insider Trading: Next Up: A Crackdown on Outside-Expert Firms', *New York Times*, May 12, 2011: B1.

Sassen, S. (2004) 'The Local and Institutional Embeddedness of Electronic Markets' in M. Bevir and F. Trentmann eds., *Markets in Historical Context*, 224–46. Cambridge: Cambridge University Press.

— (2005) 'The Embeddedness of Electronic Markets: The Case of Global Capital Markets' in K. Knorr Cetina and A. Preda eds., *The Sociology of Financial Markets*, 17–37. Oxford: Oxford University Press.

— (2006) *Territory, Authority, Rights: From Medieval to Global Assemblages*. Princeton, NJ: Princeton University Press.

Schmidt, P. (2004) 'Law in the Age of Governance: Regulation, Networks, and Lawyers' in J. Jordana and D. Levi-Faur eds., *The Politics of Regulation in the Age of Governance*, 273–95. Cheltenham: Edward Elgar.

— (2005) *Lawyers and Regulation: The Politics of the Administrative Process*. Cambridge University Press.

Scott, C. (2001) 'Analyzing Regulatory Space: Fragmented Resources and Institutional Design', *Public Law*, 329–53.

— (2004) 'Regulation in the Age of Governance: The Rise of the Post-Regulatory State' in J. Jordana and D. Levi-Faur eds., *The Politics of Regulation in the Age of Governance*, 145–74. Cheltenham: Edward Elgar.

Scribner, R. (1986) 'The Technological Revolution in Securities Trading: Can Regulation Keep Up?' in A. Saunders and L. J. White eds., *Technology and the Regulation of Financial Markets: Securities, Futures, and Banking*, 19–29. Toronto: Heath, Lexington Books.

Securities and Exchange Commission (2009) *Investigation of Failure of the SEC to Uncover Bernard Madoff's Ponzi Scheme*. Report No. OIG-509. Office of Inspector General. Washington, DC: Securities and Exchange Commission.

Selden, S. (2006) 'Self-Policing the Market: Congress's Flawed Approach to Securities Law Reform', *Journal of Legislation*, 33(1): 57–98.

Shapiro, S. (1984) *Wayward Capitalists: Targets of the SEC*. New Haven, CT: Yale University Press.

— (1987) 'The Social Control of Impersonal Trust', *American Journal of Sociology*, 93(3): 623–8.

— (2001) *Tangled Loyalties: Conflict of Interest in Legal Practice*. Ann Arbor, MI: University of Michigan Press.

Shearing, C. (1993) 'Towards a Constitutive Conception of Regulation' in J. Braithwaite and P. Grabosky eds., *Business Regulation and Australia's Future*, 67–80. Sydney: Australian Institute of Criminology.

Sliter, J. (1994) *A Policy Review of the Role of the Royal Canadian Mounted Police in Securities Fraud Enforcement*. Burnaby, BC: Simon Fraser University.

Small Investor Protection Association (2004) *Five Year Review: The Small Investors' Perspective of Investor Protection in Canada*. Toronto: SIPA.

Smith, R. and I. Walter (2006) *Governing the Modern Corporation: Capital Markets, Corporate Control, and Economic Performance*. Oxford: Oxford University Press.

Snider, L. (2009) 'Accommodating Power: The "Common Sense" of Regulators', *Social and Legal Studies*, 18(2): 179–97.

Spalek, B. (2001) 'Policing the UK Financial System: The Creation of the "New" Financial Services Authority and its Approach to Regulation', *International Journal of the Sociology of Law*, 29: 75–87.

Sparrow, M. (2000) *The Regulatory Craft*. Washington, DC: Brookings Institution.

Standing Committee on Government Agencies (2010) *Report on Agencies, Boards, and Commissions: Ontario Securities Commission*. Toronto: Government of Ontario.

Standing Senate Committee on Banking, Trade, and Commerce (2005) *Evidence of the Meeting of May 18, 2005*. Ottawa: Government of Canada.

Stenning, P., C. Shearing, S. Addario and M. Condon (1990) 'Controlling Interests: Two Conceptions of Order in Regulating a Financial Market' in M. Friedland ed., *Securing Compliance: Seven Case Studies*, 88–119. Toronto: University of Toronto Press.

Stewart, S. (2008) 'U.S. Regulators Target Short Sellers', *Globe and Mail*, 15 July 2008: B9

Stromberg, G. (1998) *Investment Funds in Canada and Consumer Protection*. Ottawa: Office of Consumer Affairs, Industry Canada.

Sutherland, E. (1983) *White-Collar Crime: The Uncut Version*. New Haven, CT: Yale University Press.

Szockyj, E. (1993) 'Insider Trading: The SEC Meets Carl Karcher', *Annals of the American Academy of Political and Social Science*, 525(1): 46–58.

Taibbi, M. (2011) 'Why Isn't Wall Street in Jail?', *Rolling Stone*, 3 March 2011: 44–51.

Task Force to Modernize Securities Legislation in Canada (2006) *Canada Steps Up: Final Report*. Toronto: Task Force to Modernize Securities Legislation.

Terpak, F. (2001) 'Objects and Contexts' in B. Stafford and F. Terpak eds., *Devices of Wonder: From the World in a Box to Image on a Screen*, 143–364. Los Angeles: Getty Research Institute.

Thrift, N. (1994) 'On the Social and Cultural Determinants of International Financial Centres: The Case of the City of London' in S. Corbridge, N. Thrift and R. Martin, eds., *Money, Power, Space*, 327–55. Oxford: Basil Blackwell.

— (2000) 'Pandora's Box: Cultural Geographies of Economies' in G. Clark, M. Gertler and M. Feldman eds., *The Oxford Handbook of Economic Geography*, 689–704. Oxford: Blackwell.

— (2002) 'Performing Cultures in the New Economy' in P. du Gay and M. Pryke eds., *Cultural Economy*, 201–34. London: Sage.

Thrift, N. and A. Leyshon (1994) 'A Phantom State? The De-Traditionalization of Money, the International Financial System and International Financial Centres', *Political Geography*, 13: 299–327.

Tinker, T. and C. Carter (2003) 'Spectres of Accounting: Contradictions or Conflicts of Interest?', *Organization*, 10(3): 577–82.

Tombs, S. (2002) 'Understanding Regulation?', *Social and Legal Studies*, 11(1): 113–33.

Tsing, A. (2000) 'Inside the Economy of Appearances', *Public Culture*, 12(1): 115–44.

Underhill, G. (1997) 'Private Markets and Public Responsibility in a Global System: Conflict and Cooperation in Transnational Banking and Securities Regulation' in G. Underhill ed., *The New World Order in International Finance*, 17–49. New York: St. Martin's Press.

— (2001) 'The Public Good versus Private Interests and the Global Financial and Monetary System' in D. Drache ed., *The Market or the Public Domain: Global Governance and the Asymmetry of Power*, 274–95. New York: Routledge.

Valverde, M. (2003) *Law's Dream of a Common Knowledge*. Princeton, NJ: Princeton University Press.

— (2005) 'Authorizing the Production of Urban Moral Order: Appellate Courts and Their Knowledge Games', *Law and Society Review*, 39(2): 419–55.

— (2006) 'The Sociology of Law as a "Means Against Struggle Itself"', *Social and Legal Studies*, 15(4): 591–7.

— (2008) 'The Ethic of Diversity: Local Law and the Negotiation of Urban Norms', *Law and Social Inquiry*, 33(4): 895–923.

— (2009) 'Jurisdiction and Scale: Legal "Technicalities" as Resources for Theory', *Social and Legal Studies*, 18(2): 139–57.

White, H. C. (1981) 'Where Do Markets Come From?', *American Journal of Sociology*, 87: 517–47.

White, H. V. (1987) *The Content of the Form: Narrative Discourse and Historical Representation*. Baltimore, MD: Johns Hopkins University.

Wickham, G. and H. Freemantle (2008) 'Some Additional Knowledge Conditions for Sociology', *Current Sociology*, 56(6): 922–39.

Williams, J. W. (2005) 'Reflections on the Private versus Public Policing of Economic Crime', *British Journal of Criminology*, 45(3): 316–39.

— (2006) 'Private Legal Orders: Professional Markets and the Commodification of Financial Governance', *Social and Legal Studies*, 15(2): 209–35.

— (2008a) 'The Lessons of "Enron": Media Accounts, Corporate Crimes, and Financial Markets', *Theoretical Criminology*, 12(4): 471–99.

— (2008b) 'Out of Place and Out of Line: Positioning the Police in the Regulation of Financial Markets', *Law and Policy*, 30(3): 306–35.

— (2009) 'Envisioning Financial Disorder: Financial Surveillance and the Securities Industry', *Economy and Society*, 38(3): 460–91.

Williams, J. W. and R. Lippert (2006) 'Governing on the Margins: Exploring the Contributions of Governmentality Studies to Critical Criminology in Canada', *Canadian Journal of Criminology and Criminal Justice*, 48(5): 703–20.

Williams, K. (2000) 'From Shareholder Value to Present-Day Capitalism', *Economy and Society*, 29(1): 1–12.

Williams, T. (2007) 'Empowerment of Whom and for What?: Financial Literacy Education and the New Regulation of Consumer Financial Services', *Law and Policy*, 29(2): 226–56.

Willis, A. (2005) 'Brown Expects National Agency for Markets Within Five Years', *Globe and Mail*, 21 June 2005: B8.

Wilson, D. (2008) Testimony Before the Ontario Standing Committee on Government Agencies. 2 December 2008. Toronto: Government of Ontario.

— (2009) 'The Role of Securities Regulation in the Fight Against Economic Crime', Speech to the 2009 McMaster World Conference. 14 January 2009. Hamilton, Ontario.

Wise Persons Committee (2003) *It's Time. Committee to Review the Structure of Securities Regulation in Canada.* Ottawa: Department of Finance Canada.

Wolburgh Jenah, S. (2008) 'What Lies Ahead', Paper Presented to the Canadian Institute's 18th Annual Securities Superconference. 22 February 2008. Toronto, Ontario.

Yudelman, D. (2001) *The Scorpion and the Frog: A Report Prepared for the Consumers Council of Canada for Presentation to the Office of Consumer Affairs Industry Canada.* Ottawa: Consumers Council of Canada.

Zaloom, C. (2003) 'Ambiguous Numbers: Trading Technologies and Interpretations in Financial Markets', *American Ethnologist*, 30(2): 258–72.

— (2006) *Out of the Pits: Traders and Technology from Chicago to London.* Chicago: University of Chicago Press.

Zey, M. (1993) *Banking on Fraud: Drexel, Junk Bonds, and Buyouts.* New York: Aldine de Gruyter.

— (1998) 'Embeddedness of Interorganizational Corporate Crime in the 1980s: Securities Fraud of Banks and Investment Banks', *Research in the Sociology of Organizations*, 15: 111–59.

Zorn, D., F. Dobbin, J. Dierkes and M. Kwok (2005) 'Managing Investors: How Financial Markets Reshaped the American Firm' in K. Knorr Cetina and A. Preda eds., *The Sociology of Financial Markets*, 269–89. Oxford: Oxford University Press.

Cases

BC Securities Commission v Branch [1995] 2 SCR 3.

Hercules Management v Ernst and Young [1997] 2 SCR 165.

Markarian v CIBC World Markets Inc. [2006] JQ no 5467.

R v Cartaway Resources Corp. [2004] 1 SCR 672.

R v Jarvis [2002] 3 SCR 757.

R v Ling [2002] 3 SCR 814.

R v Stinchcombe [1991] 3 SCR 326.

Conferences and seminars

Capital Markets Institute (2008) Advancing the Enforcement Agenda Part II: What's the Solution? Capital Markets Institute Symposium on Enforcement of Securities Law. 2 May 2008. Toronto, Ontario.

Crime and the Corporation (2006) Osgoode Hall Law School Professional Development One Day Canadian National Forum. 30 September 2006. Toronto, Ontario.

Dialogue with the OSC (2004) Ontario Securities Commission. 1 November 2004. Toronto, Ontario.

Dialogue with the OSC (2006) Ontario Securities Commission. 10 November 2006. Toronto, Ontario.
Dialogue with the OSC (2007) Ontario Securities Commission. 27 November 2007. Toronto, Ontario.
Securities Litigation (2006) Annual Conference. 27–28 November 2007. Toronto, Ontario.
Securities Superconference (2009) 17–18 February 2009. Toronto, Ontario.
Twelve Minute Securities Lawyer (2005) Law Society of Upper Canada. 25 January 2005. Toronto, Ontario.
Understanding and Managing Regulatory Investigations (2007) Osgoode Hall Law School Professional Development Course. 23 April 2007. Toronto, Ontario.
Understanding and Managing Regulatory Investigations (2009) Osgoode Hall Law School Professional Development Course. 20 April 2009. Toronto, Ontario.

Index